THE SPIRIT AND THE CHURCH

Mary E. Abhold
150 E. Wis. Ave., Apt. 4
Oconomowoc, Wis. 53066

AUG. 17-19 Notre Dame 1979

"Called to Serve"

National Conference
Renewal in the Catholic Church

THE SPIRIT AND THE CHURCH

A Personal and Documentary Record of the Charismatic Renewal, and the Ways It Is Bursting to Life in the Catholic Church

Compiled by
Ralph Martin

PAULIST PRESS
New York/Paramus/Toronto

Copyright©1976
Charismatic Renewal Services, Inc.

All rights reserved. No part of this book may be reproduced or transmitted in any form or by any means, electronic or mechanical, including photocopying, recording or by any information storage and retrieval system, without permission in writing from the Publisher.

Library of Congress
Catalog Card Number: 76-9366

ISBN: 0-8091-1947-1

Published by Paulist Press
Editorial Office: 1865 Broadway, N.Y., N.Y. 10023
Business Office: 400 Sette Drive, Paramus, N.J. 07652

Printed and bound in the
United States of America

Contents

INTRODUCTION *by Ralph Martin* 1

PART ONE: BEGINNINGS AND GROWTH

ARE YOU READY?
   Patti Gallagher 4

GOD BREAKS IN
   Paul and Mary Ann Gray 11

BEFORE DUQUESNE: SOURCES OF THE RENEWAL
   James B. Manney 21

A WOMAN AND THE POPE
   Fr. Val Gaudet 42

MOVING ON
   Cindy Conniff 48

CATHOLIC CHARISMATIC RENEWAL:
THE FIRST SEVEN YEARS
   Kevin Ranaghan 56

A TURNING POINT
   Mary Ann Jahr 66

GOD IS RESTORING HIS PEOPLE
   Ralph Martin 74

Contents

PART TWO: RESPONSES OF BISHOPS AND THEOLOGIANS

INTERVIEW WITH BISHOP JOSEPH MCKINNEY
Msgr. Hugh Behan 86

REPORT OF THE AMERICAN BISHOPS, 1969 105

CHARISMATIC RENEWAL IN THE
CATHOLIC CHURCH: AN EVALUATION
Bishop Joseph Hogan 108

NEW OPENNESS DEVELOPS AMONG U.S. CARDINALS 117

INTERVIEW WITH BISHOP PAUL ANDERSON 119

COME, HOLY SPIRIT
Cardinal Leo Josef Suenens 123

INTERVIEW WITH CARDINAL SUENENS
Ralph Martin 130

INTERNATIONAL LEADERS MEET WITH POPE PAUL 145

A JOYFUL PILGRIMAGE:
THE 1975 INTERNATIONAL CONFERENCE
Bert Ghezzi 147

POPE PAUL ADDRESSES THE CHARISMATIC RENEWAL 158

RIDING THE WIND
George T. Montague, S.M. 167

AN INTERVIEW WITH HERIBERT MÜHLEN,
THEOLOGIAN OF THE HOLY SPIRIT
Ralph Martin 174

THE BAPTISM IN THE HOLY SPIRIT:
THEOLOGICAL AND PASTORAL QUESTIONS
Fr. Salvador Carrillo Alday, M.Sp.S. 182

Contents

THE BAPTISM IN THE HOLY SPIRIT AND CHRISTIAN TRADITION
Fr. Basil Pennington and Fr. Francis Sullivan 192

A STATEMENT OF THE THEOLOGICAL BASIS OF THE CATHOLIC CHARISMATIC RENEWAL 199

RESTORING THE FULL SPECTRUM OF THE CHARISMS 214

PART THREE: A RENEWED CHURCH

THE CHARISMATIC RENEWAL AND CHURCH RENEWAL
Bert Ghezzi 226

RENEWAL OF THE CHURCH
Archbishop James Hayes 232

A CHURCH REBORN
Fr. Graham Pulkingham 237

MARRIAGE, COMMUNITY, SERVICE: INTERVIEW WITH FR. GRAHAM PULKINGHAM 245

A BISHOP, A DIOCESE, AND THE CHARISMATIC RENEWAL
Dr. Bill Burnett 254

THE FIRST PENTECOSTAL ABBEY
Mary Ann Jahr 261

THE ULTIMATE TEST
Mary Ann Jahr 266

RENEWAL AND AN AMERICAN MISSION
Fr. Richard Jones 271

THE CHURCH: A CHARISMATIC COMMUNITY
Rev. Ken Pagard 280

Contents

THE LORD, THE SPIRIT, AND THE CHURCH
Kevin Ranaghan 290

GOD IS SHAKING THE CHURCHES
Rev. Charles Simpson 304

THE POWER IN PENANCE: CONFESSION AND THE HOLY SPIRIT
Fr. Michael Scanlan 315

COVENANT COMMUNITIES: A NEW SIGN OF HOPE
Fr. John O'Connor, C.S.C. 319

NOTES ON THE CONTRIBUTORS 338

Introduction

Anyone who is familiar with the history of renewal movements in the Church will marvel at how quickly the charismatic renewal has become a significant force for the renewal of the Catholic Church. In only eight years, the charismatic renewal has spread to almost every country in the world. Many bishops and Church officials, even at the highest level, have given their approval to this movement. Some are personally involved in it.

The articles that appear in this book were originally published over a period of five years in NEW COVENANT, a monthly magazine in English for the worldwide charismatic renewal. Here, they are gathered together in one volume in order to present a concise history of the relationship of the charismatic renewal to the Church. The book is divided into three parts and each one represents a different phase of the renewal.

The first part of this book presents the amazing picture of the origins of the charismatic renewal in the Catholic Church. It shows that, even when the great pentecostal revival began among American Protestants at the turn of this century, the Pope at that time was already dreaming about a "New Pentecost" for the Church. It shows how the renewal began, not apart from the Church, but amongst a group of men and women with a deep commitment

Introduction

to the Church and to the renewal that was advocated by Vatican II. And finally, it shows that throughout its brief history the ultimate concern of those who are active in the charismatic renewal has been to promote a renewal that is in and for the Church.

The second part of this book examines the renewal from a different perspective, that of bishops and theologians. From the earliest times, it has been the prerogative of the bishops of the Church to discern what is from the Holy Spirit and what is not. This section of the book traces the history of how this prerogative has been exercised in the Church from the first report on the charismatic renewal that was issued by the American bishops in 1969, to the warm reception and encouragement that Pope Paul VI gave to those pilgrims who journeyed to Rome for the 1975 International Conference on the Charismatic Renewal in the Catholic Church. It also gives us a glimpse of the support the charismatic renewal has received from several outstanding theologians.

The third part of this book furnishes a prophetic vision of where the renewal is headed. It describes in concrete terms how the Holy Spirit is renewing various aspects of Christian life. This is probably the most important part of the book. It shows that the significance of the renewal is not in its growth in numbers or in approval that it receives from the hierarchy, but rather in the contribution it makes to the renewal of the entire Church.

Ralph Martin
Ann Arbor, March 1976

PART ONE
Beginnings and Growth

Are You Ready?

By Patti Gallagher

"What no eye has seen, nor ear heard, nor the heart of man conceived, what God has prepared for those who love him, God has revealed to us through the Spirit" (1 Cor. 2:9-10).

"Are you ready for what the Spirit can do in your life?"

This was the question Dr. Storey asked a group of us from Duquesne University during a retreat in February, 1967. I can still remember feeling a little afraid, yet filled with anticipation, as I heard his words. I wasn't sure if I was "ready" for what the Spirit would do, but I knew I needed a deeper relationship with God, and I had come that weekend hoping the Lord would change my life.

After Dr. Storey's question, I put a note on the bulletin board at the retreat house that read, "I want a miracle!" Little did I know how powerfully and dramatically the Lord would answer me and manifest himself in those next days.

To better understand what happened that weekend, it would be helpful to know something about the group of students who attended this retreat. We were all part of a Scripture study group that met weekly with the help of a few professors from

Are You Ready?

Duquesne to discuss God's Word and to pray. Although Christ was important in our lives, we were still trying to follow our own plans. Many of us had not yet surrendered fully to him as our Lord. Although prayer was important to us, few of us knew what it meant to pray deeply under the inspiration of the Holy Spirit. Charity toward others and witnessing to the Gospel were of concern to students from this group also, and yet we seemed to lack true unity and love in the Lord and the power to proclaim Jesus to others.

I, for one, came to that retreat knowing that I needed more than what my own prayer life, theology classes, and even this Scripture study had provided.

The Duquesne Weekend

In preparation for this weekend we read *The Cross and the Switchblade* and the first four chapters from the Acts of the Apostles. During the discussion periods on retreat, we asked one of the professors to explain what it meant to receive the Spirit. Don't we know Jesus already? Haven't we received the Spirit in confirmation? He assured us that our baptism and confirmation had put us into a relationship with God, and yet he asked us if we knew Jesus in a deep, personal way and if we experienced the power of his Spirit working in our lives.

As the weekend proceeded many of us were confronted with what it would mean to surrender our lives completely to Jesus as our Lord and Master and to open ourselves to the power of his Spirit. Jesus was asking us to let him reign, not simply to acknowledge him as an important person, but to allow him into the very center of our lives.

By Saturday afternoon, many of us realized that we needed to commit ourselves more deeply to Jesus. One of the young men, David Mangen, suggested that at the close of the retreat we make a personal renewal of our confirmation and ask the Holy Spirit to be released in us.

It was at this point that Dr. Storey asked if we were ready for what the Spirit would do. We students didn't know that a month before our retreat, he and three others from Duquesne had attended a prayer meeting in Pittsburgh and had received the baptism of the Holy Spirit. I remember telling David after his suggestion that even if no one else from the group wanted to renew his confirmation, I did.

That Saturday evening, February 18, 1967, was an important night in my life and in the Catholic charismatic renewal. During a birthday party at the retreat I wandered up into the chapel to see if any of my friends were there. I didn't plan on praying myself. I was simply going to call my friends down to the party.

But as I entered and knelt in the presence of the Lord in the Blessed Sacrament, I trembled with the awareness that it was God himself, in all his holiness, before whom I had come. I found myself praying from the depths of my being a prayer of total surrender to the Lord. "Yes, your will be done. I accept whatever it will mean to follow you. Only teach me how to love."

In the next few moments I found myself prostrate before the altar and filled with an awareness of God's personal love for me; a love that is so completely undeserved, so utterly foolish, so lavishly given. The only word that came to my mind in those

Are You Ready?

moments was "stay." I often think of Augustine's prayer when recalling that night. "You have made us for yourself, O Lord, and there is no rest until we rest in you."

Even though I wanted to remain in the chapel and enjoy the presence of the Lord there and within me, I knew that what I had experienced was meant to be shared. Without fully understanding what had happened, I was convinced that God intended for all his people to know his love and presence in a deep, personal way.

I left the chapel and told our chaplain what I had just experienced. I learned from him that David Managan had just been in the chapel an hour before. Dave, also, had encountered the Lord in a more powerful way than ever before. I asked this priest which people I should tell about what had happened, and he simply said that the Lord would show me. How often those words have echoed in my ears, "The Lord will show you," as the Lord has led me to share his love with brothers and sisters from different parts of the country and the world.

Before the end of the party, all the students were drawn into the chapel. It was as though Jesus were walking among us as we knelt there and touching each person in some special way. Some said they experienced a deep peace or joy, or the desire to praise God.

Dr. Storey, looking upon the group that night, commented that the bishop would be surprsied when he found out all these students had been baptized in the Holy Spirit. I wondered what he meant. The term "baptism of the Spirit" was still new to us. We didn't fully understand that what was happening among us was a release of the power of God's Spirit and that we would become known as the first Catholic charismatic prayer group.

After the Weekend

When I think of those weeks and months following our retreat, I remember the words of Psalm 126. *"When the Lord brought back those who returned to Zion, we were like those who dream. Then our mouth was filled with laughter, and our tongue with shouts of joy; then they said among the nations, 'The Lord has done great things for them.' The Lord has done great things for us; we are glad."*

So many wonderful things began to happen, things we never dreamed were possible! The Lord began to pour out the gifts of his Spirit. Some students found themselves praising him in tongues. There were healings. The Lord was speaking to us powerfully through his Word in Scripture and in prophecy. We were witnessing to Jesus with real power, even though at first we were often imprudent. We could not help but speak of what we had seen and heard. Many of us found the Lord leading us to work in ways we had not planned. Within a short time I cancelled a summer trip to France because the Lord was making it clear that he was calling me to serve him in the direct apostolate.

In mid-March Ralph Martin, Steve Clark, Gerry Rauch, and Jim Cavnar came to visit our group at Duquesne. I kept a journal during those early days of the renewal and at the time of this visit I made the following entry: "National leaders of the Cursillo are coming tomorrow. Ralph and Steve. Should be big happenings this week. Praise you,

Are You Ready?   9

Lord. Praise your name! When you come to them, you'll come to the States and to the world." It amazes me that I wrote this before I ever met these men or even knew their last names!

Little did I know how God would indeed use them. After our group prayed with these four visitors, they returned to Michigan State University and to Notre Dame and the charismatic renewal began to spread. At first it was university students who discovered this deeper life in the Spirit, but before long adults, lay and religious, began to pray for a fuller release of the Holy Spirit and God answered their prayer.

How powerfully the Spirit is moving among his people today! This past June at the Catholic Charismatic Conference, as I looked out at the 11,000 people gathered, I couldn't help but remember my first conference at Notre Dame in September, 1967. At that time there were about 50 of us.

I believe the charismatic renewal has spread so rapidly in the Church these past six years because it is God's work. He desires to reveal himself to his people. As he spoke to us during the June conference in prophecy, "What you see before your eyes is just the beginning."

At times I have hesitated to share about our experience at the Duquesne Weekend. It's wonderful to recall a glorious encounter with Jesus from the past and to remember the excitement of those early days in the Spirit. But what is even more wonderful is to meet Jesus *daily* in all the circumstances of our lives and to learn to walk *daily* in his Spirit, discovering greater and greater depths of his love.

What happened six years ago was just the beginning of a life of discipleship in which Jesus tells me that if I want to be his follower I must renounce myself, take up my cross daily, and follow him. I now understand that being baptized in the Spirit is a continual process of deeper immersion in the life and love of God. The more I grow in the Lord, the more I see of his greatness and goodness and of my poverty and need.

My prayer for all of us who have come to know Jesus as our Lord and to experience the power of his Spirit in us is that we would be faithful to him always. May Mary's hymn of praise be truly our own:

"My soul magnifies the Lord, and my spirit rejoices in God my Savior, for he has regarded the low estate of his handmaiden. For behold, henceforth all generations will call me blessed; for he who is mighty has done great things for me, and holy is his name" (Luke 1:47-49).

God Breaks In

By Paul and Mary Ann Gray

Mary Ann and I were puzzled by Ralph and Bobbi Keifer as we sat at their kitchen table that night in late December, 1966. They obviously shared some secret that caused them to bubble with laughter even more than usual. Finally Ralph responded to the question voiced only in our glances with another question: "What if I were to tell you that the New Testament is true?" Again Mary Ann and I looked at each other; what was he intimating? We had come to know Ralph when he taught us a theology course two years earlier. What initially attracted our attention had been his obvious commitment to and joyous participation in all that he taught. What was he now trying to say? What new depth had he discovered?

Ralph and Bobbi were everything we wanted to become. Because of him, I was going off to graduate school to pursue my master's degree in theology; Mary Ann and I dreamt often of one day teaching theology and living a simple life in a big old house with Salvation Army furniture, celebrating family liturgies around the table with happy children. That night we wanted to know what new source of joy the Keifers had discovered, but we didn't specifically ask, and they didn't specifically tell us.

A few weeks later, Ralph, Mary Ann and I, and several other students sat in Dr. Bill Storey's office solidifying plans for the Spring Weekend of Renewal for the Chi Rho Society. Chi Rho, founded years earlier by Dr. Storey for students to renew the liturgy, study the Scriptures, pray together and experience Christian community, was going through an identity crisis and hope for its survival hinged on the success of the weekend. Our best efforts to create Christian community and renew the world had failed. We had set out to add some meaning to the despair-filled alcoholics in Pittsburgh's Hill District Ghetto, and had wound up questioning our own meaning. Bill and Ralph suggested a change in the theme of the weekend from "the Beatitudes: or how to act like Christians" to "the Acts of the Apostles: or how to become Christians." Without fully realizing the significance of this change, we all agreed.

I went off to graduate school in February more excited and more apprehensive about the Weekend of Renewal than about graduate studies. During those first weeks in February, I searched every commentary in the Manhattan College and Union Theological Seminary Libraries in preparation for the talk I was to give on Acts 1. I wanted to return to Pittsburgh showing everyone how much I had learned in only three weeks of Graduate Theology, but as I flew out of LaGuardia on February 16, I had so many notes that there was no possibility of organizing them into a clear talk.

After three weeks in New York City, it was good to arrive at The Ark and the Dove, where the retreat was to be held, for an entire weekend with Mary Ann and our friends from Chi Rho. But the unprepared talk hung over me like a dark cloud. At least it would all be over by Saturday morning, and then I could really enjoy the weekend. I sat through Saturday breakfast unable to eat a thing as the scattered thoughts I was about to deliver raced through my mind.

As the others entered the room where the talk was to be given, I sat at the speaker's table more nervous than ever. We all stood and began to sing "Come Holy Ghost." The strangest experience in my life up to that time occurred as I felt my nerves calm and my hands grow warm. The hymn finished, and I began to speak. I heard myself being not only calm, but coherent; I surprised myself as I heard statements that I hadn't found in any commentary and didn't have anywhere in my notes.

After the talk, Ralph and Bill both told me I had really become a teacher. The very approval I had spent so many hours of research and anxiety hoping to gain for myself now was given by the two men from whom it meant the most; but now I knew that I didn't deserve the credit. Jesus did: I bowed my head and thanked him.

The talk on Acts 2 was given Saturday afternoon by an Episcopalian woman who had experienced Pentecost in her life. We don't remember what she said, but she gave us a hunger for the reality of Pentecost in our lives. In the discussion following the talk, Dave Mangan summarized the attitude of the students by asking Fr. Healy if we could renew our confirmation in the Sunday liturgy in order to experience something more than we had when first confirmed.

After "quiet time" and while dinner was being

prepared, Mary Ann and I went to Ralph Keifer and told him we wanted him to pray for us that we would experience whatever he had. The three of us went up to his room. Amidst sleeping bags and tossed pajamas, Mary Ann and I knelt on the floor while Ralph laid his hands on each of our heads and prayed, first in English, then in tongues. It was the first time we had heard tongues and neither of us quite knew how to take it. We gave our lives to Jesus, and he gave us his Holy Spirit.

As Ralph was praying, the tip of my tongue lifted and then began to move up and down, making a clicking sound as it hit against the roof of my mouth. Mary Ann felt a joy well up within her like a tremendous balloon that totally filled her and then settled in her throat; "I just had to smile and smile and praise Jesus," she recalls.

That joy very likely would have erupted into the gift of tongues if she had known how to cooperate with the Holy Spirit. Instead she got up somewhat bewildered: she had heard me begin to yield to tongues, but had not experienced the same thing herself. "I thought I didn't have the baptism if it was what Ralph and Paul had, yet I felt a bursting but inarticulate joy. I kept suppressing a holy laugh: it was as though I knew a wonderful secret though I wasn't sure what it was. Had someone asked, I probably would have told them I knew for sure that Jesus loves me. Since no one did ask, I kept quiet as we went down to dinner."

As we were eating dinner, one of the nuns from The Ark and the Dove came in to tell us that there was no water in the well and that we would have to leave Saturday evening. Ralph went to the chapel to

God Breaks In

pray; Mary Ann and I and a few others joined him. We all knelt on the chapel floor as Ralph began to pray aloud. He asked the Father in Jesus' name for water; then he began thanking God for the water. He continued for some time singing about the water and praising the Lord for it.

Unlike the rest of us, he obviously believed God had provided the water. When we later asked how he could thank God for the water before it was evident he explained that when Jesus said on the cross, "It is finished," he meant not only his life, but his work. Jesus had completely obeyed the Father in everything and his kingdom was now established through the blood he had shed.

It was left for us to believe God for the specific manifestations of that kingdom. Knowing it was God's will that we experience him on the weekend, Ralph saw clearly that it was not of God that the well go dry at such a strategic time. The faith exercised turned Satan's obstacle into the Lord's miracle. Our faith was such that, after Ralph's somewhat lonely prayer, we were still resigned to going home that night.

We came together for an apparently final Bible vigil. When it was over, Dave Mangan, momentarily forgetting the problem, went downstairs to get a drink. When he turned on the faucet, the water gushed out.

Mary Ann and I were just leaving the chapel when David came back in. He fell prostrate before the tabernacle; Mary Ann and I did also. God had all the time been close enough to hear that prayer for water, and now had shown that he was powerful enough to answer it.

Fear of the Lord welled up within us; a fearful awe kept us from looking up. He was personally present and we feared being loved too much. We worshiped him, knowing for the first time the meaning of worship. We knew a burning experience of the terrible reality and presence of the Lord that has since caused us to understand at first hand the images of Yahweh on Mt. Sinai as it rumbles and explodes with the fire of his Being, and the experience of Isaiah 6:1-5, and the statement that our God is a consuming fire. This holy fear was somehow the same as love or evoked love as we really beheld him. He was altogether lovely and beautiful, yet we saw no visual image. It was as though the splenderous, brilliant, personal God had come into the room and filled both it and us.

David, by this time, was so in love with the Lord that he needed more room to show it and began rolling about; I knelt worshiping, as Mary Ann went to her room to write the outline for her talk on Acts 3.

Others were now coming into the chapel by twos and threes. Within a short time, almost all of the students were in the chapel, kneeling, holding hands, and worshiping the Lord. Mary Ann returned. The others, like us, were not accustomed to kneeling long or praying simply. Worship had meant standing up, reading poetry, playing guitars and singing, unfurling banners; now we were totally occupied by saying nothing more than "Jesus" or "Yes, Lord" over and over, addressing him who was there. "I love you, Jesus" came forth from kids whose faces shone with gladness.

Bill and Ralph went down the line of kneeling

converts, praying for the Baptism for each one. We have never since seen such a spontaneous and universal move of the Spirit. Ralph said he felt as though fire was engulfing him; some of the students were saying "it's getting brighter" as he was saying "it's getting hotter." The Holy Spirit who appeared as tongues of fire on the first Pentecost again manifested himself as a consuming fire. Singing and speaking in tongues could be heard as we knelt there loving Jesus and being loved by him until 3 a.m. when the good sense of the chaplain and the nuns sent us to bed.

When Mary Ann got to her room, all she could do was worry about the next day's talk. "I had failed repeatedly before the weekend to find a worthwhile commentary on Acts 3. I had been terribly concerned about giving a good talk, wanting very much to impress my peer group and Paul. I had spent hours planning what I would wear, and had arrived at The Ark and the Dove with a carefully chosen dress in my suitcase, but almost no talk in my hand or head," she recalls.

"Even though I had just witnessed the Lord's glory, I didn't realize how able the Lord is. Since the others were speaking in tongues, I didn't realize I was even baptized; knowing so little, I didn't recognize the joy, fear of the Lord, love, and the quickly outlined talk as manifestations of the Holy Spirit." Patti Gallagher laid hands on Mary Ann, prayed for her, and then hung a note on the door saying "Jesus loves you!" With that Mary Ann fell asleep, and awakened the next morning, her first thought being, "Praise the Lord," and her second, "Oh my God—I have to give that talk."

"I told the Lord I was proud, but though I confessed it, it seemed to remain. I was thinking of how good I wanted to look for Paul and began to get dressed. The dress seemed to epitomize my concern for myself. Then I saw the clothes I had thrown into the suitcase four hours earlier, wrinkled slacks and a very wrinkled blouse. I said, 'Lord, I am proud inside; I can't seem to make that go away. I want to be different; I want to give that talk for you. When you look at me, Lord, know by these clothes that I don't want to be proud. The clothes are all I can change, Lord; you, please, change my spirit.'

"I dressed in the wrinkled clothes and, with only a few backward glances at the dress and heels, I met dressed-up friends and walked over to the big house with them for breakfast amid some curious looks. I knew the Lord's gaze was upon me, too, and my clothes were a constant plea for help."

As in the matter of the well, Mary Ann had little faith in the matter of the talk. Her knees knocked both under the breakfast table and under the speaker's table. "As my brothers and sisters sang 'Come, Holy Ghost,' however, he did, sovereignly. I knew what it means to be saved by grace! The cold, clammy fear faded; I felt warm all over and began to speak wisdom that was not mine."

The talk was interrupted several times by prayer and praise, and was followed by a conspicuously long period of applause. "That applause that I had so greatly desired no longer gratified anything inside. It could only touch off in me praise for my Father. I knew he did it. I opened my mouth to thank him while the applause (for him) continued; I began speaking in tongues, realizing that I, too, was a part of what God was doing."

God Breaks In 19

It was so good of Jesus to give Mary Ann and me such similar experiences of him, down to the detail of learning to depend on him for our talks. The Lord was preparing us for our life with him together. After I returned to New York, the Lord continued to teach us separately things that later he would fit together into one ministry. I was led to the Reverend Harald Bredesen, who immediately took an interest in my story of the "Duquesne Weekend." Harald had me sharing my testimony everywhere he could. It was quite a new experience, standing in front of large groups of Protestants telling them what God was doing in the Catholic Church. The greatest surprise was the enthusiasm with which they received the news.

Meanwhile, Mary Ann was learning about charismatic prayer meetings and community with the other students in Pittsburgh. We shared our experiences daily by letter, and when we were married in June of 1967, the Lord manifested the first fruits of our experiences. For three months, the Lord gave us the Kingdom experience of living in community with Harald and his family, six students from Duquesne, and a number of Spirit-filled Protestants.

There we experienced on a communal level what the Lord was desiring to do in us as individuals as he set about *"breaking down the dividing wall of hostility . . . that he might create one new man in place of the two by reconciling us both to God in one Body through the cross"* as we both came to have *"access in one Spirit to the Father"* (Ephesians 2:14-18). As we witnessed our Protestant brothers and sisters so willingly laying down their lives for us, giving up even their style of praying if it offended us, we learned the depth of love the Spirit gives through

Jesus' Body. We, too, learned to love the total Body of Christ as they loved us.

In September of 1969 the Lord directed us to Erie where he opened a teaching position for me at Gannon College. He was true to his word that he would raise up a community here. What began with Mary Ann and me praying together soon grew, and now 250 people gather each week at Villa Maria College to worship him.

Even here the Lord continues to remind us of our dependence on him. Our second child was born only through his grace and the prayers of his body. Mary Ann was not supposed to be able to conceive, or carry if she did conceive, or deliver the baby if she did carry. In the midst of the gloomy medical expectations, Dorothy (meaning "Gift of God") Joy was born.

To this day, as we continue our walk with him, the Lord continues to show us the depth of the love he first showed us when he called us to and for himself six years ago.

Before Duquesne: Sources of the Renewal

By James B. Manney

In the months following the retreat at Duquesne University a group of young men working in campus apostolate in Lansing, Michigan, and Notre Dame, Indiana, received some remarkable and disturbing letters from their friend, Ralph Keifer. Some had known Keifer while they were all students at the University of Notre Dame and they had remained in touch with him after he went to Duquesne to teach theology in 1965. They knew him as a sober, sophisticated lay theologian with a deep love for the Church and a commitment to its service.

These letters were extraordinary coming from such a balanced man, for they excitedly announced a spiritual transformation with little precedent in historic Catholicism. He and about 25 other faculty and students had received a baptism of the Spirit, he said, and it had altered their lives. In one such letter, he said: "We have found ourselves on a plane of Christian life all the textbooks call normal and all practice and expectation seem to deny. Our faith has come alive, our believing has become a kind of knowing. Suddenly, the world of the supernatural has become more real than the natural. In brief,

Jesus Christ is a real person to us, a real living person who is our Lord and who is active in our lives. (Cf. the New Testament and read it as though it were literally true *now,* every word, every line.) Prayer and the sacraments have become truly our daily bread instead of practices which we recognize as 'good for us.' A love of the Scriptures, a love of the Church I never thought possible, a transformation of our relationships with others, a need and a power to witness beyond all expectation, have all become part of our lives."

The letter was not entirely unexpected. Some of the men in Michigan and Indiana knew that Keifer and William Storey, his friend and a Church historian at Duquesne, were investigating the baptism of the Spirit. Two books—*They Speak with Other Tongues* by John Sherrill and *The Cross and the Switchblade* by David Wilkerson had aroused their mutual curiosity. Some of them shared Keifer and Storey's conviction that contemporary Church renewal must restore the power of the early Church if it was to succeed.

When Keifer's initial letter arrived, his friends were surprised, but they were also prepared to look into it. After some hesitation and investigation of their own, most of them sought and received the baptism of the Spirit themselves. They included Steve Clark and Ralph Martin, workers on the staff of St. John's Student Parish at Michigan State University in East Lansing and staff members of the National Secretariat of the Cursillo Movement; George Martin (no relation to Ralph), working in adult education for the diocese of Lansing; his colleague Jim Rauner; Paul DeCelles, professor of physics at

Before Duquesne: Sources of the Renewal 23

Notre Dame; and a group of teachers and students at Notre Dame which included Kevin and Dorothy Ranaghan, Bert Ghezzi, Jim Cavnar, Gerry Rauch, and Kerry Koller.

These men, and others who soon joined them, have deeply influenced the development of the charismatic renewal. Other groups and individuals have had considerable impact, but these men are particularly responsible for developing the organizational structure and support services which have made it an effective and cohesive movement. They serve on or advise the Service Committee of the Catholic Charismatic Renewal which operates the Communication Center at Notre Dame. *New Covenant* magazine and Word of Life publishers in Ann Arbor, the newly opened International Communications Office, and the national and regional conferences which some 20,000 persons attended in 1972.

Through these services, and as prominent leaders of their own communities and prayer groups, these men have influenced the charismatic renewal in the same way that an earlier group of leaders shaped classical Pentecostalism in the first decades of the 20th century. The early Pentecostal leaders emerged from 19th-century holiness movements; they stressed holiness of personal life, taught a Wesleyan doctrine of post-conversion sanctification, based church structure on the priesthood of the faithful, and were quick to leave the established churches when non-Pentecostal Christians criticized them. The leaders of the Catholic charismatic renewal, on the other hand, were formed in movements which stressed renewal of the Church. They were trained to evangelize nominal Christians and to encourage them to make a deeper commitment to the Lord, to integrate this new commitment into a vital Christian community, and to form leaders who would draw others to Christ.

Although their backgrounds are varied, they shared at least two common interests before experiencing the baptism of the Spirit: a fervent concern for a fundamental renewal of the Church along evangelical and communitarian lines, and a high degree of theoretical agreement about the right shape and strategy for this renewal. All were deeply influenced by the Cursillo Movement; they all shared an intense experience living and working together in a unique Christian community they formed at Notre Dame in 1964-66.

The Duquesne weekend was not an isolated event, a sudden eruption of Pentecostal fervor in the Church of Rome which spread through sheer uniqueness and force. We call it the beginning of the charismatic renewal because the baptism of the Spirit first experienced there quickly spread to these men. It animated the renewal movement they had long been advocating.

The men who formed around the Cursillo Movement at Notre Dame in the mid-1960's came from varied backgrounds with some significant common threads. They were all highly educated intellectuals who achieved considerable academic distinction. Most professed a Catholicism of an orthodox type. They were concerned about liturgical and personal spiritual renewal, although several had acquired progressive theological educations and most had worked in social-action and civil-rights movements. Steve Clark and Dr. William Storey, a leader of the Duquesne group who later came to Notre Dame,

Before Duquesne: Sources of the Renewal 25

were converts. They had the convert's appreciation for a Church examined and entered as an adult. George Martin's first conversion experience occurred at the age of 18 while he was making an abbreviated three-day version of St. Ignatius's Spiritual Exercises. After graduation from college, he joined the national staff of the social-action-oriented Young Christian Students, then came to Notre Dame to study philosophy because he felt YCS's theoretical underpinning was vague. He did his doctoral thesis on Kierkegaard, as did Ralph Johnson, another leader of the group.

Bert Ghezzi had been drawn into renewal activity while an undergraduate at Duquesne and became the first president of the Chi Rho Society, the group which later made the famous retreat. Chi Rho was active in local civil-rights movements in Pittsburgh and brought a number of progressive speakers to the campus, the theologian Hans Küng among them. Ghezzi was also concerned about a renewal in spiritual life and prayer generally. He brought these interests to Notre Dame when he enrolled as a graduate student in 1963.

There were some exceptions to this pattern. One was Ralph Martin, a brilliant philosophy student (specialty: Nietzsche) and crusading campus editor, who had no concern for the Church at all. By early 1964, he finally felt free from the repressions of his Catholic upbringing, and had gained a reputation as an argumentative atheist around campus. The first time Martin met Steve Clark, they got into an argument about Christianity in a student restaurant near campus.

Martin's conversion occurred suddenly and dramatically during the second Cursillo at Notre Dame. It was a conversion so dramatic that Bert Ghezzi, who was there, at first doubted its authenticity. "I never saw such a complete U-turn in my life," Ghezzi says. "I didn't believe such things were possible." For his part, Martin describes his conversion as a radical breakthrough to existential truth, an awareness of his sinfulness and his full, gratuitous salvation in Jesus Christ. "I saw that I had arranged my search for truth in such a way that I would never find it. As soon as I got close to something that might be true—like Christ—I decided to try another direction."

A leader of the Notre Dame group was Steve Clark, a New Yorker, who had become a Catholic by 1960 while an undergraduate at Yale University. Clark was the organizer, theoretician, and, to many, the model during his two years as a graduate student in the philosophy department. The search for the elusive sources of the evangelical-communitarian Catholic Christianity which have congealed in the charismatic renewal may profitably begin with Clark. Says Bert Ghezzi: "Steve Clark came to Notre Dame with an amazing vision of pastoral renewal. I don't know where it all came from."

One important key to Clark's thinking is his experience of conversion to Catholicism. "I approach Christianity in an evangelical way because becoming a Christian made a big difference in my life and I wanted to share it with others," he says. "I knew that Christianity was true and I could see that other people who were in trouble needed it. My first big distress came when I discovered that other Catholics at Yale didn't agree. Like many people raised as

Before Duquesne: Sources of the Renewal 27

Christians, they tended to feel that everyone was basically a Christian and that all that was needed was an improvement in society's moral tone. I didn't see things that way at all."

Clark noticed another tendency from the beginning: Catholics at Yale who associated with each other and joined Newman activities usually grew in faith and holiness. Those who took an individualistic stance and avoided specifically Christian involvements usually had a rough time spiritually and often fell away from the Church. This seemingly self-evident observation, which is surely true of any movement or religion, was the pragmatic basis for Clark's vision of the Christian community. A person will grow as a Christian if he is among a group of Christians who take a lively concern for each other's well-being. Left alone, his spiritual prognosis is gloomy. In a loose Christian environment—the average parish, for example—the Christian is more likely to be shaped by the dominant secular environment around him.

Over the years, this stress on the importance of community became much more than a principle of good pastoral practice. It became the keystone of an audacious strategy aimed at the radical Christian transformation of whole environments. In 1966, Clark and Ralph Martin, then on the staff of St. John's Student Parish at Michigan State University, proposed the creation of a network of small and large community groupings to make the secular university an environment where Christians would flourish. The difference between what they proposed to do and what frustrated priests thought was possible is spelled out in this statement of goals for MSU:

It is not enough to see the problems... We believe that it is possible to handle *all* the problems effectively... Most priests and lay workers are resigned to the fact that they are not going to do very much to "stem the tide." They therefore have resolved to do the best they can, to make some contribution. But they have not actually decided to "win," that is, to cope successfully with the whole situation, perhaps because they do not know how. We feel that this is the initial mistake that is made... The problems can be effectively handled, and it is necessary to begin by aiming consciously to solve them all.

If the seeds of this vision can be found in Clark's first weeks and months as a Christian, his later apostolic experiences nourished and refined them. While still an undergraduate, he joined a student social-action group and spent two summers working on projects in Mexico and Latin America. There, he saw that the most successful attempts at renewal in an area where the Church was under great pressure involved a restoration of the primitive Christian community described in the Acts of the Apostles. After graduation from Yale, he took a Fulbright Scholarship and spent a year studying theology at the University of Freiburg in Germany. Vatican II was underway in Rome at the time, and Clark welcomed the new pastoral ideas and approaches then emerging. He found the Church's traditional pastoral attitudes inadequate and personally frustrating to work with. Yet the progressive styles had their own limitations and dangers. "I was clearly a pre-Vatican II liberal," he says, "but one with faith."

By the time he returned to the United States, he

was uneasy about the state of the Church. He was eager to develop a strategy for fundamental renewal, test it with others and put it into practice. "I guess my travels and background gave me a special view of things," he says. "When I got back to America, I felt the Church was probably in the first stages of a nervous breakdown. Nothing really worked. There were only piecemeal solutions instead of effective plans. The edifice was starting to crumble."

The religious situation at the University of Notre Dame in 1963 was complex and gloomy. Some fresh progressive currents were there, but Clark, who had expected the premier American Catholic University to be in the vanguard of renewal, was shocked to discover that the dominant trend was toward spiritual collapse. Loyalty to the Church was ending, and students mocked and resented the traditional Catholicism that still ruled. Many students exhibited a Joycean psychology in their attitude toward the Church: a snobbish intellectual rejection masking an almost pathological fascination with Catholic forms, rituals, and taboos. Almost the only teacher at Notre Dame who was making an effort to affect students' faith strongly was an English professor named Frank O'Malley. However, his "Catholic Renaissance" approach consisted entirely of an intellectual appreciation of significant Catholic writers. It was pastorally ineffective.

In a paper, Clark and George Martin identified another problem at Notre Dame. They called it "renewal confusion." They wrote: "A person looks at Christianity as he knows it and finds it bewildering. He listens to a variety of opinions and finds them conflicting or confusing. Then he instinctively takes the part of Christianity that makes sense to him and says that this part *is* Christianity. . . All of these distortions of Christianity . . . involve a turning away from the reality of God and his love."

Almost as soon as he moved into an apartment near the campus, Clark left again, this time to make a Cursillo in East Chicago, Indiana. He saw immediately that this movement, still very new in the United States, was a practical instrument to bring about the changes he thought were desperately needed. The Cursillo offered the evangelical focus, communitarian emphasis, and carefully structured technique necessary for a fundamental renewal. When Clark started to work on Cursillos at Notre Dame, he found others who felt the same way. Bert Ghezzi, George Martin, and Phil O'Mara made the first Cursillo in South Bend in December, 1963. Ralph Martin and Paul DeCelles made the second. As the Cursillos unfolded, the Christian community at Notre Dame came into being.

The Cursillo Movement is a rarity in Church history: a unique approach to the formation of Christians, based on a fresh analysis of pastoral realities, devised by a group of prayerful, dedicated men in an almost entirely original manner. The Movement originated in the improbable locale of post-World War II Fascist Spain among a group of clerics and lay intellectuals. The founders were Juan Hervas, a Catholic bishop, Eduardo Bonnin, a psychologist and heir to an export-import fortune, and Juan Capo, a theologian. They were influenced by progressive European thinkers such as Cardinal Suenens, Abbé Michonneau, and Yves Congar, yet the strategy they devised was a new approach. The

Before Duquesne: Sources of the Renewal 31

first Cursillo was offered in 1949, around the time that Billy Graham and Oral Roberts began their ministries in the United States.

The founders of the Cursillo felt that the actual state of the Church in the modern world was so grave that men "had no choice except either to abandon Christianity or to live fully a militant and conquering Christianity." The mass of men were no longer Christian in the sense that Christianity was the operative ideal in their daily lives. The compromising and routine position of the Christian Church was doomed, "since it will inevitably be swept away by the intellectual and moral currents of a de-Christianized world and by the general state of minds and customs." The urgent work of the Church was to teach Christians to live their Christian lives intensely, by restoring a fundamental understanding of what it means to be a Christian.

They found their model for a restored Christianity in the New Testament. The primitive Church was characterized by love and unity, a powerful apostolate, common life. The Church was a visible sign to the heathen world and conquered it by a radical personal and social transformation. In his book *Questions and Problems* Bishop Hervas said the re-Christianization of the world was possible if the Church returned to the same sources of life which animated the early Christians. He named these sources as "the life of grace truly lived, centered in the adorable person of Jesus, in daily contact with Him, as with a living Person . . . Life in the Presence of the Most Holy Trinity as sons of the Father, brothers of Christ, temples of the Holy Spirit, heirs of everlasting happiness and glory . . . By the spectacle of the early Christians' lives and their ardent zeal, they continued their evangelization and transformed the world."

The renewal the Cursillo founders foresaw was essentially a new Pentecost. Eduardo Bonnin said this explicitly in his analysis of the Church's failure:

Christianity, afterwards as before, is essentially an outpouring of the Holy Spirit. It is essentially the miracle of Pentecost. And where you cannot see the outpouring of the Spirit, there the "Counselor" has not passed. There you might find men who believe in the Father, and, because of an ingenious egocentricity, are convinced about a practice of Christianity when they go to beg gifts from the Father. You might also have men who believe in the "Word" and in the sense of all the things which have been revealed in Him. Inspired by their newly acquired ideal of Him, these men try to model their lives on His with a laborious fidelity. They are industrious men of moral probity. But they are not men of the Holy Spirit of overflowing love; they are not men with flashing eyes. For them, Pentecost has not yet come.

In more theological language, Bishop Hervas said that "it is necessary not only 'to receive Christ,' but also 'to receive the Holy Spirit,' and to submit to his influence, in order to be 'one in Jesus Christ.'"

When Steve Clark first heard about the Cursillos, this charismatic, Pentecostal element was evident. He was attending an orientation session on Latin America at the Maryknoll headquarters in Ossining, New York, before leaving for apostolic work in Mexico. At lunch, a Maryknoll priest told him about a Cursillo he had observed in Mexico City. Says Clark, "He described it in Pentecostal terms:

men were filled with the Holy Spirit and became strong, dedicated apostles. Later I met some Mexican students who were cursillistas. They impressed me as being stronger Christians than the Americans I was with. I remembered the Cursillo as something that would probably be good for Americans too."

The strategy of the Cursillo founders was to form a body of mature Christian men who would be able to influence their environments, reach out and draw others to Christ, and thereby create a movement which would ultimately restore the Church. The founders' method was to draw men to an intense, compelling vision of the Christian ideal during a three-day weekend and then to sustain and nurture their faith through Christian community afterward. The three-day weekend was a comprehensive and highly structured presentation of a scriptural Christianity using a sophisticated understanding of group dynamics. Yet this was only the instrument to open men to the work of renewal. The whole strategy was aimed toward the formation of leaders, both in the choice of candidates before the weekend, and in the follow-up afterward.

The Cursillo Movement spread rapidly, at first in the Spanish-speaking world, then throughout the Church. In 1957, two Spanish jet pilots in training near Waco, Texas, conducted the first Cursillo in the United States. In 1961, the first English Cursillo was held in San Angelo, Texas, and the movement is now established in most American dioceses. Bishop Hervas played a leading role at Vatican II; he was a member of the Liturgical Commission, and his writings on the Cursillo strongly influenced certain Council documents.

However, the Cursillo was also very controversial and, in America at least, received criticism which people active in the charismatic renewal will find familiar. Many found the Cursillistas' zeal, dedication, and intense spiritual life suspect. Fr. George Montague, professor of Scripture at St. Mary's University in San Antonio, Texas, recalls telling a priest friend in New York that he was in town to give an address on the theology of the Cursillo Movement. "My friend said, 'that's too bad. There isn't any theology is there? It's all emotion, isn't it?'"

This remark is revealing, for it highlights one of the problems the movement encountered in the United States. The Cursillo Movement tended to be identified with the three-day weekend, a powerful and often shattering experience of the reality of Jesus. The follow-up part—Christian community—was less dramatic and much harder to sustain. Other problems centered around many liberal Catholics' distaste for the evangelical orientation of the movement. Bishop Hervas was very clear about the need to stress fundamentals. He wrote: **"The Cursillo offers a radical and basic solution of all man's problems . . . there is no direct and express treatment of the social, family, economic, or political questions and of their Christian solutions, but of fundamental Christianity, the basis that is the essential and radical principle of every human and Christian solution."** Nevertheless, some used the tool of the three-day weekend to promote non-Christian and partially Christian ideas. The hackneyed cliché, "find Christ in other people," first gained currency through the Cursillo Movement.

Among the most vocal opponents of these

Before Duquesne: Sources of the Renewal 35

trends in America were none other than Steve Clark and Ralph Martin. As staff members of the National Cursillo Secretariat, they gave dozens of leaders' workshops throughout the United States from 1965 to 1970. Their main purpose was to defend and develop the founders' original conception of an evangelical movement locating Christian life within community. They insisted that the Cursillo was a comprehensive renewal of fundamental Christianity, and that the basic task, as the founders properly claimed, was creation of a Christian environment.

The impact of this Cursillo experience on the development of the charismatic renewal has been decisive. From the beginning Clark, Martin, and the other leaders have hammered away at the need to integrate the experience of the baptism of the Spirit into the community where the Christian grows, receives healing and support, and draws others into the joyous life that he lives.

The haphazard, almost accidental Christian community which emerged at Notre Dame realized the Cursillo founders' ideal. The men who comprised it were busy, often troubled, young graduate students who worked on Cursillos and worried about Church renewal in their spare time. They would drive 400 miles to attend a Cursillo closing one night, worry about the job market for Ph.D.s in philosophy the next. Their personal relationships were often tense as personalities and egos clashed. Yet the Lord was unmistakably at work. Through the life of this little community, a group of highly educated Catholics experienced a life together for the first time, refined a new strategy for renewal of the Church, and heard a call for radical commitment to Christian leadership.

Their pastoral development was solid and impressive. Soon after they began to work together, some of them realized that the Cursillos could not reach most college students effectively. The founders intended Cursillos to open mature men who were already recognized Christian leaders in their communities to a grand strategy of general Church renewal. On the other hand, college students usually experienced a variety of problems with basic Christian commitment. In an environment like Notre Dame, where tradition-minded complacency coexisted with powerful secularizing forces, the content of the "average" student's faith could neither be guessed nor assumed.

A group of the early cursillistas decided to write an entirely new weekend for college students incorporating elements of the Cursillo and some materials George Martin had developed while on the national staff of the Young Christian Students. Martin and Clark wrote the first draft. Fr. Charles Harris, C.S.C., and Jim Cavnar were among those who did the revision. The weekend was originally called the Study Weekend, but was renamed the Antioch Weekend after some of the leaders, while praying for a new name, asked the Lord for direction from Scripture. One of them opened to Acts 11:26 which tells about the founding of the Church at Antioch. "It was at Antioch that the disciples were first called 'Christians,'" the verse concludes.

The Antioch Weekend is notable for its insight into student psychology. Consider this characterization of the student intellectual's attitude: "(Students) will be developing a kind of scepticism about whatever is said to them, a pride in their own minds, and a self-sufficiency. They will each have the habit of taking everything that is said in a detached way as something 'out there,' something to be contemplated and understood, something to be discussed and argued about, but probably not something they have to appropriate." To students imbued with the intellectual ideal, the Antioch Weekend presented the Christian ideal, "a call to give up all previous ideals for the sole ideal of following Christ and of serving him." The Antioch Weekend was the cornerstone in a pastoral plan to restore Christianity to a healthy place in the university's life.

The plan was never implemented. Spiritual life at Notre Dame continued to decline. Peter Collins, who later conducted highly successful Antioch Weekends at the University of Colorado, thinks the official Catholicism of the university rendered most undergraduates impervious to the need for renewal. "Most of them were still in the womb," he says. "They didn't experience tension between their faith and the secular world, and they weren't particularly looking for answers in their lives. Things have changed since, but Notre Dam then wasn't a promising situation for evangelism."

Yet the small community's vigorous life attracted many, if only by contrast to the prevailing complacency. Frank Amalfitano, a graduate student in philosophy at the time, remembers that hundreds of students would drop by the weekly Cursillo Mass, curious to see a liturgy which communicated a sense of worship. After the Mass, cursillistas and hangers-on would eat together in tables commandeered in one corner of the university's public cafeteria. It was a casual community life, dominated by the prevailing student life style. People saw each other frequently, crossed paths in the library and cafeteria, or went out for a beer together. Yet commitments went deeper. Members of the group increasingly took serious responsibility for each other's spiritual welfare. They tackled some serious personal problems as well.

The cursillistas were creative and wide-ranging. To list their activities is to recall the heady optimism of the post-Vatican II, pre-Vietnam Church. Kevin and Dorothy Ranaghan became involved in the group partly because one of its emphases was on liturgical renewal. Bert Ghezzi helped organize a graduate students' Sunday liturgy: Fr. Edward O'Connor of the theology faculty usually celebrated the Mass and delivered the homily. Ghezzi, Ranaghan, and others also organized experimental Eucharists, vespers, and other liturgically progressive events. Richard Giloth was the leader of the cursillistas' social-action efforts. Several members of the group participated in Martin Luther King's march in Selma, Alabama, and many others were involved in local civil-rights projects. A number were also active in efforts to loosen the restrictions on student life at Notre Dame and at the adjoining St. Mary's College, an all-girl school.

The most novel of these developments was a growing interest in spontaneous prayer meetings. A desire for shared, spontaneous prayer first emerged among several of the Cursillo leaders who felt that their common life should grow deeper than their regular business and fellowship meetings allowed. They began to meet in Phil O'Mara's small apartment over the university art gallery, much to the irritation

Before Duquesne: Sources of the Renewal 39

of O'Mara's then-unconverted roommate, Ralph Martin. Soon the meetings attracted a heterogeneous crowd of nearly 50 persons, including priests and nuns, Protestants and Catholics, men and women, cursillistas and non-cursillistas. Their sharing and prayer was often quite formal; the spontaneous prayer was typically offered by one person at a time. Yet many felt the meetings were a breakthrough of some kind and, when circumstances permitted, the formality was overcome. One evening, in 1965, there was an instance of glossalalia. It was stopped by the leader of the meeting, who did not understand it.

Ultimately, God's work among these men involved a break with the academic environment which nurtured them. They were influenced by the Cursillo founders' conviction that a fundamental renewal of the Church would succeed only if a group of men dedicated themselves to it as their primary apostolate. One of the most influential books among them was *Dedication and Leadership* by Douglas Hyde, a British Communist who abandoned the Party for Christianity. Hyde found his model for the Christian leader in the Communist Party worker, a man so dedicated that he would eat and sleep so he could live to work for the Party, and whose first thought in the morning was joy at the prospect of doing something to build Communism that day.

Steve Clark and Ralph Martin eventually took the boldest step. During the Christmas holidays in 1965, the two met at Martin's parents' home in Teaneck, New Jersey, and agreed to spend the summer together at Mount Savior Monastery in Elmira, New York. While there, they felt the Lord was leading them to leave graduate school and make themselves more available for direct Christian work. Clark had remained at Notre Dame while Martin had begun work on a philosophy doctorate at Princeton University. After they made their decision, they were invited to give the opening and closing talks at the National Cursillo Convention in Kansas City. Subsequently, they joined the staffs of both St. John's Student Parish at Michigan State University and the National Secretariat of the Cursillo, also located in East Lansing.

The other men at Notre Dame struggled with the questions of careers and commitments as they searched for ways to serve the Lord adequately. Some entered the seminary, others joined lay apostolic groups; many completed their degrees and became college teachers.

Many of them emerged from their experiences at Notre Dame with commitments to serve the Lord in a direct way. George Martin is now director of religious education for the Catholic diocese of Oklahoma City-Tulsa. One of his major projects is to oversee the integration of Catholic schools in both cities. Bert Ghezzi is a philosophy professor at Grand Valley College in Michigan and chairman of the Service Committee of the Catholic Charismatic Renewal. Kevin Ranaghan is executive director of the Apostolic Institute in Mishawaka, Indiana, an organization which trains laymen for the diaconate. William Storey is professor of Church history at Notre Dame and a prominent liturgist. Kerry Koller teaches philosophy at the University of San Francisco and is one of the leaders of the charismatic renewal on the West Coast. Phil O'Mara teaches English

Before Duquesne: Sources of the Renewal 41

at Tougaloo College in Mississippi, a predominately black school, and is a leader of the charismatic renewal in the South. Ralph Keifer is executive director of the English-speaking section of the International Liturgical Commission. He is charged with preparing definitive English texts of missals, Mass texts, and other liturgical materials.

While they were students at Notre Dame, no one knew exactly what their experiences and commitments amounted to. Today we can see God breaking through. Miraculous events—healing, discernment of spirits, answered prayer—accompanied the Cursillos they ran. Most of them had personal encounters with Jesus during this time at least as intense as their later experiences with the baptism of the Spirit. By February, 1967, they realized, clearly or dimly, that God had knit them together for a purpose.

Perhaps George Martin sums up the meaning of these early days most accurately. He calls them simply "incredible grace-filled times."

A Woman and the Pope

By Fr. Val Gaudet

When Catholics began to enter into pentecostal spirituality, many people claimed that it was a providential answer to the prayer of Pope John XXIII asking the Holy Spirit to renew the wonders of Pentecost in today's Church. We can reasonably imagine that Pope John had some source of inspiration for his idea of a new Pentecost. It is interesting to note that the first person to be beatified by Pope John XXIII, Sister Elena Guerra, was a forerunner of today's charismatic renewal in the Catholic Church.

Elena Guerra, foundress of the Oblate Sisters of the Holy Spirit, was born in Lucca, Italy, on June 23, 1833. Elena broke away from her sheltered Christian upbringing at the age of 19 to work in the countryside of Lucca among the victims of cholera. She later dedicated herself to an intensive lay apostolate and was responsible for the foundation of a "Pious Union" that grew to 500 persons.

In 1872, with several close friends from this group, Elena experimented with a contemplative life centered on the Blessed Sacrament. She soon realized, however, that she and her companions were better suited for the active life. At that time, a fierce anticlericalism was rampant in Italy, especially in

A Woman and the Pope

schools. To fight this trend, Elena and her companions dedicated themselves to educating young middle-class girls from Lucca. They made their first vows as members of a diocesan community.

By the age of 50, Elena had matured as a noted educator and as a writer of devotional books. At this time, she felt inspired to write to Pope Leo XIII to urge him to renew the Church by means of a return to the Holy Spirit. She revealed her secret inspiration to only one "good person." "Preposterous!" was the answer. To do that would be pride." Thus, she kept her secret to herself, "waiting for better days and hoping that more light would come to her about this project."

It came eight years later. In 1893, a humble and devout woman from the kitchen staff, Erminia Giorgetti, felt she heard the Lord tell her to go to Mother Elena to reveal what the Lord wanted her to do. She told Elena that she must write to the Pope urging him to unite all the faithful in a continuous prayer to the Holy Spirit asking him to bring all hearts back to God. She also predicted that the Pope would soon write an encyclical on the Holy Spirit. Elena confided all this to her spiritual director, Bishop Giovanni Volpi, and with his help Elena Guerra was able to send 12 confidential letters to Leo XIII between 1895 and 1903.

In her first letter to Pope Leo, Elena called for renewed preaching on the Holy Spirit, "who is the one who forms the saints." In the last paragraph, she says that Satan's empire will be broken by the Spirit, and that God would "grant us a long-awaited renewal of the face of the earth." Pope Leo answered indirectly by publishing *Provida matris caritate,* in which he required the whole Church to celebrate a solemn novena to the Holy Spirit during the nine days before the feast of Pentecost. At this time, Elena began to form prayers groups, called "Permanent Cenacles," with their own structure and organization.

In a subsequent letter to the Pope, Elena expressed her desire to see the whole Church united in a continuous union of prayer in the same way that Mary and the Apostles were united in prayer in the Upper Room before Pentecost:

". . . (because) it is said that Your Holiness places great hopes in a religious effort of prayer to the divine Paraclete, I take on myself to insist that this union of prayer to the Holy Spirit is exactly that which I dare to ask, but even more, that it be a permanent union, organized and proclaimed for the whole Church."

She goes on to say that even though she calls this union a "Universal Cenacle," she does not care much about the name. The important thing is that "the faithful are being united in a unanimous and ceaseless prayer to the Divine Spirit," bringing unbelievers and dissenters back to Christ. She ends with the wish: "Oh, if ever the 'Come, Holy Spirit' which, since the Cenacle and after, the Church has not ceased repeating, could become as popular as the 'Hail Mary'!"

The prophetic mission of Elena to Leo XIII, and through him to the whole Church, was to see the Church transformed into a praying Cenacle. Her deepest desire was that the whole clergy be the first

A Woman and the Pope

to pray to the Holy Spirit, to "reform also their lives, since it is only the holy pastor who can render holy his flock."

In 1897, Bishop Volpi returned from a visit to Rome and told Sister Elena that the Pope had promised that he would do everything so that the Holy Spirit would be honored. Shortly afterward, the Pope published his encyclical *Divinum illud munus,* the richest doctrinal treatise about the Holy Spirit any pope produced. In this document, Pope Leo XIII explicitly recommends to all Christians a devotion to the Spirit. He sees in it the efficacious and indispensable means of a renewal for contemporary society, for the family, and for individuals: it will bring about Christian unity among churches and the conversion of the universe. Again he prescribed the celebration of the novena for Pentecost in all parish churches.

However, in September 1898, Elena could not hide her painful disillusion: "I do not know if the solicitude and application of the episcopacy have produced among the Christian people the good fruits that Your Holiness has reason to expect, but it seems to me, if these fruits were ripe, in some way or other they could have been seen." In this letter, she said that, while many bishops had thanked the Pope for his 1897 encyclical on the Spirit, it would have been better for them to obey.

In a letter dated October 15, 1900, she suggested that Pope Leo begin the first new year of the new century by singing "Come Holy Spirit," in the name of the whole Church, which he did. (It is an interesting coincidence that also on the night of December 31, 1900, in Topeka, Kansas, the Rev. Charles Parham prayed with Agnes Ozman to be baptized in the Holy Spirit—an occasion generally accepted as the beginning of the Pentecostal movement.)

Probably because Elena complained that bishops and priests showed little enthusiasm to implement *Divinum illud* in their dioceses and parishes, Leo XIII shortly thereafter sent a private letter to the bishops of the world, along with an extra copy of the encyclical. In this letter he deplored that many of the clergy had thought that the novena was to be held only for the year 1897. It ended by saying: "His Holiness nourishes the sure hope that the bishops and the clergy will respond, with God's help, in such a matter, with industry and alacrity."

When Leo XIII died, on July 20, 1903, Sr. Elena was 70 years old. She had written extensively about spreading the Good News and had sent her nuns as missionaries to distant countries. Her next 10 years were a time of trial and decline. She was deposed from her superiorship by the local bishop at the instigation of three younger sisters, and after five months of excruciating pain she died on Holy Saturday, April 11, 1914.

The prayer to the Holy Spirit for the success of the Vatican Council that John XXIII issued in September, 1959, ended: "Renew Thy wonders in this our day as by a new Pentecost." Pope John used the very same expression speaking to pilgrims from Lucca who came to Rome to attend Elena's beatification on April 26, 1959: "Her [Elena's] message is always relevant. We are all aware, in fact, of the need for a continued effusion of the Holy Spirit, as of a new Pentecost which will renew the face of the earth." Pope John repeated his call for a "new Pen-

A Woman and the Pope 47

tecost" on numerous occasions.

Today, as we see that the charismatic renewal has reached so many shores, we might infer that Elena's dream of a Universal Cenacle of prayer is finally being implemented. The triumph of the Holy Spirit for which Elena Guerra worked is, without doubt, the deepest objective of hundreds of prayer groups all over the world. These prayer groups are not the same as the ones formed by Elena Guerra and her nuns; yet, as she had hoped, they are substantially making of the Church a permanent Cenacle of praise and expectancy.

We can praise the Lord for spiritual leaders such as Elena Guerra, whom Pope John called "the Apostle of the Holy Spirit"; we also thank him for Pope John himself, the promoter of a new Pentecost in the Church. Pope Paul VI continues to promote this vision. As he said during a general audience in November, 1972, "The Church needs her perennial Pentecost: she needs fire in the heart, words on her lips, prophecy in her vision." Like Leo XIII, Elena Guerra, and Pope John, who all knew how difficult it is to surrender completely to the will of the Lord, Pope Paul has this moving appeal which he directs to all: "Living men, you, young people, and you consecrated souls, you, brothers in the priesthood, are you listening to us? This is what the Church needs; she needs the Holy Spirit: the Holy Spirit in us, in each of us, in all of us together, in us who are the Church!"

Moving On

By Cindy Conniff

International, dynamic, and growing steadily within all the Christian denominations, the charismatic renewal is one of the most surprising works of the Spirit in the 20th century. In an effort to estimate the dimensions of the neo-pentecostal movement, *New Covenant* conducted a survey among national leaders of the renewal in the various denominations. While the survey revealed a certain amount of information, it also indicated that in most churches the movement is just beginning to assume form and cohesion.

Historically, neo-pentecostalism is young. It stems primarily from two sources: the experience of charismata in 1901 at Bethel Bible School in Topeka, Kansas; and the Azuza Street revival in Los Angeles, California in 1906. In January 1901, a student at Charles Parham's Bethel Bible School received the baptism in the Holy Spirit, accompanied by the gift of speaking in tongues. After hearing Parham speak of this experience, William Seymour, a Holiness preacher, took the pentecostal doctrine to Los Angeles and there led the Azusa Street revival. From Azusa Street the movement spread rapidly in the United States and abroad. However, as members of the traditional denominations tried to introduce the pentecostal experience into their churches they were either forced out of the congregations or simply left in discouragement. As Vinson Synan points out, "From 1895 to 1925, 38 distinctively pentecostal denominations began in the United States alone, not to mention thousands of rural 'brush arbor' and urban 'storefront' independent congregations" (*New Covenant,* May 1973). Today there are an estimated 13-15 million classical pentecosts in the world. Not only are they the largest Protestant denominations in Italy, Portugal, Brazil, Argentina, Puerto Rico, and Chile, but in North America they are growing from 9-15 times faster than the other mainline churches (*New Covenant,* May 1972).

In 1960 the second stream of pentecostalism began, this time within a traditional Protestant church. The Rev. Dennis Bennett, rector of St. Mark's Episcopal Church in Van Nuys, California, received the baptism in the Spirit while praying with friends. Several months later during Sunday services, Bennett told his congregation about the charismatic renewal that he and about 70 of his parishioners were experiencing. All went well until the end of the second service when the assistant "snatched off his vestments, threw them on the altar and stalked out of the church crying, 'I can no longer work with that man'" *(Nine O'Clock in the Morning).* Bennett resigned his position, and shortly afterward the Bishop of Olympia, Washington, invited him to assume the pastorate of St. Luke's Church. ". . . And bring the fire with you," the bishop told him.

Following this initial outpouring of the Spirit in the Episcopal Church, the neo-pentecostal movement spread within traditional Protestantism. In August, 1961, the Rev. Larry Christenson, a pastor within the American Lutheran Church Synod, received the baptism in the Spirit. He invited about 60 Lutheran pastors to hear David du Plessis speak, and the movement began to take hold in Southern California. Although Christenson encountered some opposition within both his congregation and synod, they did not accept his offer to resign.

Throughout the 1960s, Presbyterians, American Baptists, and Methodists all saw the beginnings of charismatic renewal within their denominations. The attitudes of church leaders ranged from hostility to indifference, with only a few expressing interest or support. Misunderstanding or fear of the charismatic experience resulted in actions such as that taken against a Presbyterian minister in Oklahoma. After a struggle within his church, the local presbytery (a regional governing body) removed him from his pastorate. Finally, he became a layman, and continued serving the renewal within the Presbyterian Church. In all denominations, despite official resistance, the movement gained ground.

In 1967 the third stream of the charismatic renewal emerged when a group of Roman Catholic faculty members at Duquesne University in Pittsburgh received the baptism in the Spirit. These laymen had been praying and talking together for several months trying to determine what was missing in their individual Christian lives. Eventually they attended a charismatic prayer meeting in the area. Two of them returned the following week and received the baptism in the Spirit. They in turn prayed with the others who had been unable to attend and by February, 1967, all of them had received this infilling of the Spirit. Shortly thereafter the movement

Moving On 51

spread among about 30 Duquesne students and outward to faculty and students at Notre Dame University in Indiana. From that small core group, the charismatic renewal began to penetrate the Catholic Church.

ATTITUDE OF THE HIERARCHY

The *New Covenant* questionnaire tried to assess the attitude of the hierarchy toward the renewal.

Presbyterian

"We are convinced that the work of the Holy Spirit is a neglected area of our thinking and practice. It is very possible that the Holy Spirit is preparing a renewal of our church that may come in surprising ways and through unexpected channels" (Report of the Special Committee on the Work of the Holy Spirit, 1970). That report, adopted by the General Assembly of the United Presbyterian Church in the United States of America, indicates the beginning of a more positive attitude toward the renewal. Similarly, in 1971 the Presbyterian Church in the United States adopted a generally positive "Report on the Person and Work of the Holy Spirit." Since these studies serve mainly as reference works and pastoral guidelines, their acceptance on a practical level varies according to the disposition of the individual minister. And in fact a large number of synod executives, presbytery leaders, and ministers have not paid much attention to the renewal. However, more and more are becoming interested and even open to the movement.

Lutheran

Within the American Lutheran Church Synod,

the attitudes of the bishops vary; some are quite open while others remain opposed. The ALC members of the Lutheran Coordinating Committee have established good contact and an open door of communication with their synod president, Dr. David Preus. In 1963 the ALC conducted a synod-level study that was critical of the renewal in certain areas. However, it did not prohibit its spread. Since that time the movement has gained momentum. In light of that growth, in 1973 the ALC Council of Bishops approved a set of guidelines for those having pastoral responsibility within the renewal among Lutherans. In essence, the guidelines encourage ministers to take a positive, supportive attitude toward those involved.

In July, 1974, the Lutheran Church of America submitted a report on the charismatic renewal to its annual convention. The study, which at this writing is for information only and not necessarily for formal adoption, is primarily pastoral in design. Essentially it is a very positive statement encouraging mutual support and respect among LCA officials, pastors, and congregations as they attempt to understand and respond to the renewal.

The bishops within the Missouri Synod, the more conservative of the three synods, vary from negative to interested. In January, 1972, the synod issued a report on "The Charismatic Renewal and the Lutheran Church." The study is ambiguous, but as one member of the synod noted, "in some ways this has kept the Spirit free to move."

Episcopalian

In relation to the charismatic renewal, the Episcopalian bishops have not issued any statements as an official body. However some bishops, such as William Frey of the diocese of Colorado, have become either personally involved or supportive. In general they are becoming less guarded and more open to the movement.

Baptist

The American Baptist Charismatic Fellowship reports that they have a very good relationship with their national headquarters. In fact, in March of 1974 the director of the American Baptist division of communication spent a weekend at a charismatic Baptist church in California. He then wrote a favorable article, "An Experience of Joy" for *The American Baptist,* the denomination's national magazine. Generally the regional executive ministers range in attitude from favorable and supportive to cautious and negative.

Methodist and Orthodox

Neither the Orthodox nor the Methodist Churches have issued official statements regarding the renewal in their churches. However one neo-pentecostal leader of the Methodists estimates that 70-75 percent of the bishops are interested; 10-15 percent are tolerant; 5-10 percent are very favorable; and 5-10 percent are opposed to the movement.

Roman Catholic

In November, 1969, the National Conference of Catholic Bishops issued a report on the renewal in the Catholic Church. Noting that "theologically the movement has legitimate reasons for existence," the bishops stated that it should "not be inhibited but allowed to develop" (*New Covenant*, September 1971). In 1972 another report was sent to the bishops, based on a survey taken among them earlier that year. This genuinely positive report led Bishop McKinney to estimate that "90 percent of the bishops have the impression that the charismatic renewal is a good thing in the church" (*New Covenant*, June 1972). Since then, leaders such as Cardinal Suenens of Malines, Belgium, and Archbishop Hayes of Halifax, Nova Scotia, have become personally involved in the movement. Cardinal Krol of Philadelphia, Cardinal Dearden of Detroit, and Cardinal Carberry of St. Louis all recently celebrated liturgies for the charismatic prayer groups in their diocese. Also, many bishops have asked leaders in the renewal to act as liaisons between the bishops and charismatic communities in their diocese. And nearly every American cardinal has sent letters to the priests in his archdiocese urging them to provide support and guidance for those involved.

In 1971, the Vatican entered a five-year dialogue on pentecostalism with leaders of the Pentecostal and neo-pentecostal movement. The dialogue centers on the theological and experiential aspects of the renewal, and will result in a report intended for wide distribution. The meetings are not immediately concerned with "the relationship of Catholic pentecostals to the Roman Catholic Church." Rather, the members hope "to share in the reality of the mystery of Christ and the Church, to build a united Christian testimony, and to indicate in what manner the sharing of truth makes it possible for us to grow together" (*New Covenant*, January 1972).

In October, 1973, Pope Paul held a special audience with 13 participants of the International Leaders Conference in Rome. The Pope spoke encouragingly of the renewal, noting certain common aspects that appear among those involved: "the taste for deep prayer, personal and in groups; a return to contemplation and an emphasizing of praise of God, the desire to devote oneself completely to Christ, a great availability for the calls of the Holy Spirit, more assiduous reading of Scripture, the will to make a contribution to the service of the Church" (*New Covenant,* December 1973).

In considering the last 10 years, the leaders who responded to the survey noted a steady growth and acceptance of the renewal within all the denominations. In some churches the movement has spread against considerable hierarchical opposition; in others, such as the Roman Catholic Church, the leaders have supported and encouraged it. In the future, the respondants agreed, a greater attempt must be made to work closely with the hierarchy.

Catholic Charismatic Renewal: The First Seven Years

By Kevin Ranaghan

I would like to reflect with you on the lessons of our experience over the last seven years in the charismatic renewal. I would also like to discuss what we have learned through practical experience about some of the basic pastoral problems within the charismatic renewal.

First, let me explain to you what I felt the Lord saying to us last night. The Lord assured us that he has his hand stretched out over us and over every country, diocese, and parish in his Church throughout the world. I feel the Lord wants us to make a real assent of faith to that. I believe the Lord is telling us that his Spirit is fully in the Church: in all those who bear the name Christian, in all those who have been baptized into his body. I believe that he wills now to bring this Spirit fully alive all over the world, in every place, in every heart.

And he calls us today to acknowledge that this renewal is *his* work and that it goes completely beyond our capabilities. The Lord wants to tell us that we must decide to be pliable in his hands, that we must be his instruments. He has not called us together to be leaders of a movement we ourselves are constructing. God himself will lead his people. He asks us simply to be bearers of his word and his love.

I feel the Lord calling all of us to a new and deeper sense of personal repentance. I feel that Jesus is calling us to go before him more broken-hearted than ever about our inadequacies and our sinfulness, and to lay ourselves again at the altar of his mercy so that we can be continually purified by his grace and become more pliable in his hands.

Renewal of Christian Initiation

I want to summarize some of the main ideas we have come to understand in the last seven years. I believe that there are three principal thrusts which form the center of the charismatic renewal. The first thrust is to personal conversion. In the charismatic renewal, the Lord is calling us all to enter into a deep personal relationship with him, to accept him personally as our Lord and our Savior, and to turn our lives over to him as completely as we can. Jesus is calling us to come to him and to accept his death and resurrection as the very center of our lives. In that process of conversion, the Lord is calling us to a life which is primarily one of worship and of praise.

The second thrust is toward what we might call radical discipleship. In the charismatic renewal, the Lord is speaking to each individual, "Not only accept me but follow me. Come in my footsteps, walk as I have walked. To give you confidence to do this, I want you to know for sure that my Spirit is within you. You have the power for worship, for love, and for service because I the Lord have planted my

Spirit deep within your heart." We have conceptualized this idea of radical discipleship around the notion of being baptized in the Holy Spirit. We have understood that we are all called to be continually plunged into and overwhelmed by the Spirit of the risen Lord, which gives us the power for Christian life.

Thirdly, the charismatic renewal is gathering us together. A chief result of people being baptized in the Spirit is that they spontaneously come together. They begin to share their lives, their prayer, and their work. Just as the experience of the first Pentecost led the three thousand to group together into community, there is also a communal aspect to the charismatic renewal. People all over the world feel that God is calling his people together into a life of corporate witness, corporate sharing; corporate service to the Church and the world.

We have come to explain these three thrusts—conversion, discipleship—and gathering together, as a renewal of our Christian initiation. What has been done for us objectively in baptism, in confirmation, and in our entrance into the eucharist community has become a real experience of power in the lives of individuals in the charismatic renewal.

Renewal of the Whole Church

Some basic convictions flow from these three basic thrusts. In the past seven years the Lord has been saying to and through us that a real, personal, conversational encounter with God in Christ is meant to be a normal and regular Christian experience. This kind of encounter with Jesus is for everybody and is available to all Christians. It is not just something limited to the few or the elect, to those who have been given some special mystical grace; it is meant to be a normal part of Christian life. We have said that the agent of this encounter is the indwelling and empowering of the Holy Spirit. And as a result of his work there is meant to be in the daily life of all Christians an existential encounter between Jesus and the individual believer. We are to be together with Jesus in a very personal way by the power of his Spirit.

We have also come to a new understanding of prayer, especially prayer of praise. We are not praising a Lord who is far away, but a Lord who is present in our personal lives. As we experience him as present we are somewhat overwhelmed, so we lift our hearts and voices to praise him. This new gift of praise has become, I think, the dominant theme of worship in the charismatic renewal. "Praise the Lord" is not just a slogan or a cliché, it's a way of life.

In the past seven years we have also all reassessed our personal concepts of Church renewal. Although we in the charismatic renewal have come from the far right, far left, and every position in between, a fairly unified view of Church renewal has emerged among us. On the one hand, we believe that the structural and liturgical reforms of Vatican II are truly of the Holy Spirit. Through these reforms, the Church is better equipped for its work in the world. At the same time, we see that the Holy Spirit is working to renew the hearts of his people. We see that the charismatic renewal is perhaps the Holy Spirit's most powerful agent for this work in the modern age. Also, a whole variety of new social institutions in the Church are emerging from the charismatic renewal—prayer meetings, the core group, the pastoral team, the service committee, the day of renewal, the covenant community. These structures may well replace those which are no longer adequate for what the Lord is doing today in his Church.

We have come to one principal conclusion: that the charismatic renewal is in the Church, for the Church, for the renewal of the Church. We reject the idea that the charismatic renewal is some kind of para-ecclesiastical structure; it is not a movement which exists for itself. It is not a grouping of the elect or the wonderful spiritual elite who have been called out of a carnal, dying structure. God has given us the grace to understand that he is not creating the Thursday night devotions to the Holy Spirit, that he is not founding a new kind of piety for those who enjoy that kind of thing. The Movement is not an end in itself, but its purpose is to spend itself for the renewal of the whole Church.

We who are on the first wave of the charismatic renewal in the Church must realize that we are called to lay down our lives in service. We are to do this so that what the Lord has shown us and what we have experienced of his grace may spread, take root, blossom, and grow throughout the Roman Catholic Church and in every other ecclesiastical communion. I think the Lord has shown us that he intends by his Spirit to renew the face of the earth from within the Church, the divinely established sacrament of his presence. The Lord has also shown us that we must be men and women deeply in love with the Church, servants who are loyal and obedient to the Church which is his very body.

That call to service of the Church includes the responsibility to relate rightly to our bishops and pastors. We need to learn how to properly respect their authority as shepherds, which the Lord has given them. At the same time we should be free to talk plainly and honestly with them about the truth and authenticity of what God has been doing among us in the charismatic renewal. We have to examine what it means to be obedient in a mature way.

Instruction

Now I'd like to speak about some of the problems we have all experienced from within the movement. My wife and I were renewed in the Holy Spirit on March 5, 1967, at the first Catholic charismatic prayer meeting in South Bend, Indiana. Within weeks, hundreds of people were coming to our weekly prayer meetings to look at this "strange thing." At the end of each prayer meeting we would ask, "Does anyone want to receive the baptism in the Holy Spirit?" Lots of hands would go up. Then we would spend one or two hours wandering helter-skelter around the room laying hands on anyone who was sitting down and praying with them that the Lord would baptize them in the Holy Spirit. Many of those people were renewed in the Spirit, but some were not. We discovered that there was a real precondition to being baptized in the Spirit: faith in Jesus Christ. We were so naïve at the beginning that we thought we could just pray with anybody.

Secondly, we discovered very quickly that people had a better chance of receiving a lasting empowering of the Holy Spirit if they were prepared to understand what they were asking for and what they were claiming in faith. Competent instruction does not deny or limit the sovereign action of God and of the Holy Spirit. It is simply a prudent and effective measure. As time went on in the early years, we moved from a 15-minute explanation at the end of a prayer meeting to a separate hour-long instruction after which we would pray with people. Then we instructed people one week and told them to return the next week to be prayed with. Finally, we began using a six or seven week Life in the Spirit seminar program. In the seminars, those who are most experienced in the Life in the Spirit present conversion and renewal in the Spirit in the overall context of a full Christian life.

Even now, we occasionally experience a problem of a too rapid, too free praying with people to be baptized in the Spirit. As a result, many people seem to be satisfied with what I would dare to call a shallow experience, which blooms for a while and then fades.

Need for Teaching

Besides initial instruction, we have also found a real need for teaching on a continuous basis in our prayer groups and communities. We discovered, to the shock of some, that not everyone who claimed to be exercising a spiritual gift was in fact doing so. We found that grace indeed builds upon nature and that unsound gifts often come from unsound persons. There is false prophecy and false teaching. Not everything that happens at a prayer meeting is automatically authentically of God. One of the ways the Lord has led us to respond to that is through the development of a real teaching ministry. I don't mean simply teaching of ideas, or a short course in dogmatic theology for 15 minutes every week. Rather, it is the kind of charismatic teaching where the teacher listens to what God is doing in the group and brings that truth into the light, integrating it with the best scriptural and theological traditions of the Church. In that way the people can have a mature understanding of what God is doing among them.

Ecumenism

We have also had to address some sticky ecumenical questions. From the beginning of the charismatic renewal, we have seen that God is pouring out his Spirit among his people regardless of denominational or ecclesiastical boundaries. While one can distinguish the charismatic renewal in the different churches, I do not see any essential difference between the outpouring of God's Spirit in the Roman Catholic Church and the outpouring of God's Spirit in any other denomination. There is one Lord and one Spirit; we all are sharing in significant unity the light of one Lord. We need to acknowledge very deeply in our hearts that this is one renewal.

At the same time, a number of ecumenical problems have emerged over the last seven years. We have had to consider how we relate to our brothers and sisters of other ecclesiastical communities. How do we pray together, how do we respect each other's differences both in doctrine and in practice? How do we simultaneously form our fellow Catholics in a way that is rooted in our own tradition? I present these as questions because the area of responsible ecumenism is one of great challenge in the charismatic renewal today.

Leadership

I'll make one last point. I think we have come

to learn that the charismatic renewal needs leadership. It seems to me that the turning point in the stability of any prayer group or community comes when they recognize and respect the gift of leadership among them. Sometimes people say, "We don't need any leadership, the Lord leads us as he wills: we have no leaders because the Spirit just moves freely without any kind of structure." This ignores the clear teaching of scripture that Christ leads his people through gifts and ministries that he gives to men and women in the body.

But leadership in the charismatic renewal can be filled with danger. Our whole experience of leading or being led has been formed by very worldly models. Leadership in the world is equated with authority, and authority is equated with domination and manipulation of people. We see this in politics, business, education, and it has not been unknown in the life of the Church. However, the leadership that is a gift of the Spirit is meant to flow from the cross of Jesus, for it was through his cross that he became fully anointed as Messiah and Lord. It is quite different from worldly leadership.

Yet none of us who have become leaders is free entirely from worldly ways; we experience emotions and drives within ourselves to come to the top, to lead; to run things according to our plans. We envy people whom the Lord raises up to leadership. "Why shouldn't it be me?" we say, "Don't I have better training, better background?" Yet where the gift of leadership doesn't really emerge, prayer groups wobble and begin to disintegrate. We and hundreds of other people are faced with the challenge of exercising the pastoral gifts of leadership and of teaching and counseling in the way of service rather than in the way of domination and control.

Finally, in the last seven years we have come to know that Jesus is Lord. While we grapple with the problems in the renewal, we have to remember that Jesus is Lord. After all, we are not the board of directors of General Motors, we are not running some great multi-national corporation. Let us be humble, repentant; open to the continual anointing of his Spirit and always acknowledge that he is our Lord, that he is our leader and that he himself is renewing his Church.

A Turning Point

By Mary Ann Jahr

Munching an apple, he sat cross-legged on the grass leaning against his backpack. The name tag stuck in his leather visor encircling his shoulder-length hair read, "Mel Balk. Jesus is Lord. I love you." "I've been jumping from Jesus group to Jesus group," proclaimed the 24-year-old, "but something was always missing. This weekend I met the Holy Spirit . . . I'm not waiting anymore. I'm so happy."

After finishing their sausage and eggs, Teri and Karl Young from Philadelphia paused at the long cafeteria before wandering across campus to the next session. "The Lord has really worked in our lives this weekend," declared the Montessori teacher and father of two. "He healed the relationship between another couple and ourselves. We are becoming a little body of Christ—more committed to one another."

Black-haired and moist-eyed Gwen Savage from Dublin, Ireland, swayed to the music that filled the stadium, her arm around the person standing next to her. "It's magnificent. Beautiful. I feel really close to God," she said.

For many of the 30,000 people who attended the Eighth International Conference on the Charismatic Renewal in the Catholic Church June 14-16, the

A Turning Point

weekend proved to be a turning point in their lives. But on a broader level, it also proved to be a turning point in the worldwide charismatic renewal.

"We are moving from an apologetic phase to a prophetic phase," Ralph Martin emphasized during the main talk at the conference. ". . . It is time to begin to speak out his Word to the nations. . . God is moving to restore New Testament Christianity to all his people, and that is more than a renewal—that is restoration. . . He doesn't just want us to have a nice experience in the Holy Spirit. He wants us to change the face of the Church and the face of the earth."

Thunderous applause and cheers greeted this new call, which climaxed the weekend.

The three-day conference focused on Jesus as the healing light, the call to be his light among men, and proclaiming Jesus Christ as the light of the world.

Healing Light

At about 6 p.m. of Friday, a steady rain settled over the Notre Dame campus. Despite the downpour, about 30,000 people—soggy from the rain, but with smiles on their faces—crowded into the south half of the stadium. On the blue platform on the playing field, a group of musicians, draped in borrowed jackets and raincoats, sang and swayed to the music with their arms around each other. At one point the enthusiastic, expectant crowd burst out with shouts and applause in response to a loud thunderclap.

One man in a sport jacket and tie commented about the rain, "I came here tonight looking sharp.

Look at me now!" he grinned. "The Lord sure did humble me. I guess that's when healing can really happen."

At 7:40 p.m. the rain stopped and a healing service, which proved to be a historic moment in the life of the modern Catholic Church, began. "It was the first time a large group of Catholics with their pastors prayed to God for the healing gifts of the Holy Spirit to be manifest, and we saw God heal before our very eyes," exclaimed Ralph Martin in his concluding talk.

And the Lord did heal. Twenty-six-year-old Mary Iscaro from Ann Arbor, Michigan, blind from birth, began for the first time in her life to see the people around her. Sr. Anne Kearney of Adrian, Michigan, was healed of severe arthritis. Ralph Wilkerson from Melodyland in Anaheim, California, was cured of severe spinal arthritis and a smashed disc he had had for five years. About 70 physical healings and hundreds of inner healings were reported.

Before the healings began occurring, the Lord through prophecy spoke to the multitude: "I have mercy. I have wonderful mercy. I want to wash your feet. I want to heal you. I want to come into your heart. Open yourself to me and let me come in. I want to heal you tonight. I have mercy. I have mercy on you. Open yourself to me and let me heal you, forgive you. I love you. I love you."

A healing team of Fr. Mike Scanlan, Fr. Francis MacNutt, Barbara Shlemon, Sr. Jean Hill, and Fr. Tom Forrest conducted the healing service.

In a brief talk Fr. Scanlan encouraged the crowd to "throw off darkness and let Jesus Christ, the light of the world, free you and heal you."

As the service continued with an inner healing prayer by Fr. MacNutt, the word gift section on the platform began sensing through the word of knowledge that people were being healed of arthritis, cancer, blindness, back problems, deafness, blood disease, and other physical afflictions.

Those who were healed reported to special locations around the stadium. People whose arms and legs had been stiff for years with arthritis danced in place and rotated their arms above their heads without any pain; people with poor vision could see clearly without glasses; people with deafness listened to the ticking of their watches. Others, who experienced healing of cancer, kidney problems, blood diseases, and other afflictions, were instructed to have their doctors verify their healings when they returned home.

Sr. Kearney, who feared she would have to quit teaching because of her severe arthritis, told the crowd, "I thank the Lord I have great new life and I can continue to serve him. I can continue to teach."

His Light Among Men

Beginning at 6:30 on Saturday morning, individuals and clusters of people praying and singing dotted the campus lawns. After breakfast and prayers 17 prayer groups and communities witnessed to the power and effectiveness of the Holy Spirit. Groups from Ann Arbor, Michigan; Augusta, Georgia; Canada; Chicago, Illinois; Convent Station, New Jersey; Dallas and El Paso, Texas; Ft. Lauderdale, Florida; Minneapolis, Minnesota; New Orleans, Louisiana; Philadelphia, Pennsylvania; Providence, Rhode Island; Puerto Rico; San Francisco, California; and Washington, D.C. presented half-day and day-long workshops.

A half-day charismatic film festival emerged as a popular feature. Movies on the charismatic renewal, healing, and individual charismatic communities were shown to an overflowing crowd.

After dinner the 30,000 conferees again assembled in the stadium for a Eucharist led by Cardinal Leo Josef Suenens, Archbishop of Malines-Brussels, Belgium.

At dusk a dramatic procession of more than 700 white-robed priests and bishops wound its way from the north end of the stadium to join the multitude at the south end. Four abreast, the clergymen progressed, outlining the football field in white. Singing, clapping, and grinning, they occasionally extended a hand or stopped to hug someone in the crowd.

On the field near the 40-yard line, an altar was erected as the focal point for the night's activities. After the homily by Fr. Faber McDonald of Prince Edward Island, Canada, more than 100 ushers and several hundred priests filed up the stairs to direct and distribute communion to the thousands in the stands.

After the Eucharist, the lights in the stadium darkened. A hush covered the field as a grill in front of the altar was ignited. One-by-one, candles were lit from the flame and carried into the stands. Gradually the light spread throughout the stadium as each person lit the candle of the person next to him, until the stadium glowed with thousands of tiny flames. With joyful praise the participants acknowledged the ceremony as symbolic of the fact that Jesus Christ is the light of the world and that his light is spreading.

At the close of the service Fr. George Kosicki of Detroit, Michigan, called the brothers and sisters to "please take these candles home with you. Take them home around the country, around the world. Take them home and share this light ceremony with your families, with your prayer groups, with your communities and parishes, so that the light of Christ we have shared here may reach out to the ends of the world."

Jesus Christ, the Light of the World

A cold, misty day greeted the conferees Sunday as they stood in the breakfast line or wandered off to the designated locations for worship services. Baptist, Catholic, Episcopalian, Lutheran, Orthodox, and Pentecostal denominational services were held.

At 10 a.m. each conferee attended one of 25 talks on various aspects of the charismatic renewal, including presentations on the Holy Spirit in Australia, Ireland, and the Orient. For the first time talks in French and Spanish were offered.

The call for the participants to assemble in the stadium came at noon as four music groups presented a program of popular Christian music.

Again a persistent drizzle failed to dampen the enthusiasm of the multitude. "I have sat through many a football game in this stadium in rain and snow," declared moderator Kevin Ranaghan of South Bend. "I think this is a beautiful opportunity to let loose a cheer for God. Praised be Jesus!" Cheers of praise erupted as the 30,000 leapt to their feet.

After a time of joyful prayer and praise, the

crowd listened attentively to testimonies of healing that occurred at the Friday healing service. As the drizzle continued, Fr. Francis MacNutt walked to the podium and called on the 30,000 to pray that the rain would stop. Soon after the rain and mist subsided.

In a brief talk Cardinal Suenens read the prayer of Pope John XXIII during Vatican II calling on the Holy Spirit to "renew thy wonders in this our day, as by a new Pentecost." He noted that the prayer is for the whole Church, and reflected on how Peter and Mary were a source of balance for the Church.

Following enthusiastic rejoicing in the Lord, Protestant layman Dr. Robert Frost told the assembly that God is calling his people to be one as the Father and Son are one to be a witness to the world. "I feel in my spirit we're on the edge of something, perhaps far greater than we can realize and anticipate," he stated.

In the principal talk of the conference Ralph Martin stated that God is bringing his people together. Three mighty pentecostal rivers (Classical Pentecostal in 1900; Neo-Pentecostal in 1957; and Catholic Pentecostal in 1967) have begun flowing, he said, but God wants to bring them together.

"I believe in a very deep way God is beginning to move to change the course of these three mighty rivers—rivers that have been flowing separately. God is beginning to work on the riverbeds to make them be able to flow together to present a united witness to the Church and to the world," he proclaimed.

Interrupted more than 20 times by applause, Martin's talk was called "prophetic" and a "significant statement of what the Lord is doing among his people."

"The darkness is growing darker," he declared, "and the light must grow brighter."

God Is Restoring His People

By Ralph Martin

Seven years ago, at the first international conference, the Lord gave us a passage from Isaiah which he brought back to my mind during the last couple of days. *"Behold, I am doing a new thing; now it springs forth, do you not perceive it? I will make a way in the wilderness and rivers in the desert. The wild beasts will honor me, the jackals and the ostriches; for I give water in the wilderness, rivers in the desert, to give drink to my chosen people, the people whom I formed for myself that they might declare my praise"* (Isa. 43:19-21).

That word gives us a perspective about what we are involved in: the Lord is doing a new thing, and he wants us to notice it as it springs forth.

The last 400 years of Christianity have seen a process of disintegration. Where there used to be at least some measure of unity in the Body of Christ there has been an incredible fragmentation. There are hundreds and hundreds of groups of Christians that don't talk to one another; that have split again and again because they can't agree on certain things. This fragmentation has had an effect on the world's being able to perceive who God is and who Jesus the Messiah is. It's shattered and fragmented something of the image of himself which God intends to be in the world so that the world can come to faith.

It's also had a tremendous effect on society. Nation after nation that still has the name of Christian is being unmasked as spiritually bankrupt and lacking any vital truth or power at the heart of its national life. Just the other day, I read a report from a Catholic bishop in France. He reported that during the last seven years, 20 percent of the French priests had left the active ministry, and over the last four years there was a 68 percent decline in seminarians. He said that the situation of the Catholic Church in France in 20 years would be catastrophic.

This decay isn't just true in the Catholic Church. The Church of England has 28 million members in the British Isles. On Easter Sunday last year 1.8 million showed up at church, little more than five percent. In 1963 in the Anglican Church, 636 men entered the ministry; 10 years later 373 entered. That isn't a picture of the Church of Jesus Christ. That's a picture of churches that are badly in need of the action of God.

What we are seeing isn't the result of a few years of negligence, but a process that has been going on for a long time. In the middle of the 19th century Nietzsche, the German philosopher, saw that something had gone out of the heart of Christianity —he said something had died in it and hardly anybody could perceive it yet, but in the 20th century it was going to be manifest. He proclaimed "God is dead." He also said, "You Christians are going to have to look more redeemed for me to believe in your redeemer." That's the world speaking to us. Something has got to happen to the body of Christ to bring it to that place of overflowing vitality of life where a world which is rapidly growing dark can begin to see the light.

Jesus tells us what needs to happen in John 14-17. He is talking here directly to his disciples. He promises to send the Holy Spirit upon them and he prays for their unity so that *"the world may believe."* We need to take with utter seriousness God's word through Jesus just before he dies. I believe that God has begun to do something significant in our day to accomplish his purpose of unity, and I want to describe how I see it.

Although God has been working in a variety of ways to renew and unite his people, I think he began to move in a centrally significant way at the turn of the century, when the Pentecostal movement broke out. In that farmhouse in Topeka, Kansas, when a small group of people were baptized in the Spirit, a stream of God's life broke forth that has since gone on to become a mighty river. There are now about 13 million classical Pentecostals around the world.

But when they came with their message to the historic churches they were told: "Our theology has already taken care of this problem, and these things can't happen today. They were just for the early Church, we don't need it." God, do we need it! The stream went forth with power and might, but it was cut off from the institutional churches. But that didn't stop God, because wherever the message of Pentecost has come, millions of people all over the world have come to a living relationship with Jesus Christ and have received the power of the Spirit. Praise God for the classical Pentecostals!

The second stream began in about 1957. People

God Is Restoring His People 77

in the historic churches began to be baptized in the Spirit and felt like they could hang in there; they didn't need to leave their church. It wasn't a happy relationship; there was a lot of hurt and a lot of pain. The churches weren't particularly happy, and the people who were staying weren't particularly happy. But God was honoring the hanging-in-there, and from 1957 to 1967 another stream broke forth that we now call the neo-pentecostal movement. Many of the people who stayed in their churches during this time stayed because of strategy. They believed that would be a good place to be to help the whole church come into the experience. Groups like the Full Gospel Businessmen and various Christian centers are expressions of this stream, and now millions of people are flowing in this river of God's Spirit.

The third stream broke out in 1967 among a very few people and now is a mighty river with hundreds of thousands of people involved in it around the world. God has been moving and working for a long time to lay the groundwork for what we are experiencing in it now. On the very day at the turn of the century that we now recognize as the beginnings of the classical Pentecostal movement, Pope Leo XIII issued a letter to all the bishops of the world begging them to encourage their people to pray for the outpouring of the Holy Spirit. At Vatican II, one of the cardinals stood up and said, "Let's not have any references to the gifts of the Spirit, because they aren't for today." But Cardinal Suenaens read the Scriptures, talked with theologians and came back the next day and said, "Charisms are for today; leave the references in the document," and they were left in the document. The fact that the first group of Catholics involved happened to be theologians, or happened to be connected with Catholic universities was providential. They were in a unique position to articulate to the church what was happening. Another significant thing is that this first group of Catholics didn't come to Christianity for the first time then. They had experienced a vital Christian life in the Catholic Church for a number of years. They were Catholic, not out of tradition, not out of strategy, but because they perceived and discerned in the Catholic Church the body of Christ and the anointing of God. They were able not only to "hang in there," but to know that what had happened was something for the whole Church of Christ.

The growth of the renewal in the Catholic Church has been extraordinary, with about 350,000 involved now worldwide. This year our directory of prayer groups lists over 2,400 groups from 54 different countries. The charismatic renewal has become quickly and significantly international. There are now 10,000 Catholics in France baptized in the Spirit. This is happening in country after country.

Also, over the past year almost every American Cardinal has made a positive pastoral response to the charismatic renewal. Cardinal Medieros of Boston and Cardinal Manning of Los Angeles have both encouraged priests to get acquainted with the movement. Cardinal Carberry of St. Louis meets every month with a group of leaders in the charismatic renewal to talk about how it is developing in his archdiocese. Both Cardinal Dearden of Detroit and Cardinal Krol of Philadelphia celebrated special Pentecost charismatic liturgies in their archdiocese this year. So much is happening that you don't even notice it. God is moving in an active, powerful way to renew the whole Catholic Church.

A group of Canadian bishops have prepared a document that goes beyond the 1969 statement of the American bishops. It is even more positive and more encouraging about the charismatic renewal. They expect to have it adopted in the course of the summer. Just a few weeks ago some of us were in Malines with Cardinal Suenens working on a document that will be made available to the bishops of the whole world. It will help them know how to respond when the charismatic renewal breaks out in their diocese, and how to respond to it in a creative way.

But we're not just seeing a growth in numbers, we're seeing God doing something in those who are getting involved. About a month ago, during the liturgy at a meeting of the Catholic Charismatic Renewal Service Committee, somebody prophesied. I turned around, and who was it but Bishop McKinney giving a prophecy. In Malines we were celebrating the Eucharist and all of a sudden somebody started singing in tongues. It was Cardinal Suenens. As I see the kind of thing that God is doing, I just want to bow my head in awe before God our Father who is doing amazing things and preparing amazing things to happen in the Church.

This Friday night was a historic moment for the modern Catholic church. It was the first time a large group of Catholics with their pastors prayed to God for the healing gifts of the Holy Spirit to be manifest and saw God heal before their very eyes. *"The Spirit of God is upon me. He has anointed me to preach good news to the poor; to proclaim release to the captives, to give sight to the blind"* (Isa. 61:1). That prophecy of Isaiah, applied to Jesus, is now applied to the body of Jesus Christ—the Church. We have been anointed by the Holy Spirit to preach the gospel to the poor, to make the blind see and the deaf hear and to make the sick well. It is this power of God which is breaking out in the Body of Christ today, and we saw the first fruits of it Friday night. Gifts of healing and prophecy aren't to happen just at Lourdes and just through canonized saints, but through the whole people of God. God has brought us into a new realm of freedom in his Holy Spirit where we can with confidence know that, as we preach the Gospel, Jesus wants to reach out his hand and confirm it with signs, and he wants to do this in every city where his people gather to praise him.

We are just at the beginning. The breadth of God's plan is beyond our imaginations. I think that through these three mighty pentecostal rivers that are flowing in separate channels, God is bringing together. I see him beginning to do it.

What is happening among the classical Pentecostals today is something we can call an ecumenical shockwave. It is a shock to the Pentecostal churches to see what God is doing in the Catholic Church. When all your life you have been trained to look at the Catholic Church as the whore of Babylon, and when the whore of Babylon preaches Jesus, what are you going to do? It shakes up your whole world view. Among the leaders in the classical Pentecostal churches now, there is a tremendous reassessment taking place. They want to see how to flow into the new thing that God is doing.

God Is Restoring His People

Something is also happening in the neo-pentecostal movement. With men like Derek Prince, Bob Mumford, Don Basham, and Charles Simpson, new things are beginning to happen. They are teaching important things like unity in the Body of Christ and authority and submission. For a tradition of Christianity that is very individualistic, it's a new thing to have the Spirit of God talk to you about submission and authority. Along with that, a tremendous spirit of openness and friendship to the Catholic charismatic renewal is beginning. God is opening a new door for us in the Catholic charismatic renewal. We are moving from an apologetic phase into a prophetic phase. Over the last five years God has given us great wisdom about how to relate to our fellow Catholic laymen and our Catholic bishops so that we can all move together as a church. God has spoken to us about loyalty as Catholics and commitments of obedience and submission to our bishops. That has been a very important thing. Now with that as a foundation, I believe that God is saying that it is time to speak out his word boldly. He has a word to speak for the Church and for the world through what we are experiencing. Renewal is too weak a word for what needs to happen in the Christian church. "Renewal" can give us a sense that we will just polish something up a little bit. Rather, I think God is moving to *restore* New Testament Christianity to all his people—that is more than renewal. Restoration means reform as well as renewal for everything that God wants to happen in his people. Much has been lost, much has been distorted. He wants to change the face of the Church and the face of the earth.

I was talking with some reporters yesterday, and they asked: "Why did you have to blow it Friday night by having a healing service? You were just getting respectable. Last year you reached the point of respectability, and this year we were ready for more of that." Praise God for the surprises of the Holy Spirit! God is directing the movement of the Spirit to accomplish his personal aims and designs in our time. We need to be in a personal union with him, wanting to hear his voice and wanting to move on with him. I believe that he is leading us as he led the people in the Exodus. He is as sure a guide as the pillar of fire and the clouds were to the Israelites in the desert. We run the risk of wanting to go back to Egypt. We run the risk of wanting to stay where we are. We're happy with our prayer group as it is right now. We're happy with our Catholic Church as it is right now. Let's not rock the boat. To stop short of God's full purpose is to run the risk of us being left behind to die in the desert. A good thing of God can be the enemy of the next thing of God. If we clutch on to today's gift and say it's so nice, I want to stop here, we are going to become the enemy of the next thing that God wants to do. In the past, even the Bible became for some people the thing with which they defended themselves against God. Jesus spoke to Jews who loved the Bible and said, *"You search the Scriptures because you think that in them you have eternal life; and it is they that bear witness to me; yet you refuse to come to me that you may have life"* (John 5:39-40). This is also true with the sacraments. If we love the form and culture of the sacraments more than the person we meet in them, we protect ourselves from that person. Today, if we love

God Is Restoring His People

the Catholic Church as it is so much that we won't let Jesus make it what he wants it to be for today, we become the enemy of the Catholic Church.

I believe that in a very deep way God is moving to change the course of these mighty rivers. They have been flowing separately, but God is working on the riverbeds to enable them to flow together, to present a united witness to the Church and to the world. I don't know *how* God is going to do it, and I don't know *when,* but I know he's begun, and he'll complete it. I don't necessarily think we ought to do one thing differently than we've been doing because of this. But I hope that this will make us want to listen to God more, and look for the movement of the Spirit so that when he gives direction for our local situation, we will be ready to move. What we're experiencing in the Holy Spirit is not something that's private and personal, just for us; it's something that's cosmic in scope. What's unfolding is a mighty plan from God. The darkness is growing darker, and the light must grow brighter.

The spirit that we've received as a movement is not a spirit of timidity and not a spirit of fear, but a spirit of sonship: we're sons and daughters of God. He wants us to live in that and to walk in boldness and confidence as his sons and daughters.

God is moving to bring his people together in the bonds of deep love and commitment so that the world may believe. Let's follow him and not be left in the desert. Let's go on with him and enter the promised land.

PART TWO
Responses of Bishops and Theologians

Interview with Bishop Joseph McKinney

By Msgr. Hugh Behan

The following is a record of a conversation between Bishop Joseph McKinney, auxiliary bishop of Grand Rapids, and Msgr. Hugh Behan, pastor of St. Mary's parish in Grand Rapids, where the charismatic community meets. Msgr. Behan is also Diocesan Director of Radio and Television.

B From my own personal acquaintance with you, Bishop McKinney, and from what I've heard, the charismatic renewal for you is something pretty important. You are a lifelong Catholic, an ordained priest, and an ordained bishop and yet is appears that the charismatic renewal has meant something special to you.

McK It has. I find great help in my prayer life through association with charismatic prayer groups and I am experiencing more than ever before the power and guidance of the Holy Spirit in my life.

B Can you give some examples of what you mean? What about your practice of tithing your time

Interview with Bishop Joseph McKinney

for prayer? Is it true that you began to do this as a result of your involvement in the charismatic renewal?

McK Yes. I had been doing some background reading on the movement, and one of the books mentioned someone tithing one-tenth of each day to the Lord in prayer. I sensed a power working there and could tell from the fruits of this kind of prayer life that there was really something there. It really hit me and caused me to ask some fundamental questions about my own life. I asked myself, "What is the top priority in my life? Am I really sincere about wanting to be a man of prayer? Is there anything I want to be more than a man of prayer?" It was tough to face questions like this. But I was finally able to say, "Nope, there's nothing I'd rather be known for than as a man of prayer." Then I had to do something about it.

B What did you do?

McK I decided to give the Lord two hours and twenty-four minutes a day in prayer. This includes the Mass I celebrate, and takes advantage of all the times during the day when I could possibly pray. My car is now what I call a house of prayer on wheels and I say the Jesus prayer while driving quite frequently. When I'm preparing a homily, I pray about it. When I'm reading the Scriptures or doing some spiritual reading, I pray about the reading as well as simply read. And now when I get up in the morning I usually start singing a hymn, because that makes it easier to get into prayer.

B   You're not going to room next to me, that's all I can say! What is this Jesus prayer you talked about?

McK Well actually, in addition to the traditional ways I still use to pray I've found three new ways. The Jesus prayer is one of them.

B   Can you briefly explain what they are?

McK Sure. The first is the kind of prayer described in Matthew 18:19-20: *"If two of you on earth agree to ask anything at all, it will be granted to you by my Father in heaven. For where two or three meet in my name, I shall be there with them."* I have found great help in solving problems in my diocese by praying with priests first.

The second is the Jesus prayer from the Eastern tradition. This consists of repeating the name of Jesus over and over again, sometimes putting in other words, sometimes just breathing out the name of Jesus slowly with every breath. I have discovered that there is great power in the name of Jesus.

The third is the prayer of listening. At the end of every day, I ask the Lord, "What were you trying to tell me today?" and I just listen for a few minutes. Sometimes things that seemed insignificant earlier in the day take on greater importance then.

B   Do you still find difficulty sometimes in prayer?

McK Yes. It's still shaky in many ways and I don't want to give the impression that it's not difficult sometimes, but in the year since I was prayed over I can safely say that I know how to pray better and that I do pray better. And it's improving, more in terms of month-to-month, than day-to-day or week-to-week. It's certainly easier to pray than it was before. It's kind of a healing process, and I'm getting healed too. I can face myself now and at least say, "Well at least you're trying to be a man of prayer." Before I couldn't face myself.

B You mentioned that you were experiencing more than ever before the power and guidance of the Holy Spirit in your life. Can you explain this more fully?

McK I think I can best do so by giving some examples. This power of the Holy Spirit that has been released in my life through the charismatic renewal became particularly clear to me when I had to give a retreat for priests. As you know, giving a retreat for priests these days is quite a challenge. I think I spent two months preparing for it and had eighteen talks ready. But then I felt I should go away for a day just to pray and fast to prepare for it. During that day the Spirit began to show me that, in addition to preparing talks, I had to be open too and expect His help and guidance on the spot. The Spirit said that I had to be open to Him helping me understand where the men were and what their real needs were. And the experience of that retreat was tremendous for me because I found priests listening.

At the end of the retreat an older priest came up quietly just to say, "Bishop, I'm deeply grateful for this retreat. I don't recall in fifty years ever having attended one that had this kind of power with me. We really needed this." My reaction was one of "Isn't this wonderful! Praise the Lord!" but at the same time, I wondered if the young priests had been reached. Then three young priests came to me after the retreat to say they felt they were beginning to find their way out of confusion. They attributed this feeling primarily to the insistence during the retreat that we must center our lives on Jesus Christ as our Lord, and be men of prayer.

I had a similar experience giving a retreat at a seminary where the seminarians were terribly divided and the community fragmented. On the retreat I preached the basic gospel message, of the living person of Jesus as Lord. Afterward the rector said that the results of the retreat could be summed up in the remarks of one student who put it like this: "Before the retreat I didn't think that even Jesus Christ could unite this community, but somehow He did it through the bishop."

These are results of a power working through us that we can't claim originates with us; it is the power of the Holy Spirit Himself, and it produces results far beyond what merely human effort alone produces. It is this working of the Spirit through me, in preaching, in counseling, in prayer, that I've begun to experience in a new way through the charismatic renewal.

One more example: There are times now when all of a sudden I just do something with a conviction that this is what must be done. And it is something that is completely contradictory to my personality. For instance, up until recently I've never been naturally stern or strong with a priest, but in one situation I felt that was what the Spirit wanted. It involved a delicate problem which the priest had to face and I spoke to him very directly about it. This isn't my nature. The man responded very well, and what opened him up was that he knew it wasn't just me that was speaking to him; he sensed something else working in my life, an authority, a conviction, that came from God Himself. I know this can be explained in human terms, but I don't explain it that way. In the year since I was prayed over I have found a sense of intuitive conviction that I never had before when I have to face difficult situations. I really depend very strongly on the power of the Holy Spirit in these situations.

"Baptism in the Spirit"

B What is this "baptism in the spirit" that I've heard spoken about as the key to a renewed life in the Spirit, and this "praying over?"

McK This ties in with a question that is often asked. Why is it that in Confirmation and Baptism we do not experience much of the life in the Spirit that is being experienced by many in the charismatic renewal? I don't presume to have the full answer, but I'm led very strongly toward the conviction that we don't have an expectant faith, we don't wait for what God has for us, we're not really open to it. Baptism in the Spirit, as I see it, is prayer in expectant faith for a renewal of the sacraments of Baptism and Confirmation. It is a prayer that the Spirit given to us in these sacraments becomes more active and free to work in our life.

This event is frequently best prepared for and

experienced in a community of vital faith by prayer with the laying on of hands. But it can come to people praying on their own. If you consider the question of priests' involvement, I think the key is having the guts to experience strangeness and awkwardness a few times, and to be open to the Spirit beginning to mean something.

B You've referred to being prayed over and the life of the Spirit becoming more active and manifest in you since. What led you to become involved in the charismatic renewal? What led you to the Baptism of the Spirit?

McK For me a bishop is someone who has to unite a local church. As I began to experience the pluralism, indeed division, in the church today, I started looking for an answer, some way to make the church one. I noticed how St. Paul handled the problem of polarization between the Hellenists and the Jews in the early church. He didn't approach it directly but rather drew their attention to the person of Jesus, insisting that in Jesus we find the key to the answers we are seeking to all our problems. I knew that what I was looking for as a key to the unity of the church had to do somehow with centering our lives on Christ.

I went to a theological institute on Jesus Christ and listened to theologians. I came back feeling sad because I didn't find the answer, only questions. But then in the experience of a prayer retreat, led by—a priest who was deeply involved in the charismatic renewal—Fr. George Kosicki, I found the key. It is centered in the realization that Jesus Christ is Lord. Our whole theology can be plugged into that statement, and it pulled things together for me. At the end of that retreat I asked to be prayed over for a deeper work of God's Spirit in me. That began my contact with the charismatic renewal, and the deepening of my own prayer life and experience of the working of the Spirit.

Future Direction

B What do you see as the future direction of renewal in the Church? How do you see the polarization being overcome?

McK I've got a book here called *Unless the Lord Builds the House* by Ralph Martin, published by Ave Maria Press. I've just finished it and I'm really going to get copies of it around because I think it's *very* perceptive about what's going on in the Church today. Ralph Martin is a layman, deeply interested in the Church, who has worked in many forms of the apostolate. He gives examples to support the point that we in the renewal have made a mistake of assuming that people have a personal relationship with Jesus Christ, and that this is at the core of everything. This book has helped me develop a vision of how the Lord wants to make the Church one, both the Catholic Church and the other Christian Churches. Christ is the center and Lord of all, the center for all *authentic* Christianity. He is the center, the core, that makes unity possible. The Church has to be open to a certain pluralism, a certain variety in the ways of expressing this one thing. But we had better have only one theme, one central core, from which all things flow. That core is commitment to the living person of Jesus.

B Do you see problems with this commitment understood in today's renewal?

McK Quite frankly, I do. I think we're taking the heart of Christianity—the person of Jesus—for granted. When we're attracted to that person, in personal union with Him, then He will teach us the truths that keep us in unity. He will communicate His vision of reality to us. Sometimes even in statements that we bishops put out we're a little heavy on "the Church teaches." Sometimes we don't quite make clear the centrality of commitment to the person of Jesus that is needed to make the teachings make sense and to motivate people.

This particular book really hits the nail on the head in many ways. And it's especially helpful, I think, if you are bewildered like I am about the supposed "Christian humanism" that is so rampant today. Ralph makes it clear that there is a Christian humanism, but that there is also a humanism, quite common today, that bears the name of Christian, but which basically denies that we need a savior. It is a humanism which is basically contradictory to everything we stand for and believe in, a humanism which implies that Jesus Christ would never really have had to come to this earth. He didn't use that exact expression, "Jesus Christ would never have had to come to this earth"—that's my own—but when I try to follow the reasoning, that's where I end up.

B   Can you see what could happen to the Church?

McK   I don't really try to. I have thoughts here and there, but what I know for sure is very simple: the more authentically we are one with Christ, the more authentic the future will be. I can't predict what His action will be, but I did feel the Council was saying in essence that if we surrender ourselves to Christ, all will come together and we will find that unity. I'm really inspired by the way they started the document on the Church: "Christ is the light of all nations." His name was the first word in the most important document.

B   From what I know, the charismatic renewal started spontaneously and is very much a grass-roots movement. In other words, it hasn't come down from above but began among the people. Doesn't this fact make bishops suspicious about it?

McK   I have certainly had bishops come to me who were concerned and at a loss about what to think about it. But I think studying the facts clears up most suspicions immediately.

What Should Bishops Know?

B   What kind of things do you feel are important for bishops to know about the renewal?

McK   Well, first of all, I think it's important for bishops to see the charismatic renewal in the context of the renewal called for by Vatican II. One of the most amazing things is that if you study the Council documents—the documents on the priesthood and others—there's a description of this renewal. The priests are requested to prepare the people for the liturgy by developing their prayer life. Everything is there. It's almost a guideline to what has happened. In the document on the laity the fuller role of the laity within the Church is described, along with a need for a renewal of their life and prayer so they can take more effective action. The charismatic renewal appears to me to be God's way of making real what the Vatican Council called for in the renewal of the spiritual life. As with other authentic renewals from the Lord, the form in which it appears is sometimes startling and foreign to us.

B Have the bishops that you've talked to expressed an openness to the charismatic renewal?

McK I think most bishops, very wisely, have two reactions. One is that they sense that there is some real good in it, with perhaps the potential of meeting many of the problems we face in today's Church. The other is that they're concerned about people being misled and not being firmly grounded in sound theology. A growing number of bishops are having firsthand experience of the charismatic renewal's effects, both good and bad. One bishop mentioned that he was impressed when he learned that a priest who was planning to leave the priesthood went to a charismatic meeting at Notre Dame and had a change of heart after being prayed over in faith. This priest was able to lead another priest to a similar change of heart by praying over him. Bishops also hear about the "strange" incidents that indeed exist on the fringes of the movement. But by and large, I think that the vast majority of bishops are open to the charismatic renewal or soon will be.

B What would you suggest to bishops interested in tapping the potential of the renewal?

McK In order for the Church not to lose the benefits the movement has to give, I would suggest two things.

One is that the bishops must get well-balanced priests involved, not as observers but as participants, because the priest plays an important role in guidance. These people need and want—indeed, are looking for—pastoral guidance. They need people who can see mistakes coming up and can explain how to avoid them. Priests have an important contribution to make here. If priests have hang-ups about celibacy or authority or about the physical resurrection of Christ or these kinds of things, they should go to the prayer meetings but not take a leadership role until their own lives are in order.

The other suggestion is the importance of regional and national groups and conferences, as I mentioned before. It's here that the soundest leadership is learning through their mistakes, and helping the movement develop within the Church.

Emotional Aspects of Renewal

B What about the emotional aspects of the renewal. Aren't there dangers there?

McK I think we've had some hang-ups with our emotions. A person is considered perfectly normal if he jumps up and down at a football game or if he enjoys a good party, but if he does this in connection with religion we think he's rather strange. It's my growing conviction that if the life in Christ means so much to people that they're enthusiastic about it and can use their whole being in giving praise to God—emotions and body as well as will and intellect—more power to them.

B Isn't there a danger that emotionally unstable people will be attracted to a movement like this?

McK Of course they would be attracted, as they would to any group of people who showed love and concern for them. As one of the priests in the renewal said, "Our Lord didn't say, 'Suffer every well-balanced person to come to me.'" Of course, understanding how to help people like this can often be difficult, and there's no question that they can cause problems. The leaders I know are quite aware of the dangers and are working, praying, consulting to find solutions and safeguards for them. People who aren't sound psychologically or theologically will be gently but firmly asked not to share at meetings, to recognize the problems they have and to accept the various ways of dealing with them.

B Is it true that in addition to professional help, which I know the leaders respect, there are instances of people with problems being healed emotionally through the contact with God they've had in the prayer groups?

McK Yes, that's true. Over a period of time many

experience improvement, gradual healing in the area of their emotional life. There are also some physical healings for which there is no natural explanation. This has convinced me that one of the ministries we haven't developed within the Church very much is the healing ministry, especially the healing of the conflicts within the soul, the things that tear people apart. Some priests that are working in this area, particularly in connection with the sacrament of penance, are experiencing some wonderful things.

Soundness of the Leaders

B What is your opinion of the soundness of the leaders you know in the movement?

McK I have real respect for and confidence in the leaders I know best. These are a number of the national leaders, and the ones right here in Grand Rapids. Among these leaders there is good solid thinking and theology, and the fruits of the Spirit— especially joy, peace, and love. You can't find bitterness among these people. You can't find ill will toward the institution. They love the Church. I'm impressed with how they're handling some difficult situations and how they're working to hold things together and keep this renewal firmly within the Church. The national leadership I know I think is very good. That's why I think it's important that all the prayer groups continue to come to leadership training conferences, regional days, and the national meetings, because there's real danger in every movement of going off in the wrong direction if you operate on your own. The communication and cooperation within the movement as manifested in the national conferences is very important.

As I got in touch more with the leaders emerging in the movement, I found the fruits that we as bishops look for. They are attracting old and young alike, from all walks of life. They have a deep conviction that we have the answers in the Church. There is no theology being proposed that is not consonant with what we have learned in the past, but there is a beautiful development of what we mean by being temples of the Holy Spirit, of how the Holy Spirit enlightens, enlivens and empowers us, making it possible for us to accomplish the work of the Lord that none of us could presume to accomplish on our own.

B Would it be fair to say that you see the movement making an important contribution to the Church, but that there are some real dangers that must be avoided and problems that must be worked out?

McK Yes, that would be fair. Something I learned through a book on business management is applicable here. In progressive business management the executives don't focus on men's faults, but identify their strengths and put them to work. The same thing is true about this movement: it would be a mistake to focus on what could go wrong or the isolated incidents that have gone wrong. There's tremendous strength and power from the Lord here, and we have to learn how to tap it and put it to work for renewal. The faults will be cleaned out in the process.

Priests and the Movement

B Now that we've spoken about the bishops and

the movement, could we speak for a while about the priests and the movement?

McK Yes, what do you have in mind?

B You and I both know there are priests who are definitely gun-shy, who perhaps have experience with one element of the renewal and have turned off the whole thing. What has been your experience in talking with priests about the charismatic renewal who are not themselves involved?

McK I share their difficulties. I myself experienced problems opening up to what the Lord had for me through the renewal. Even though our present prayer life may not be very vital, we still find it hard to open up to new dimensions of prayer, new forms, because it involves us expressing ourselves more openly and from the heart. But I think *all* of us have something to learn about prayer from the charismatic renewal, and that it's worth persevering through the difficulty and awkwardness to come to it.

B Can you develop this more, Bishop?

McK I think one clear illustration of what I'm saying is a situation I became aware of while visiting New Orleans. I stayed with a group of Poor Clare sisters who had been cloistered for years, always praying. From the point of view of most members of the Church these are the people who really know how to pray. Now this particular community has had contact with the charismatic renewal groups in New Orleans and the nuns told me time and time again all they had learned about prayer from that prayer community, and how they were able to share things in return.

B I think many priests—and this would describe something of my own experience—are or were just a little bit afraid. I'm not sure I'm able to put my finger on it, but I think it is a fear of breaking out of the "John Wayne syndrome" where men—in this country, at least—are not supposed to show any emotion except anger. That's an acceptable masculine emotion, but anything else is a threat to your masculinity. To express love to one another, to touch each other, to let our positive emotions show in any way is forbidden. Then would your suggestion to priests who make an inquiry be: "Go and experience it?"

McK Yes, and also get to know the people involved. Invite them to your Mass. If they make mistakes, feel free to talk to them about it in a gentle way; they want to know. There's something to be said for priests praying together, but not as a substitute for the mixed group. They've got a longer history and there are things there we have to learn. I know we're supposed to give praise and thanksgiving, for example, but I'm still not very good at it, and I know these people have got a lot of lessons to teach us.

B I know one thing that strikes people as strange at first is that murmur of prayer when everyone prays softly out loud all together; I believe they sometimes call it a "word of prayer." What do you think about that?

McK I find it very helpful. Remember how we used to have a rule that when you say the Office you were supposed to move your lips. Also, if you have ever experienced singing in the shower, if you actually use your mouth and lips to express the things that are on your heart, I've found that they become more a part of me, and I think this is the great value of the word of prayer. But how to express prayer is really secondary; it's the fruits that it produces which are important.

Judging Its Fruits

B A few last questions. If someone were to say, "Well, how do I know that this is genuine and real, and not a mere passing emotional religious fad?" Would you say to judge it by its fruits?

McK Yes, that's it basically. Within the movement is developing what, for me, is a clear contemporary understanding of an old spiritual truth: it's called "discernment of spirits." It's beautiful to hear people talk about the criteria for judging an authentic work of the Spirit. They put in today's language the same things that Ignatius and St. Teresa of Avila said. Things like: if there's bitterness involved you should seriously question if it's a work of the Spirit; or, if it isn't helping the common good, the community, etc. This spiritual sensitivity, this discernment, is something that develops in most people after some time of experience with both true and false expressions of the Spirit.

B What about the question of polarization in the parish where those who do not belong to the prayer group feel alienated? What would your response be if I as a pastor were to throw this at you?

McK I have no doubt that there will be some whose enthusiasm will turn people off. But I think that a person who's "turned off" should really ask some hard, personal questions, because often we're victims of jealousy. There is something like a conviction that develops that perhaps we're in contact with something really big and important, and instead of saying "Why not for me?" we react against it. Sometimes it's a resistance to changing our lives in ways which we know a deeper contact with the Lord would require. Sometimes it's an actual hardening of our heart, a refusal of repentance. What most Catholic Pentecostals are saying is that you have to start with repentance, you have to change your heart; the Holy Spirit doesn't work freely in our life until we've entered into repentance. If the graces of Baptism and Confirmation are to be renewed in baptism of the Spirit, we must start with repentance. Well, many people do not want to face this issue. They would rather cover up things that need changing with words like "Someone else is at fault."

One of the things that's happened to me in the renewal is that where I used to point fingers at others and blame them, I'm starting to point the finger at myself. And this is really where the ballgame is played. With wisdom and understanding in all quarters, with openness to the Spirit in all quarters, there doesn't have to be division.

Report of the American Bishops, 1969

The following is the report of the Committee on Doctrine of the National Conference of Catholic Bishops submitted to the bishops in their meeting in Washington, D.C., Nov. 14, 1969. The report was presented by Bishop Alexander Zaleski of Lansing, Michigan, Chairman of the Committee:

Beginning in 1967, the so-called Pentecostal movement has spread among our Catholic faithful. It has attracted especially college students. This report will restrict itself to the phenomenon among Catholics. It does not intend to treat classic Pentecostalism as it appears in certain Protestant ecclesial communities.

In the Catholic Church the reaction to this movement seems to be one of caution and somewhat unhappy. Judgments are often based on superficial knowledge. It seems to be too soon to draw definitive conclusions regarding the phenomenon and more scholarly research is needed. For one reason or another the understanding of this movement is colored by emotionalism. For this there is some historical justification and we live with a suspicion of unusual religious experience. We are also face to face with socially somewhat unacceptable norms of religious behavior. It should be kept in mind that this phenomenon is not a movement in the full sense of the word. It has no national structure and each individual prayer meeting may differ from another.

Many would prefer to speak of it as a charismatic renewal. In calling it a Pentecostal movement we must be careful to disassociate it from classic Pentecostalism as it appears in Protestant denominations, such as the Assemblies of God, the United Pentecostal Church, and others. The Pentecostal movement in the Catholic Church is not the acceptance of the ideology or practices of any denomination, but likes to consider itself a renewal in the spirit of the first Pentecost. It would be an error to suppose that the emotional, demonstrative style of prayer characteristic of the Protestant denominations has been adopted by Catholic Pentecostals. The Catholic prayer groups tend to be quiet and somewhat reserved. It is true that in some cases it has attracted emotionally unstable people. Those who come with such a disposition usually do not continue. Participants in these prayer meetings can also exclude them. In this they are not always successful.

It must be admitted that theologically the movement has legitimate reasons for existence. It has a strong biblical basis. It would be difficult to inhibit the work of the Spirit which manifested itself so abundantly in the early Church. The participants in the Catholic Pentecostal movement claim that they receive certain charismatic gifts. Admittedly, there have been abuses, but the cure is not a denial of their existence but their proper use. We still need further research on the matter of charismatic gifts. Certainly, the recent Vatican Council presumes that the

Spirit is active continuously in the Church.

Perhaps our most prudent way to judge the validity of the claims of the Pentecostal Movement is to observe the effects on those who participate in the prayer meetings. There are many indications that this participation leads to a better understanding of the role the Christian plays in the Church. Many have experienced progress in their spiritual life. They are attracted to the reading of the scriptures and a deeper understanding of their faith. They seem to grow in their attachment to certain established devotional patterns such as devotion to the real presence and the rosary.

It is the conclusion of the Committee on Doctrine that the movement should at this point not be inhibited but allowed to develop. Certain cautions, however, must be expressed. Proper supervision can be effectively exercised only if the bishops keep in mind their pastoral responsibility to oversee and guide this movement in the Church. We must be on guard that they avoid the mistakes of classic Pentecostalism. It must be recognized that in our culture there is a tendency to substitute religious experience for religious doctrine. In practice we recommend that bishops involve prudent priests to be associated with this movement. Such involvement and guidance would be welcomed by the Catholic Pentecostals.

Charismatic Renewal in the Catholic Church: An Evaluation

By Bishop Joseph Hogan

I would like to attempt to share with you some reflections on the most recent evidence of the continuing presence of the Spirit of Christ in the world of the 70's. I refer to what is called the Pentecostal Movement among Catholics—I speak of its hopes and promises and its potential dangers.

The Catholic Pentecostal Movement began as a spark in 1967 at Duquesne University in Pittsburgh, and since then has grown with amazing speed throughout the Midwest and the entire country, and increasingly throughout the whole world.

Briefly, the Catholic Pentecostal Movement might be described as a group belief that the Holy Spirit will manifest himself in the daily life of the average, sincere Christian. He will make Christ present, even *experientially,* to anyone seeking Him through the power of the Holy Spirit. Ordinarily, this experience of Christ and the working of the Holy Spirit come through an act of faith in an informal rite called "the baptism of the Spirit."

The baptism in the Holy Spirit is essentially a part of our Christian initiation, the sacrament of

Baptism and its ongoing actualization in our celebration of the eucharist and living the Christian life. What purpose then is there, one might ask, in a Catholic Pentecostal Movement seeking a baptism in the Holy Spirit with the gifts and fruits of the Holy Spirit? The answer lies in the fact that baptism in the Holy Spirit, as we use the term, has been poured out in the Church since Pentecost Sunday and through every complete baptism celebration still today. The Church is filled with the Holy Spirit; as the Body of Christ, it has already received all the gifts and fruits of the Spirit. What this new Pentecostal Movement seeks to do through faithful prayer, and by trusting in the Word of God, is to ask the Lord to actualize in a concrete, living way what the Christian people have already been given so that his life, his gifts, and his fruit may be actualized in the lives of the members of Christ's Body.

A Renewal in Faith

Among Catholic pentecostals this baptism is neither a new sacrament nor a substitute sacrament. Like the renewal of baptismal promises, it is a renewal in faith of the desire to be everything that Christ wants us to be. For Catholics this experience is a renewal, making our initiation as children in the sacrament of baptism concrete and explicit on a mature level.

The men and women, clerics and lay people who have sought and received the baptism in the Holy Spirit are by and large ordinary Catholic people from every walk of life, profession and socio-economic bracket. They have shared the desire to be good Catholics and to grow in the life and love of

Christ. Serious about their religion, concerned for the spiritual welfare of others, anxious for constructive renewal in the Church, they have been equally involved in their civic communities and employment, entering fully into all the normal activities which mark this period of our national life—human rights, law, justice, good government, peace. They seem to be a healthy cross section of American Catholicism. But they have been united in one Lord, one faith, and one baptism by the desire to be more fully the type of Christian that Jesus wants them to be. They share, for all their differences of opinion, the belief that the Lord knows best what's right and needed in his Church. As a group they have the characteristics of serious Christian dedication, openness to the will of God, and the willingness to yield to Him.

Yet this is not the complete picture, for there have been a number of people who have come face-to-face with the Pentecostal Movement as persons with minimal faith, or lost faith, or nominal Christian observance. These people have been touched by the witness of a friend or by a prayer group, and being attracted by it they have found for the first time real faith in Christ and the richness of life in the Spirit.

Renewed Life in the Spirit

To renew their baptismal commitment, to live concretely in the Spirit of Christ, thousands of American Catholics have prayed to be baptized in the Holy Spirit. There is no set form or formula or setting for this type of prayer. It takes place in small or large prayer groups, with a friend or alone—but always with Jesus. It takes place with the laying on of hands or without this gesture, at home, at school, at work, at Mass, in the car—but always in expectant faith.

New, Richer Faith

In fact if there is any one thing which most strikingly characterizes Catholic pentecostals it is not tongues or singing or prayer groups; it is that they came to seek a renewal in the Holy Spirit in simple faith, and having received the answer to their prayer, they begin to walk in a newness of faith. The people involved in the charismatic renewal are basically men and women of new, richer faith.

Faith, of course, is a gift of God, a grace, an unearned favor. It comes to one, in the plan of redemption, by hearing and believing the word of God, by witnessing the life of the Word lived out in the lives of Christians, by seeing the results of faith in the beauty of those around us. The life of witness is the life of the Church, it is the lived out proclamation of the good news of salvation. Through preaching in action, the Spirit draws men to God in Christ and the life of faith is born.

When men of faith pray with expectation, Christ's answer builds up their faith. A man may come to seek baptism in the Holy Spirit because he has seen and believed the work of the Spirit in the life of a friend. He then trusts Jesus in prayer and expects that the Lord will renew in him the gifts and fruits bestowed in baptism but not fully actualized in a living way. In the answer to that prayer, Jesus often becomes more real to the believer. He is much closer, more present and active in one's life. He is not only enthroned at the "right hand of the Father," but He, the risen Lord, is also really alive among the members of His body. Our old belief becomes a new awareness, becomes really real to the believers. The relationship of faith between this man and the Father through Christ has deepened, transformed, and has become the center of personal existence. It would be false to characterize this new-found faith-life as a purely emotional experience. Certainly human emotion is involved in any act of love, and people respond emotionally according to their temperament. But it seems better to speak of this new faith-life on the level of a penetrating and all-encompassing awareness and conviction which involves the whole body-person, with all its human qualities in a response of deep commitment.

If anything has been renewed, enlivened or rediscovered by Catholics in the Pentecostal Movement it has been this new emphasis on a life of radical faith in the loving presence of the risen Lord in our midst by the power of His Spirit. This renewal of faith seems destined to play an even greater role as it suffuses and enlivens the several movements of renewal within the Church: liturgical and scriptural, reform of clerical and religious life, the ascendency of the laity to full responsibility as the People of God, and in the broad field of ecumenical relationships. We can also expect the effect of this lively faith in Christian involvement in the vital crises of political, social, and economic development in the world.

Granting the seeming goodness of the movement, its bearing of good fruit and all that, why should it happen in today's Church, in sharp contrast to our experience in former generations? In today's whole movement of renewal, characterized by a drawing together of clergy and laity, by a mutual confession of past failings, by a desire to purify the Church's Bride of Christ, there is an openness of the whole Church to everything Jesus would have it be. In such an atmosphere Jesus is able to break through the walls of human weakness with the result that the charismatic life of the Church grows once again, alongside the growth in liturgy, scripture, and role of the laity.

Today the Church and the world are both in a time of severe crises, of religious, political, and economic revolutions. The relevance of Christianity to the world is severely challenged on all sides. The past sins of Christian people are bearing bad fruit while waves of bitterness rise up from young people and young nations in reaction to the old order. In this situation, Jesus in the life of the Spirit, is renewing the dramatic charisms of the Spirit—not only to build up the Church but to call attention to and communicate the good news of salvation.

To the Catholic Church of today, in the throes of renewal, the Lord Jesus has sent His blessings in many wonderful ways while challenging it to fuller life in Him. One of the things He is doing among His people is making them more aware of the reality and power of His Holy Spirit. He is leading thousands of Catholics to experience, perhaps for the first time, the fruits of the Spirit in their own lives and in their relationships with the Father and with all men. Also experienced today, with many other good things, are the ministry gifts of the Spirit common in the New Testament Church. This outpouring, where it is received, is renewing the People of

God. It is received by prayer in expectant faith that the Lord will renew in us His baptism in the Holy Spirit.

Dangers I see—but not sufficient to overshadow the positive values of the movement. I feel the need for a theological direction to guide sincere souls in their journey with the Spirit in order to avoid extremes. Once a person is convinced that the Holy Spirit is a guide, either through the Scriptures or prophecy or any private communication, all argument must stop. But the groups admit one safeguard inherent to their meetings—the discernment of spirits—an admission that not all messages are from the Holy Spirit and that another gift is necessary to discern the truth or fallacy of such communications.

If the movement is from God (and I have no reason to doubt it at the moment), it must be viewed in terms of many years. The humility of the pentecostals might be a safeguard for now, but the future will demand men trained in theology to steer the Movement away from subjective illusions that could repeat the historical tragedy of the past: greater disunity among Christians, all in the name of the Holy Spirit and a Christ who said: "May they be one so that the world may come to believe that you sent me" (Jn. 17:21). Such a theological need is already being felt by many Pentecostal leaders.

Spiritual Gifts are Necessary

Although I am cautious about spiritual gifts, I can accept the gifts of tongues, prophecy, interpretation and even healing that I find in these groups. In fact, I find it a strong and persuasive argument that these gifts are necessary in this neo-pagan age as they were among the early Christians who had to face the paganism of Rome.

Of all the dangers, I consider the danger of spiritual pride the most insidious, since pride becomes more camouflaged when it infiltrates the areas of prayer and good works. With the gifts comes the natural admiration of those who possess them. What person would not want to possess the powers of healing? Although St. Paul said it was a good thing to desire the gifts, he devoted a whole chapter of an epistle (chapter 13) to tell the Corinthians that spiritual gifts mean nothing if the love of God is absent.

Healing, for instance, is a gift promised to those who believe; yet that belief is not something prompted by a desire to see God's power as a desire to channel God's mercy. The devil could do no better than to tempt people to throw themselves from a temple top or to change stone into bread merely to show the power of God. It not only shows the power of God but likewise renders glory to those who were the instruments of such power. In the Acts, Simon wanted to buy this power from the apostles for that reason. Psychology has shown that we have unconscious reasons for doing things, and motives for asking miracles must be scrutinized carefully.

The same must be said about spiritual smugness and complacency for any group so taken up with spiritual gifts and supernatural intervention. The wisdom of St. Philip of Neri—"There but for the grace of God go I"—must be a constant theme lest the groups become cliques and groups within groups become the "elect." Pride will soon show itself in gifts that are just the opposite of the gifts of the Spirit—quarreling and disunity.

New Hope

I sincerely believe that the Movement offers new hope for a Church whose structures have been mercilessly critized by its own members. Vatican II foresaw more than structural changes; the renewal was aimed at its members, at changing the lives of Catholics and putting Christ at the center of Church life. The almost masochistic furor over Church structures, producing good and evil effects alike, has overshadowed the greater need for sanctity among Church members, and the pentecostals are interested precisely in that. With the guidance of the Holy Spirit and the safeguards, it could be the dawning of a new age of the Spirit as envisioned by Pope John who inaugurated the Second Vatican Council.

Whether we get involved in the new movement or not is not essential. To fail to feel attracted to it is not indicative of personal illness. For all of us, however, devotion to the Holy Spirit (the forgotten Person of the Most Blessed Trinity) is important to our spiritual vitality. For the Holy Spirit was sent by God the Father and God the Son to renew the face of this earth and joined to our spirit to bring us to the fulness of our human potential.

New Openness Develops Among U.S. Cardinals

As the charismatic renewal continues to grow, a significant openness to the renewal is developing among the Roman Catholic Church hierarchy.

In 1974, six of the seven cardinals in the United States have responded in a positive pastoral way to the renewal.

Cardinal John Dearden of Detroit and Cardinal John Krol of Philadelphia celebrated special Pentecost charismatic liturgies in cathedrals filled with worshipers. Calling the renewal an "extraordinary phenomenon," Cardinal Dearden said the renewal is "one of the very significant experiences of the Church in our time." He added that it represents "an open awareness of the rich gifts of the Holy Spirit; an explicit commitment to Christ that made possible the full operation and flowering of these gifts; and an awareness that gives expression to many works and many activities that are significant both to the individual and to the community."

At the Pentecost Mass in Philadelphia, Cardinal Krol told 2,000 worshipers, "There is a great need for awareness of the presence of the Holy Spirit. There must be a greater effort to respond to the desires of the Holy Spirit."

In pastoral letters, Cardinal Timothy Manning of Los Angeles and Cardinal Humberto Medeiros of Boston encouraged the priests in their archdioceses to become involved with charismatic prayer groups. Cardinal Medeiros said that the priests should incorporate charismatic "faith and zeal into deeper life for all of us."

Although they have made no official statements, two other cardinals have appointed liaisons to the renewal. Cardinal John Carberry of St. Louis meets each month with 15 charismatics to discuss developments in his archdiocese. Recently Cardinal John Cody appointed a liaison to the renewal in Chicago.

Interview with Bishop Paul Anderson

Q: Perhaps you could tell us how you first came into contact with the charismatic renewal?

A: The first time was in Washington, D.C. at a bishops' meeting. I knew that the renewal was taking place, but I wasn't involved. One bishop got up and asked how the bishops of the United States should regard the charismatic renewal. Someone answered that it has a basis in Scripture, and as bishops, we must be careful not to condemn, but to show an open, look-see attitude.

The next time was about a year ago in the diocese of Duluth, when I went to a prayer group in Crosby. I asked them to pray for me and I prayed for them. It was beautiful.

Then Fr. George Kosicki came to our diocese and gave two priests' retreats that involved about 60 percent of our 100 priests. They came out of those retreats with a new sense of direction.

Q: How long ago was that?

A: In May of this year. Since then much has happened. Three groups of priests have asked to come to my house to pray together at least once a month. That house has even taken a new direction.

It used to be a big, old, rambling house where I had shelter, but that always bothered me because I never felt that gave the right image to people in the church. It was too wealthy. Now I find it being used by the Lord for new purposes. A community of faith is growing up within the house itself. We have prayers now every morning. It's a community. It's beginning to grow. I didn't start it; God did. I didn't decide one day, "Let's have a community." Likewise, I see in the parishes in the diocese one thing after another that is a movement of the Holy Spirit.

My prayer for the diocese is that the "New Pentecost" comes. Father George said, "You keep praying for that because the prayers of bishops are powerful. God doesn't refuse bishops." I don't know about that, but I do know I want a revolution. I feel my part in the revolution is to be a liberator—to free people, to free the diocese, to free our priests—so the Spirit can work in the church.

Q: Could you tell us what you experienced on the retreats, and what difference it has made in your life?

A: I had wanted to make a retreat for my own spiritual health at the time. The deepest experience was that I came closer than I had been in five years to the priests who were there. The retreat was a catalyst. I saw a group of priests of all ages and all theological levels come together. A community of faith was born between these priests and myself.

Q: Were you baptized in the Spirit then?

A: I was prayed with on the retreat to be filled

Interview with Bishop Paul Anderson 121

with the Spirit and experienced it, but I had felt this in a powerful way two years previously, when people from 23 parishes had gathered in the city of Duluth to celebrate the Easter Vigil. Outside of ordination to the priesthood and to be bishop, that was one of the most moving experiences of my life. If ever I felt the person and the presence and the power of the risen Lord Jesus, it was that Easter Sunday with 7,000 people participating and 35 priests concelebrating Mass. I think part of our renewal in the diocese began at that time. The retreats with Father George, the house, the Center of Diocesan Renewal, and my being here at Notre Dame are other parts of a big picture that I see falling into place.

The result for me has been joy. I've always had hope in my heart, but not much joy. Now in the past few months there's a new dimension of joy and peace. I see the fires of the New Pentecost coming upon us. Praise God—this will enflame all of us in the diocese. I pray that this will come to all the bishops of America.

The world is in a hopeless situation. Hope and joy are what is needed now more than ever. The time is ripe for it. I've seen more joy on this campus in the last 24 hours than I've seen in five years. This has to be a sign that God is working.

Also, I find God using me in a new way. The other night I walked into a hospital to visit some patients. As I went through the cards I saw one for a priest from the Marquette, Michigan diocese. I visited him and found that he had four months to live. My first reaction was "Oh!" He said, "What do you mean, 'Oh!' I've had a good life and I'm going to see God." I spent one of the most beautiful hours of my life with this man, and did something that six months ago I couldn't have done—we spent half that time praying together.

Q: What do you see as the most crucial need for the people of God, both in your own diocese and within the church as a whole?

A: In the past five or six years we have been renewing church structures and forms. We have been caught up in programs; we've reformed the liturgy: that is, we've changed formats, we've changed altars and language and candles and churches and architecture. Yet, there is still a depression in the hearts of people, a sadness that pervades the church, a pall of gloom that has settled over the church. People are crying out for help.

We're realizing that our deep need is for renewal within ourselves. The tremendous vacuum in us needs to be filled. We need to open ourselves to God's love. That's beginning to happen, and that is the renewal—opening up people, not opening up all these external structures.

Come, Holy Spirit

By Cardinal Leo Josef Suenens

Coming to the States and speaking about Jesus, I must say this, that something is happening in America which is important for the renewal of the whole Church. I seriously think that America has some practical role to play in what God is doing today. Perhaps you are not as conscious of it as we foreigners are. It's like what happens when a visitor comes to your house and says, "What a nice picture is on your wall." Now you hadn't looked at that picture for a long while because you have become accustomed to it. So it is when we come to see you: we see that something is here in America that will bring us to a living faith in a living God. Something is happening in America, some new sign of hope, some star in the darkness: you are not only rediscovering Jesus as the Lord, you are also rediscovering that the Spirit of Jesus is alive today and working in your midst.

Certainly rediscovery of the Holy Spirit is not only happening in the United States. I feel that in many places in the Church we are rediscovering the Spirit in this time in history. We rediscovered him in a special way during the Vatican Council. The Eastern bishops insisted all the time that we should give more space and more place to the Holy Spirit. You can see as you read the Vatican Council documents that he is mentioned right and left.

The accentuation of the Holy Spirit in our time is certainly a sign of hope, but we need more than right thinking about the Holy Spirit: we need a renewed encounter with, a new surrender to, the Holy Spirit. And Americans have begun to experience this renewed contact with the person of the Holy Spirit. Among Catholics at least this began six or seven years ago here in the United States in what is now called the charismatic renewal: I seriously believe that in this charismatic renewal there is something very important for the renewal of the Church, something that will help us toward a real visible unity with God. I think that we have here one of the wonders of God today.

I suppose that you, like me, have been a bit uncomfortable when you read in the Acts of the Apostles and see, during the early days of the Church, that the Holy Spirit was at work all the time. He was calling some to be apostles, he was choosing some, he was sending them in such-and-such direction and saying, "Now stop, go elsewhere"—all the time he was at work. As you read you see him speaking to those people in signs so that they could feel his presence: all the time he was guiding, illuminating, directing. The Acts of the Apostles is really the Gospel of the Holy Spirit. When you open to the letters of St. Paul you discover even more of the activity of the Holy Spirit: there are gifts of wisdom, interpretation, gifts of knowledge, and healing, gifts of all sorts, even the gift of tongues—St. Paul speaks about all of these.

In light of all this we cannot simply say, "We cannot accept these gifts as valid or real." No. These

Come, Holy Spirit

gifts are there for us to read about in Scripture: they have been given from the very start. The problem is not whether these powerful gifts of the Spirit are possible in the lives of Christians, but rather why did they stop happening among Christians. I've always felt uncomfortable that we no longer in our own day experience the same manifestations of the Holy Spirit that the early Christians experienced. I tried, like anyone I suppose, to explain it. I'd say, "Well, in the beginning the Church needed special help from the Holy Spirit. He gave them an abundance of gifts just to give them a bit of encouragement, but later on, once you are serious, you don't need all that."

It is not exactly true to say that we didn't see any manifestations of the Spirit down through the centuries. The gifts of the Spirit were still experienced and expected in the second century. Afterward the charismatic gifts are not seen except in the lives of saints: they appear in the lives of saints at least to show the honor, the continuity of the Holy Spirit in history.

So, in any case, there is a temptation to say that charismatic gifts were for the beginning but not for now. But I say that now in our time in the charismatic renewal there is a public manifestation of the power of the Spirit which is perplexing; its very presence demands a response, demands an evaluation. We say on our part, "We have to be convinced that this is a genuine work of God." In that regard I was happy to see the statement of the American Catholic hierarchy, who are themselves very prudent men. They said, "Let us be ready to accept this where the signs of God are evident."

There are of course some things that need correcting. Pentecostalism, especially Classical Pentecostalism, tended to be very anti-church. Now, however, as the charismatic renewal is within the churches, that does not appear to be much of a difficulty. Also, one must not speak about baptism in the Spirit as if he did not believe in the reality of the sacrament of baptism.

Sometimes we have difficulties in judgment, especially judgment of the charismatic gifts and the charismatic renewal because of our own attitudes. Now I say that this is a Christian—one who has really changed, and has surrendered himself to the Father, the Son, and to the Spirit. We Christians are not called followers of Jesus; the first name given to us was "Christians," meaning, "Anointed by the Spirit of God." We must continue, then, in this way that was known to the early Christians. We are always judging Christians according to what we see today as being an average Christian. We are all average Christians, but that doesn't mean that we are normal Christians. We are all abnormal Christians, handicapped children of God, because we have not allowed the Holy Spirit to do his full work in us.

We don't trust him enough. We say, "Yes, Holy Spirit, we are open to you, but not for everything. Don't give me this grace, or don't give me that one, I will choose for myself which graces you should give me." I am a prudent man, but the Holy Spirit is very imprudent. We ask to be opened and then we put our baptism and all that it means—we put it, I dare say, in a sort of freezer. Now, I have nothing against deep freezers, but if we are to live normal, full Christian lives, the power that we received at baptism has to come out of the freezer. We need a release of the Spirit within us. We need to say, "Lord, if you are waiting to do your work in us, we accept that; have your way with us, Lord."

I have looked carefully and I think I can say with confidence that the charismatic renewal does not wish ultimately to be a separate movement. We do not wish to make it closed; we just wish to be a normal part of the renewal of the Church. Just as the Liturgical Movement, the Biblical Movement, and the Ecumenical Movement eventually disappeared as movements, so the charismatic renewal movement will someday disappear, but hopefully not before it has accomplished its task of fostering in every part of the Church a renewed expectancy and experience of all the gifts of the Holy Spirit. And I think the Holy Spirit has come to do this from the inside.

If you ask me for signs that show that the charismatic renewal is really a work of the Holy Spirit, I would give you these. First, the people in the charismatic renewal really love the Word of God. They read the Word of God diligently, meditating upon it, letting their minds be formed by it. That for me is a sign of God. I also see them discovering new sense of prayer, especially prayer of praise. Christians today are accustomed to prayer of petition: we know perfectly the second part of the Our Father, "Give us this day our daily bread"—give us this, give us that. But the first part, "May your name be held holy, may your kingdom come," is not our cup of tea, normally speaking. We are called, all of us, to rediscover that prayer of praise of God for who he is, for his great love, for his infinite greatness, for his creation, for the world of love which is present in himself. As we have discovered, not only the priests, but also the laity, have the duty to praise the Lord.

Another sign for me of the authenticity of this

renewal is that the people in it are rediscovering the worth of the sacraments. They are coming back to the Eucharist, accepting and rediscovering the meaning of penance and the sacrament of penance.

I also see among them something very striking: their coming together in the communion of prayer, in large meetings. There is even the building up of Christian communities like those recorded in the Acts of the Apostles. I have been impressed that in these groups there are conservative and liberal people, extreme right and extreme left; the wonder of it is that, although they remain extreme right or extreme left, they pray together and they have started to love each other. To me, that is a good sign.

The prayer of the charismatic renewal happens in an ecumenical setting and I think that is important. Christians of all denominations are learning here to pray together in the Spirit of God. It is true that Christians have prayed together ecumenically before, but I think we need ecumenical prayer not only during the famous Week for Christian Unity, but 52 weeks in the year. As Cardinal Bea said, we can only go through the door of unity on our knees.

I would just like to end with part of a lecture given in Uppsala by an Orthodox bishop and theologian. He made a comparison between the Church without the Holy Spirit and the Church with the Holy Spirit. He said that without the Holy Spirit, God is far away, Christ stays in the past, the Gospel is a dead letter, the Church is simply an organization, authority is a matter of domination, and the Christian is a slave to morality. But with the Holy Spirit the cosmos is resurrected. In the Spirit, the risen Christ is present, the Gospel is the Father of

Life, the Church shows forth the light of the Trinity, and authority is a liberating service. In the Spirit, mission is a Pentecost; in the Spirit, the liturgy is both memorial and anticipating; and in the Spirit, human action is divine action. So let us be faithful to what we say we believe when we say, "We believe in the Father, the Son, and the Holy Spirit."

Interview with Cardinal Suenens

By Ralph Martin

Q: For many of us, this is an unexpected visit. What brings you to America and, more particularly, to Ann Arbor?

A: The official reason for my visit was to give a series of lectures to Episcopalian priests in various cities around the country, but the unofficial reason was to come and visit you here in Ann Arbor and see at first hand a major center of the charismatic renewal in the Church. I've read a lot about the charismatic renewal and the community here and I'm convinced that something important for the whole Church is going on. Just as the Lord invited the first two apostles, by suggesting that they "come and see," I too wanted to come and see. I have come here on a pilgrimage. This is the culmination of my trip. It's so important in the Church today that we not be content to give theoretical answers to problems, but are able to point to practical, experiential examples of answers to problems. We need to be able to point to places where God is obviously acting, where God and the truth of Christianity can be experienced as lived vitally. The best way to respond to those who protest that God is dead is not by arguments but by pointing to situations where he is obviously and visibly acting. That is why I am here, to see again the Acts of the Apostles in action.

Q: When did you first start hearing about the charismatic renewal in the Church?

A: Last year, I gave 10 lectures in the United States and everywhere I went people asked me what I thought of the charismatic renewal. I began to sense that something was happening that was significant and it was a real incentive to study and find out more. Some of those who work with me in Belgium came to visit here in the States and found out more. They provided me with a supply of literature on the renewal. I've read Fr. O'Connor's book 2 or 3 times; I've read your book *Unless the Lord Build the House* and Steve Clark's booklet *Spiritual Gifts;* I've read every issue of *New Covenant* and found them very helpful. Then, when I was speaking in Philadelphia last year, some nuns from the charismatic house of prayer in Convent Station, New Jersey, came in a terrible blizzard, late at night, just to tell me about what God was doing. I promised to visit them at Convent Station next time I returned, and I fulfilled that promise a few weeks ago. The two days we spent at Convent Station in mid-March were my first real personal contact with the charismatic renewal. I was very impressed. Another contact had been with Fr. Francis Martin when I was in Rome recently. He's translated several of my books into English and he's one of the leaders of the charismatic prayer groups in Rome. After talking to him at length about this, I invited him to give a retreat at the American college at Louvain, and invited 60 other people to join in the retreat with me. Since we have an interdisciplinary group of faculty and students at Louvain studying the charismatic renewal, I was concerned that they should not only study it with their heads, but see it in action. Now I'm here.

Q: As you have become more familiar with the origins and current development of the charismatic renewal, how have you come to evaluate it? What do you think it could contribute to the renewal of the Church? What do you sense God doing in it?

A: As you know, I feel very strongly that the implementation of Vatican II involves a renewal of the structures and forms of the institutional Church, and I have spent a great deal of time and effort working in this direction. And I believe that we need to continue this work, making the structures and forms of the Church more and more conducive to the full participation of all the people of God, implementing collegiality and co-responsibility, as directed by the Council. But now I see more clearly than ever the need for the development of a grassroots charismatic renewal if co-responsibility and collegiality are ever to come to life. I see a profound complementarity between the achievement of true co-responsibility and the development of an authentic charismatic renewal among the whole people of God. We need a renewal in the widespread experience of the gifts of the Spirit for co-responsibility to become a reality. We need to stress this. We need a spiritual renewal as well as a structural renewal. The Church is the Body of Christ. The structures and forms of

Interview with Cardinal Suenens

the Body are important, but it is the Spirit that gives it life. We need to continue to work on the structures and form, but the more important thing is the renewal of the life of the Holy Spirit within the Church. I think it is very logical that my concern for co-responsibility should lead me to see an authentic action of God in the charismatic renewal. In fact, two or three years ago I decided to write a book stressing this aspect. I tentatively titled it "Holy Spirit, the Renewer." But now that I've come into contact with the charismatic renewal I prefer to wait for a while and experience more fully the Spirit at work today. I don't want it to be just a book on the theological level, but also a book about something that happens today and is real.

Q: As you have come into closer contact with the charismatic renewal have you found something in it for your personal life, as well as for the life of the Church? Have you become personally involved in it?

A: Yes, I have. I have taken very seriously what in the charismatic renewal is called the baptism of the Spirit. I have asked for it for myself. And I feel that it is precisely here, at the heart of the charismatic renewal with baptism in the Spirit, that the renewal has such an important contribution to make to the Church. As a pastor, I have been concerned for a long time with the need to make Christianity more personal for Christians who do not have much of a personal relationship to Christ. Many Christians do not experience this personal relationship as they should. Many are Christians out of custom, because their parents are, and so on. But at some point, each person should be led to make a personal commitment to Christ. Basically, I believe that baptism, confirmation, and the Eucharist should still be administered to children as they are now. I feel it is appropriate for children to be baptized in the faith of their mothers and fathers. But at some point, they have to make a personal commitment to Christ for themselves. They need to be prepared to do this, they need to be helped in doing it. What you are doing in the Life in the Spirit Seminars could perhaps be a way of preparing people to make such a mature, personal commitment to Christ. There's always a problem with terminology, but what's being spoken about and experienced in the charismatic renewal as baptism in the Spirit, is what we're looking for. It's what we need to be able to lead people to. We partake of the Spirit through Baptism and Confirmation. But there is still a need for many of us to be baptized in the Spirit, to experience a release of the Spirit, to surrender to him, to allow the Spirit of God to take over.

Q: Would it be fair to summarize what you've been saying this way: that you see a need for the structural renewal of the Church to continue and make progress, but that there's a need simultaneously for a genuine spiritual renewal such as is happening in the charismatic renewal?

A: Yes. If we stop with the structural changes with parish councils, associations of priests, pastoral councils, synods of bishops, and so forth, we have merely reached the sociological level, but not the spiritual. The people in these structures need to be alive in the Holy Spirit and sensitive to his action if they are truly to promote life, and not merely engage in sterile confrontation and the exchange of human opinion. For example, when we come to the Bishop's Synods, we bishops need to be more concerned with being open and sensitive to the Holy Spirit than with defending our positions. That is very difficult to do, but without this genuine openness to and sensitivity to the Holy Spirit, we won't be able to follow the Lord into the full renewal he really has for the Church.

Q: You've mentioned that you see some kind of profound complementarity between the present-day renewal on a wide scale of the charisms of the Holy Spirit and the development of collegiality and co-responsibility. Could you elaborate?

A: In the Council, we stressed very strongly the idea that the Holy Spirit is given to the whole people of God. That's very important. All of us are to receive the fullness of the Holy Spirit, but express it in different functions. Every Christian is to be alive, active, responsible. But since he is part of a body—the Body of Christ—he is to be co-responsible with others. The various gifts given to each Christian need to work together in harmony with the other gifts of the Spirit given to other Christians. The People of God, the Body of Christ, remain theological ideas unless they are brought to life in particular situations with the power and vitality of the Holy Spirit. Also, the priests, bishops and the pope himself are all part of the people of God along with the laity. Their functions do not remove them from their fundamental identity as baptized Christians. "The people of God" isn't just the laity, but a description of what all of us are together in the Church. But to make that a functioning reality, we need the active work of the Holy Spirit. We need the charisms to come to life in the whole people of God.

Q: One of the first things that attracts people's attention and concern when they encounter the charismatic renewal is the matter of speaking in tongues. They find it relatively easy to desire increased peace, joy, a richer prayer life, even some physical healings, but they are initially "uptight" about tongues. What do you think about the reappearance of the gift of tongues as a common gift?

A: Well, first of all, we can't say the gift of tongues is impossible or that it's crazy or doesn't make sense. It is clearly described in the Scriptures as something that God gives, that has a value. Secondly, the caution that Scripture expresses about tongues is that it should be exercised in an orderly way, not that it should be prohibited or that it is valueless. Paul says: *"do not suppress the gift of tongues, but let everything be done with propriety and in order* (1 Cor. 14:39-40). Thirdly, it seems that tongues is intended mainly as a gift of private prayer, and is therefore not suitable for public speeches in churches. It is a way of God showing us that we are not alone in prayer, but that the Spirit of God is with us to help us to pray in depth. It is the Spirit praying with us (Rom. 8:26). I also get a glimpse of an additional meaning: God is being glorified in all the tongues of the world. In the instances when actual languages are recognized, we have a glimpse of the evangelization of the world, a glimpse of mission. But in the end we must simply say that this is another of those "surprises of the Holy Spirit"—another instance where God chooses to work in a way that we humans would never have anticipated or chosen!

Q: Those of us who have been concerned with Church renewal for a long time, and are now involved in the charismatic renewal, recall your intervention at Vatican II to insure that the validity and existence of the charismatic gifts would be recognized. Many today see this as a Providential anticipation of the charismatic renewal. Could you tell us what happened?

A: Well, I didn't expect to make an intervention at that point at all. It was just that the day before I heard one of the other Cardinals proposing that the charismatic gifts were just for the early Church and not for today. I felt like I had to do something about that, because to deny the charisms seemed to undercut the possibility of a genuine awakening of the whole people of God, or at least cloud the deepest significance of the fact that the Spirit is active and vital in each person. I asked a good biblical scholar to bring together all the important texts about charisms and I made an intervention with that as the basis. I concluded by saying that if the gifts of the Spirit are given like this, lay people must be invited to the Council, including women, for women are fully half of the human race unless I am mistaken. I remember one of the Cardinals counseling me that I shouldn't insist on that point. It would be more suitable to expect to see lay people and women in some future Vatican III, he said. But as it turned out, a group of lay people, including women, were invited to attend the third session of Vatican II. It was a symbolic action, but an important one. At that time I was not aware of the possibility of what we now see as the charismatic renewal developing, but if that intervention has been of use to the Holy Spirit in this way, so much the better.

Q: It seems as though there's been a special association of the Holy Spirit with your life and service. Along with your intervention at the Council, I recall that your motto as a bishop is "In the Holy Spirit."

A: Yes, the Holy Spirit has always been important to me in my life. When I became a bishop, I was very aware from history of the tension between the Church as hierarchy and institution and the charismatic Church. You can see this tension all through history—in the Franciscans, in all movements of reform and renewal. I felt that as I became a bishop, taking part in the work of the hierarchy, the Lord was calling me first to be at the disposal of the Holy Spirit, and second to be an administrator. If God is to be free to act, we need Spirit and life first; then we give it order. Life precedes order. I felt we needed to give priority to the action of the Holy Spirit, to the reality of God's working in the Church. That was why I chose "In the Holy Spirit" as my motto.

I sensed the working of the Spirit in various ways over the years. I sensed him at work in the Legion of Mary. The main promise of the Legion of Mary is to the Holy Spirit, not to Mary. To me, this illustrates an important truth. Christ is born both of the Spirit and of Mary. We need to recognize both elements to keep the right balance. If you are only pneumatological, concerned with the Spirit, you risk remaining up in the air. There is a need also to stress the Incarnation, the way God works through our common humanity. This we find in Mary. One day I was having a discussion with Karl Rahner, the German theologian, and I asked him why he thought many Catholic Christians since the Vatican Council were so afraid of acknowledging Mary's place in the overall Christian mystery. His answer was very striking: "Christians today have made of Christianity too much of an ideology, an abstraction. Abstractions don't need a mother."

I began to meet charismatic workings of the Spirit before the movement itself blossomed. I found them not only in the Legion of Mary, but in the Focolare movement, in the Marriage Encounter, and in many other movements. The Spirit is at work in the Church today in a diverse manner.

Q: Several weeks ago, I noticed in *L'Osservatore Romano,* the official Vatican newspaper, that you had been received in a private audience with the Pope. Then, shortly after, Pope Paul gave a public talk on the relationship between the charismatic and the institutional in the Church in which he spoke positively of the charismatic. Can you say something about this?

A: Well, I can say something about the visit, but not about any connection between that and the subsequent public talk: I have no information on that. I can just say that I had a long audience with the Holy Father and I spoke to him for over a half hour of that time about the charismatic renewal. I shared with him my discoveries in that field. I know he appreciated what I shared with him and listened very sympathetically. That's all I can say about it at this time.

I am very glad that Rome is the site of the first international meeting of leaders of the charismatic renewal in the Catholic Church (in October). The link between the charismatic and the institutional is important; it is important that those in the institution who are not familiar with the renewal and who might be aloof, be assured of the complementariness of the two. The charismatic renewal is not against the institution; it is the life of the institution. Through involvement in the charismatic renewal, Christians are being brought to a love of the Scriptures, to a love of the Eucharist, to a love of the Church. These are the fruits by which we know assuredly that God himself is at work.

Q: In 1969, you gave an interview in which you spoke very frankly about the need to fully implement Church renewal as directed by Vatican II. This interview caused quite a stir around the world. Some said it made you the leader and spokesman for Catholics who wanted to move forward with renewal. But in the American press at least, some hinted at possible opposition between you and the Pope. But in our talks, I've sensed nothing but love and reverence for

Interview with Cardinal Suenens

the Holy Father on your part. What is the nature of your relationship?

A: I spent 10 days on retreat before giving that interview. I gave it only in the belief that it would make a positive contribution to clarifying the direction the Spirit is leading us. I touched on the need to continue the reform of certain structures of the Church, to implement collegiality on all levels, to see the Curia as a body at the service of the Pope and the synod. Clearly, renewal means that certain traditions of recent centuries have to change and this will cause difficulty to some who are invested in these traditions. But this conversation has always been about methods and directions, over which honest men can and do disagree. It has never involved personalities. There has never been the slightest difficulty on the personal level between the Pope and myself. We have frank discussions several times a year in which we do not always agree on everything the other says, but our love and commitment to one another has never been questioned.

Q: You've taken a real concern for the unity of all Christians and you have been deeply involved in the ecumenical thrust of Vatican II. Do you see the charismatic renewal making a contribution to Christian unity?

A: Yes, I do. In fact, I could have started talking about the charismatic renewal in terms of its ecumenical implications, for these are very important indeed. The charismatic renewal has extraordinary ecumenical implications. It's important that the ecumenical movement of the Holy Spirit happen not just in the theological discussions, important as these are, but in the daily life of the Christian people. One week each year, Christians of different Churches pray together for Christian unity. The charismatic prayer groups developing all over offer the opportunity of praying together for Christian unity 52 weeks a year. Rediscovering our common unity in the person of Jesus, experiencing the Holy Spirit together, and turning to the Lord together in prayer, are indispensable for the reunion of the Christian people and Churches. Cardinal Bea once said that the only way we can go through the door of unity is on our knees. I agree. For ecumenism to advance we need to pray together and open our arms to one another. Many important breakthroughs are happening in a wonderful way in the charismatic renewal. It will be a great impetus for Christian unity. Christians of different churches need to experience themselves as belonging to the same family, as being brothers and sisters, and that is happening in the charismatic renewal.

Q: Would you like to try to sum up the contribution you see the charismatic renewal making to the whole Church?

A: I see the key to all of today's problems summed up in the question: "Do you love me more than everything else?" That is the root question we are faced with in the renewal of the Church today. I think the charismatic renewal can contribute to this fundamental renewal on every level. It has implications for every area of the renewal of the Church. It can help bring Christians of all kinds to a fully committed Christian life. I see it offering a rich renewal for priests, a renewal in their commitment to Christ, a renewal in their spirit of prayer. It can help bring the renewal of the priesthood out of the theological discussions to a real encounter with Christ. I see great possibilities for the renewal of religious orders. Along that line, I think it is very important to share with the whole Church what you are doing in developing Christian communities, in living together in households, in the experience of the common life. What's emerging here in Ann Arbor and other places is a way of God for the future.

Q: I understand that you hope the charismatic renewal will grow in Belgium.

A: That's right. We need the Holy Spirit like everyone else. I'm asking my secretary, Fr. Wilfrid Brieven, to keep in touch with developing prayer groups, so we can support and encourage them, as well as avoid some of the inevitable difficulties in renewal movements when there is not wise pastoral leadership. You are always in danger from mosquitoes when you turn a light on in the darkness.

Q: Is there anything you'd like to say to the people of God who will be reading this interview, in closing?

A: I would just like to say this: believe in God, believe in what he has called you to be and what you are. Believe in him and his promises to you with an expectant faith. Faith is not just believing some things in general, but it is expecting that God will do what he promised to do. We need to take him at his word and expect it will come to pass. "Lord, we will take you at your word. We believe in your promise and we expect it to be true today. Today you are creating us with all your love." People of God, be open for the surprises of the Holy Spirit.

International Leaders Meet with Pope Paul

Participants in the International Leaders Conference attended a general audience with Pope Paul VI on October 10. After the general audience, 13 leaders met with the pope in a brief private audience. The pope greeted each leader, and spoke to them in French. The pope's statement was printed in the Vatican newspaper L'Osservatore Romano *on October 11. The following is a translation of that address from the English-language edition of* L'Osservatore Romano. *Sections in italics are comments the Pope informally added to his prepared text.*

We are very interested in what you are doing. We have heard so much about what is happening among you. And we rejoice. We have many questions to ask you but there is no time.

And now a word to the members of the Grottaferrata congress.

We rejoice with you, dear friends, at the renewal of spiritual life manifested in the Church today, in different forms and in various environments. Certain common notes appear in this renewal: the taste for deep prayer, personal and in groups, a return to contemplation and an emphasizing of praise of God, the desire to devote oneself completely to Christ, a great availability for the calls of the Holy Spirit, more assiduous reading of the Scripture, generous brotherly devotion, the will to make a contribution to the service of the Church. In all that, we can recognize the mysterious and discreet work of the Spirit, who is the soul of the Church.

Spiritual life consists above all in the exercise of the virtues of faith, hope and charity. It finds its foundation in the profession of faith. The latter has been entrusted to the pastors of the Church to keep it intact and help it to develop in all the activities of the Christian community. The spiritual lives of the faithful, therefore, come under the active pastoral responsibility of each bishop in his own diocese. It is particularly opportune to recall this in the presence of these ferments of renewal which arouse so many hopes.

Even in the best experiences of renewal, moreover, weeds may be found among the good seed. So a work of discernment is indispensable; it devolves upon those who are in charge of the Church, "to whose special competence it belongs, not indeed to extinguish the Spirit, but to test all things and hold fast to that which is good" (cf. 1 Th. 5:12 and 19-21) (*Lumen Gentium,* 12). In this way the common good of the Church, to which the gifts of the Spirit are ordained (cf. 1 Cor. 12:7), makes progress.

We will pray for you that you may be filled with the fullness of the Spirit and live in His joy and in His holiness. We ask for your prayers and we will remember you at Mass.

A Joyful Pilgrimage: The 1975 International Conference

By Bert Ghezzi

On the Monday after Pentecost, Pope Paul VI greeted more than 10,000 members of the Catholic charismatic renewal at a special audience in St. Peter's Basilica. This historic event was significant for the charismatic renewal and for the church. The Pope's action and words were warm, friendly, and clearly supportive. He gave his welcome to whatever contribution the charismatic renewal can make to the spiritual renewal of the church. On its part, the Catholic charismatic renewal, represented by 10,000 pilgrims from more than 50 countries, expressed dramatically its love for the church and its identity with it.

The events of Pentecost Monday in Rome were the climax of the ninth annual International Conference on the Charismatic Renewal in the Catholic Church. At 10 a.m. that day the conference participants assembled to celebrate the Eucharist in the vast Renaissance basilica which for many represents the very center of the Christian world. Pope Paul honored the charismatic renewal by granting Cardinal Suenens the privilege of celebrating the mass from the magnificent central altar which is normally reserved for the Pope alone. Approximately 700 priests concelebrated. "To each of you, welcome, welcome! . . ." was the Cardinal's joyful greeting. The crowd, obviously glad to be there, responded with cheers and applause.

The Eucharist was a wonderful blend of the old and the new, the ancient Roman liturgy providing a royal framework for a free flow of praise. The use of familiar Latin chants side by side with the songs of the charismatic renewal during the mass brought tears to many eyes. Four times during the liturgy there were prophecies announcing that the Lord had begun to work in a new way, exhorting hearers to greater trust in Jesus, and promising that Christ himself would be their joy, comfort, and deliverance in suffering. Participants expressed their love for Jesus in the Eucharist by singing in tongues, filling the basilica with glorious melodies. Some observers regarded the closing liturgy in St. Peter's as a symbol of the growing integration of the charismatic renewal into the Catholic Church.

The assembly quietly prayed and sang for half an hour after the Eucharist, awaiting the arrival of Pope Paul. When he appeared the pilgrims greeted him by singing spontaneous choruses of "Alleluia." The Pope read a message to the charismatic renewal in French (see p. 23 for the official English text) and summaries in Spanish and English. On two previous occasions the Pope has spoken specifically about the charismatic renewal, but never before with such open encouragement. He commented on the necessity of spiritual renewal for modern men who imagine that they are the rulers of their own destiny; he also expressed a warm appreciation for an experienced personal relationship with God which is typical of the charismatic renewal. Pope Paul developed three scriptural guidelines, saying that adherence to them would insure that the renewal would not veer into error and that it would make a sound contribution to the renewal of the church. All three principles were rooted in the letters of St. Paul: fidelity to the true doctrine of the faith; seeking the higher gifts which build up the community of the faithful; and the supremacy of love as the way of Christian perfection and the necessary context for the use of spiritual gifts. He also urged the conference to frequently receive the sacraments of the Eucharist and Reconciliation.

After he completed his prepared message, Pope Paul addressed a personal word of support to the charismatic renewal. The renewal he saw before him, he said, "ought to rejuvenate the world, give it back a spirituality, a soul, a religious thought; it (the renewal) ought to reopen its (the world's) closed lips to prayer and open its mouth to song, to joy, to hymns, and to witnessing." He directed a special word to pilgrims present in the basilica who were not a part of the conference, calling them to participate in spiritual renewal. As the Pope spoke, his voice grew more and more vibrant and as he ended he cried out "Jesus is Lord! Alleluia!" Before leaving, he personally greeted Cardinal Suenens, other bishops associated with the renewal, and a few representative leaders from different countries.

The charismatic renewal held its international conference in Rome as a way of joining in the celebration of the Holy Year and the conference adopted the Holy Year's theme of "Renewal and Reconciliation" as its own. Conference chairman Ralph Martin and the steering committee, composed of members from ten different countries, planned the four general sessions to help conference participants experience a personal spiritual renewal and a reconciliation with the Lord and with brothers and sisters. General sessions were held Friday, Saturday, and Sunday, May 16-18, beneath a large trapezoid-shaped canopy in a field over the Catacombs of St. Callixtus, an official place for Holy Year assemblies. Walking the same ground that was trodden by the early Christian martyrs was a constant reminder to participants of the seriousness of the call to follow Jesus.

Friday afternoon, the first general session opened with sharings by representatives from Mexico, Canada, India, and Ireland. Tom Flynn of Dublin told, amidst cheering, of the reconciliation of Catholics and Protestants who are crossing peace lines in strife-torn Northern Ireland to pray together. The heart of the first session was a service of reconciliation led by American Father Francis Martin and an international team of gifted preachers. In French, Spanish, Italian, German, and English, team members called the conference to a personal decision to work for reconciliation. They challenged participants to be reconciled with the church by no longer indulging in destructive criticism, to work for healing of relationships in families and among those living a celibate life, and for the young to re-establish their respect for the elderly. Drawing elements from the previous messages and from prophecies received by members of the international word-gifts group, Fr. Martin summarized the thrust of the reconciliation service in a moving prophetic exhortation:

> ... *My love has eyes that see the heart of every person; my love takes the initiative ... who of you deserves to be here, deserves to walk on ground sanctified by saints? ... Know how deep, strong, total my love is for you. Repent, because I love you. ... I am preparing you for Pentecost. ... This renewal is my idea, not yours. ...*

After the close of the session, participants returned to their lodgings throughout the city where they had an opportunity to receive the sacrament of Penance and join in the celebration of the Eucharist in small groups.

On Saturday morning, leaders from many different nations conducted workshops under the main canopy and in four tents nearby. Topics such as healing, sacramental renewal, parish renewal, family life, and prayer developed the conference theme in specific areas.

Saturday afternoon, the second general session opened like the first one, with sharing. "When the charismatic renewal came to France a few years ago," joked Fr. Albert de Monléon of Toulouse, France, "everyone thought it was another American gadget which would not last a very long time. But it lasts and grows." Fr. De Monléon said that the Lord was issuing a call to depth in prayer and to joy in the midst of trial. Brian Smith of Brisbane, Australia, echoed this in his sharing. He explained that the Lord was teaching three main things in Australia: greater depth in prayer, commitment of brothers to each other in Christian community, and the importance of developing unity among Christians. Then,

Fr. Mike Scanlan (U.S.) assisted by Fr. Salvador Carillo (Mexico), Fr. Jean-Michel Garrigues (France), Fr. Serafino Falvo (Italy), and Fr. Heribert Mühlen (Germany) led the conference in a ceremony which culminated in the renewal of commitments made in Baptism and Confirmation. Fr. Scanlan proclaimed a message which presented the unity of Christians as the source of salvation for a world wrapped in darkness. "The world," declared Fr. Scanlan, "says that language, nationality, tradition, and culture come first. . . . We say that what comes first is the lordship of Jesus Christ and the power of the Holy Spirit." In an impassioned presentation, he advised the group to renounce the posture of modern Pharisees who rejoice falsely that they are better than other Christians because of spiritual experience and instead to take the posture of the humble tax collector who pleaded to the Lord for mercy.

At one point in the session, the whole assembly burst forth singing "Alabaré!" a lively song in Spanish which became a theme song for the conference. As leaders on the stage, including the bishops, began to dance, the crowd, young and old, joined in, some forming circles in nearby fields. When things settled down, each team member led his group in a renewal of Baptism and Confirmation promises. In response to the oft-repeated questions, the assembly echoed with "I do," "Rinunciamo!" "Creeomos!" "Nous Croyons!" as conference participants pledged their faith anew. When all had responded, Fr. Scanlan had those present lay hands on one another to pray that Christ empower each one by the Holy Spirit to live a renewed life in union with brothers and sisters.

The 1975 International Conference   153

On Pentecost Sunday morning, the pilgrims from the charismatic renewal joined several other groups in St. Peter's to celebrate the Eucharist with Pope Paul VI. Many were overawed by the majesty of the building and the solemnity of the worship. Pope Paul seemed pleased with the spontaneous singing of "Alleluia" which greeted him as he entered and left the basilica. In his homily the Pope spoke of rejoicing, saying that the exuberant enthusiasm of St. Peter on the day of Pentecost gives the church a revelation of the inner life of the Holy Trinity. If we comprehend the church's doctrine on the Holy Spirit, he said, "we would want not only to possess the Holy Spirit, but to experience the sensible effects of his presence in us. For we know that the Spirit is light, strength, charism, infusion of superior vitality, virtues, gifts, and fruits."

The Pope then gave a description of the activity of the Holy Spirit which is close to the charismatic renewal's description of being baptized in the Holy Spirit. "The Holy Spirit, that is God-love, lives in the soul, and the soul suddenly feels itself invaded by a need to abandon itself to love, to Love; and it is aware of a surprising and unusual courage that makes us joyful and secure, a courage to speak, to sing, to proclaim to others, to all *'the wonderful works of God'* (Acts 2:11). . . ."

After the Eucharist, afternoon participants attended workshops in a variety of languages on topics such as Social Concern, Christian Unity, Christian Community, Bishops and the Renewal, and Sacred Scripture, all of which continued to elaborate the theme "Renewal and Reconciliation."

Cardinal Johannes Willebrands, President of

the Vatican Secretariat for Promoting Christian Unity, addressed the late afternoon general session on "The Holy Spirit and the Church." The Cardinal's talk was an impressive statement on the unity of the Catholic Church. He reflected on the experience of St. Paul who after his deeply personal pentecostal experience humbly went to receive baptism from the church. St. Paul's example, he said, serves as an object lesson to the participants in the charismatic renewal; it demonstrates the inseparable link between the events of Pentecost and the founding of the church:

> *Brothers and sisters, it is my conviction that the mission of the charismatic renewal is not to be a privileged group or an esoteric-group, but to remind all the people of God that we all belong with Jesus Christ, baptized in him, and with his Spirit in the community of the church—that we have received the gift of the Spirit, but that we have to manifest him in our lives, that we have to live in him and to give the joy of the Holy Spirit to all mankind.*

The Cardinal presented Vatican Council II's doctrine on the mystery of the church as the presence of Christ and his Holy Spirit among us; he declared that the church's unity is a sign which will bring about the salvation of all. It will rescue mankind from a secularized world and bring them into union with God.

Because of the fundamental unity of the Holy Spirit and the church, Cardinal Willebrands challenged the charismatic renewal to make no separation between the charisms—the special gifts of the Spirit—and the church. "A Christian is charismatic because the church is charismatic, having received the gifts of the Spirit." He developed his point by showing the connections between the sacraments of the church and the charismatic gifts. "The church cannot live on one of them alone, nor can we as individual Christians develop a Christian way of life based upon one of them alone. We need them both." He concluded by assessing the ecumenical importance of the charismatic renewal. He said that the personal, spiritual renewal of Christian living—when achieved with fidelity to the bishops and the Pope—is the very heart of ecumenism; it is here, he said, that the charismatic renewal is making a significant contribution. The Sunday afternoon session closed with several sharings about other contributions the charismatic renewal is making to the life of the church, in particular in the area of renewal of religious communities and family life.

The conference closed Monday morning with the mass at St. Peter's and the papal audience. Participants left Rome with a new sense of unity, mission, and joy. The Lord brought forth in the conference a remarkable sense of oneness in the charismatic renewal. National, linguistic, traditional, and cultural barriers seemed small obstacles in the face of the love of God which drew participants together in brotherhood. The oneness expressed in the conference is symbolic of the oneness being produced by the Holy Spirit in the charismatic renewal worldwide.

Participants, too, experienced the essential unity between the charismatic renewal and the life of the

Trinity incarnated in the church. At the very center of Catholicism, the conference participants felt the church's love for them expressed in Pope Paul's own affection toward them. Rome itself with its Catholic heritage evoked in Catholics a renewed loyalty to their church. If the Catholic charismatic renewal responds to the Lord's leading at the conference, and in particular to the words of Pope Paul and Cardinal Willebrands—and there is no reason to expect that it will not—one can expect to see soon a fuller integration of the movement into the body of the church.

The charismatic renewal also received a new sense of mission. Participants received from the Pope a commission to make a contribution to the spiritual renewal of the church. Furthermore, they heard him exhort the charismatic renewal to engage in the spiritual battle to bring the light of salvation to a secularized world which is increasingly engulfed in darkness. The Lord seems to have used the conference in Rome to impart to the charismatic renewal a new freedom to work along with him in the church and the world.

During the conference the Lord gave participants a new and more profound sense of joy which seems sure to permeate the charismatic renewal on every continent. Observers who have attended classical and neo-Pentecostal meetings for many years commented that never had they encountered such freedom in praise and worship as they saw in the general sessions. It seems more than mere coincidence that Pope Paul chose this Pentecost Sunday to release a new apostolic exhortation on the essential place of joy in the Christian life.

The Lord also spoke to the charismatic renewal

about the joyful suffering of faithful disciples. Many participants observed that they sensed the Lord leading the renewal to appreciate more deeply the mystery of the cross—to grow in experiencing the harmony of pain and joy that comes with sharing Christ's sufferings. The Lord seemed to be inviting people in the charismatic renewal to give themselves so completely to him in prayer and service that they would have nothing left except the perfect joy of embracing God himself.

All of this is of great importance for the charismatic renewal and the church. In the coming months we can expect the Holy Spirit to sharpen our understanding of the meaning of the Rome conference and the new directions in which he is leading. For now we can celebrate with observers such as Fr. Heribert Mühlen, a renowned German theologian, that the church has entered a new era of spiritual renewal. We can decide to renew our commitment to the Lord and to each other to give ourselves fully to serving him in his church.

Pope Paul Addresses the Charismatic Renewal

On Monday, May 19, 1975, the last day of the International Charismatic Conference, Pope Paul VI personally addressed the more than 10,000 conference participants at an audience in St. Peter's Basilica. The following is an official translation of his prepared text which was distributed by the Vatican Press office on May 19. The Pope gave his main address in French, followed by a summary in Spanish and English. He then spoke informally to the conference in Italian.

You have chosen the city of Rome in this Holy Year to celebrate your Third International Congress, dear sons and daughters; you have asked us to meet you today and to address you: you have wished thereby to show your attachment to the church founded by Jesus Christ and to everything that this See of Peter represents for you. This strong desire to situate yourselves in the church is an authentic sign of the action of the Holy Spirit. For God became man in Jesus Christ, of whom the church is the mystical body; and it is in the church that the Spirit of Christ was communicated on the day of Pentecost when he came down upon the apostles gathered in the *"upper room,"* *"in continuous prayer,"* with Mary, the mother of Jesus (see Acts 1:13-14).

As we said last October in the presence of some

Pope Paul Addresses Charismatic Renewal 159

of you, the church and the world need more than ever that "the miracle of Pentecost should continue in history" (*L'Osservatore Romano*, October 17, 1974). In fact, inebriated by his conquests, modern man has finished by imagining, according to the expression used by the last council, that he is free "to be an end unto himself, the sole artisan and creator of his own history" (*Gaudium et Spes* [Pastoral Constitution on the Church in the Modern World], 20). Alas! Among how many of those very people who continue by tradition to profess God's existence and through duty to render him worship God has become a stranger in their lives!

Nothing is more necessary to this more and more secularized world than the witness of this "spiritual renewal" that we see the Holy Spirit evoking in the most diverse regions and milieux. The manifestations of this renewal are varied: a profound communion of souls, intimate contact with God, in fidelity to the commitments undertaken at Baptism, in prayer—frequently in group prayer—in which each person, expressing himself freely, aids, sustains, and fosters the prayer of the others and, at the basis of everything, a personal conviction, which does not have its source solely in a teaching received by faith, but also in a certain lived experience. This lived experience shows that without God man can do nothing, that with him, on the other hand, everything becomes possible: hence this need to praise God, thank him, celebrate the marvels that he works everywhere about us and within us. Human existence rediscovers its "relationship to God," what is called the "vertical dimension," without which man is irremediably crippled. Not of course that this "search for God" appears as a desire for conquest or possession; it wishes to be a pure acceptance of him who loves us and gives himself freely to us, desiring, because he loves us, to communicate to us a life that we have to receive freely from him, but not without a humble fidelity on our part. And this fidelity must know how to unite action to faith according to the teaching of St. James: *"For as the body apart from the spirit is dead, so faith apart from works is dead"* (James 2:26).

How then could this "spiritual renewal" not be a "chance" for the church and for the world? And how, in this case, could one not take all the means to ensure that it remains so?

These means, dear sons and daughters, the Holy Spirit will certainly wish to show you himself, according to the wisdom of those whom the Holy Spirit himself has established as *"guardians, to feed the church of God"* (Acts 20:28). For it is the Holy Spirit who inspired St. Paul with certain very precise directives, directives that we shall content ourself with recalling to you. To be faithful to them will be for you the best guarantee for the future.

You know the great importance that the Apostle attributed to the "spiritual gifts." *"Never try to suppress the Spirit,"* he wrote to the Thessalonians (1 Thess. 5:19), while immediately adding: *"Test everything, hold fast what is good"* (v. 21). Thus he considered that a discernment was always necessary, and he entrusted the task of testing to those whom he had placed over the community (see v. 12). With the Corinthians, a few years later, he enters into great detail: in particular, he indicates to them three principles in the light of which they will more easily be able to practice this indispensable discernment.

1. The first principle by which he begins his exposé is fidelity to the authentic doctrine of the faith (1 Cor. 12:1-3). Anything that contradicted it would not come from the Spirit: he who distributes his gifts is the same one who inspired the Scriptures and who assists the living Magisterium of the Church, to whom, according to the Catholic faith, Christ entrusted the authentic interpretation of these Scriptures. This is why you experience the need for an ever deeper doctrinal formation: biblical, spiritual, theological. Only a formation such as this, whose authenticity must be guaranteed by the hierarchy, will preserve you from ever-possible deviations and give you the certitude and joy of having served the cause of the gospel without *"beating the air"* (1 Cor. 9:26).

2. The second principle: all spiritual gifts are to be received with gratitude; and you know that the list is long (1 Cor. 12:4-10; 28-30), and does not claim to be complete (see Rom. 12:6-8; Eph. 6:11). Given, nevertheless, *"for the common good"* (1 Cor. 12:7), they do not all procure this common good to the same degree. Thus the Corinthians are to *"desire the higher gifts"* (v. 31), those most useful for the community (see 14:1-5).

3. The third principle is the most important one in the thought of the Apostle. This principle has suggested to him one of the most beautiful pages, without a doubt, in all literature, to which a recent translator has given an evocative title: "Above all hovers love" (E. Osty). No matter how desirable spiritual goods are—and they are desirable—only the love of charity, *agape,* makes the Christian perfect; it alone makes people pleasing to God. This love not only

presupposes a gift of the Spirit; it implies the active presence of his Person in the heart of the Christian. The Fathers of the Church commented on these verses, vying with one another to explain them. In the words of Saint Fulgentius, to quote just one example: "The Holy Spirit can give every kind of gift without being present himself; on the other hand he proves that he is present by grace when he gives love" *(Contra Fabianum,* Fragment 28: PL 65, 791). Present in the soul, he communicates to it, with grace, the Most Blessed Trinity's own life, the very love with which the Father loves the Son in the Holy Spirit (John 17:26), the love by which Christ has loved us and by which we, in our turn, can and must love our brethren, that is *"not only in word or speech but in deed and in truth"* (1 John 3:18).

The tree is judged by its fruits, and St. Paul tells us that *"the fruit of the Spirit is love"* (Gal. 5:22)— love such as he has just described in his hymn to love. It is to love that are ordered all the gifts which the Spirit distributes to whom he wills, for it is love which builds up (see 1 Cor. 8:1), just as it is love which, after Pentecost, made the first Christians into a community dedicated to fellowship (see Acts 2:42), everyone being *"of one heart and soul"* (Acts 4:32).

Be faithful to the directives of the great Apostle. And, in accordance with the teaching of the same Apostle, also be faithful to the frequent and worthy celebration of the Eucharist (see 1 Cor. 11:26-29). This is the way that the Lord has chosen in order that we may have his life in us (see John 6:53). In the same way, approach with confidence the Sacrament of Reconciliation. These sacraments express that grace comes to us from God, through the necessary mediation of the church.

Pope Paul Addresses Charismatic Renewal 163

Beloved sons and daughters, with the help of the Lord, strong in the intercession of Mary, Mother of the Church, and in communion of faith, charity, and of the apostolate with your Pastors, you will be sure of not deceiving yourselves. And thus you will contribute, for your part, to the renewal of the Church.

Jesus is the Lord! Alleluia!

(The following is the English summary.)

We are happy to greet you, dear sons and daughters, in the affection of Christ Jesus, and in his name to offer you a word of encouragement and exhortation for your Christian lives.

You have gathered here in Rome under the sign of the Holy Year; you are striving in union with the whole church for renewal—spiritual renewal, authentic renewal, Catholic renewal, renewal in the Holy Spirit. We are pleased to see signs of this renewal: a taste for prayer, contemplation, praising God, attentiveness to the grace of the Holy Spirit, and more assiduous reading of the Sacred Scriptures. We know likewise that you wish to open your hearts to reconciliation with God and your fellow-men.

For all of us this renewal and reconciliation is a further development of the grace of divine adoption, the grace of our sacramental Baptism *"into Christ Jesus"* and *"into his death"* (Rom. 6:3), in order that we *"might walk in newness of life"* (v. 4).

Always give great importance to this Sacrament of Baptism and to the demands that it imposes. St. Paul is quite clear: *"You must consider yourselves dead to sin but alive to God in Christ Jesus"* (v. 11). This is the immense challenge of genuine sacramental Christian living, in which we must be nourished by the Body and Blood of Christ, renewed by the Sacrament of Penance, sustained by the grace of Confirmation and refreshed by humble and persevering prayer. This is likewise the challenge of opening your hearts to your brethren in need. There are no limits to the challenge of love: the poor and needy and afflicted and suffering across the world and near at hand all cry out to you, as brothers and sisters of Christ, asking for the proof of your love, asking for the word of God, asking for bread, asking for life. They ask to see a reflection of Christ's own sacrificial, self-giving love—love for his Father and love for his brethren.

Yes, dear sons and daughters, this is the will of Jesus: that the world should see your good works, the goodness of your acts, the proof of your Christian lives, and glorify the Father who is in heaven (see Matt. 5:16). This indeed is spiritual renewal and only through the Holy Spirit can it be accomplished. And this is why we do not cease to exhort you earnestly to *"desire the higher gifts"* (1 Cor. 12:31). This was our thought yesterday, when on the Solemnity of Pentecost we said: "Yes, this is a day of joy, but also a day of resolve and determination: to open ourselves to the Holy Spirit, to remove what is opposed to his action, and to proclaim, in the Christian authenticity of our daily lives, that Jesus is Lord."

(At this point the Pope's official text ends and his informal address in Italian begins.)

Very dear ones: It is permissible to add a few words in Italian [applause] in fact two messages. One is for those of you who are here with the charismatic pilgrimage. The other is for those pilgrims

Pope Paul Addresses Charismatic Renewal 165

who are present by chance at this great assembly.

Firstly, for you: reflect on the two names by which you are designated, "Spiritual Renewal." Where the Spirit is concerned we are immediately alert, immediately happy to welcome the coming of the Holy Spirit. More than that, we invite him, we pray to him, we desire nothing more than that Christians, believing people, should experience an awareness, a worship, a greater joy through the Spirit of God among us. Have we forgotten the Holy Spirit? Certainly not! We want him, we honor him, and we love him, and we invoke him. And you, with your devotion and fervor, you wish to live in the Spirit. [applause] This, [applause] and this should be where your second name comes in—a renewal. It ought to rejuvenate the world, give it back a spirituality, a soul, and religious thought, it ought to reopen its closed lips to prayer and open its mouth to song, to joy, to hymns, and to witnessing. It will be very fortuitous for our times, for our brothers, that there should be a generation, your generation of young people, who shout out to the world the glory and the greatness of the God of Pentecost. [Applause] In the hymn, in the hymn which we read this morning in the breviary, and which dates back as far as St. Ambrose in the third or fourth century, there is this phrase which is hard to translate and should be very simple: *Laeti*, that means "joyfully," *bibamus*, "we absorb," *sobriam*, that means "well-defined and well-moderated," *profusionem spiritus* ["the outpouring of the Spirit"]. *Laeti bibamu sobriam profusionem spiritus*. It could be a formula impressed over your movement: a plan and an approval of the movement.

The second message is for those pilgrims present at this great assembly who do not belong to your movement. They should unite themselves with you to celebrate the feast of Pentecost—the spiritual renewal of the world, of our society, and of our souls—so that they too, devout pilgrims to this center of the Catholic faith, might nourish themselves on the enthusiasm and the spiritual energy with which we must live our religion. And we will say only this: today, either one lives one's faith with devotion, depth, energy, and joy or that faith will die out.

Riding the Wind

By George T. Montague, S.M.

I was born on a Texas ranch in the summer of 1929. The stock market crashed shortly thereafter. This sequence of events has always amused me, and I used to remind my mother that my birth was so important that after it the whole country went into a post-natal depression.

That Texas ranch would have a lot to do with shaping my roots. I learned to love the moist mornings and the smell of the fields at harvest time. And at night I never tired of drinking in the skyful of brilliant stars. But often, my contact with nature produced not exhilaration but a mysterious melancholy and nostalgia. The stars and the clouds had been there for millions of years before me, and they would continue their timeless journeying when I was no longer there. They did not appear to notice me when I came to admire them, nor did they say goodbye when I had to leave. So perhaps the greatest lesson I learned from nature was that my heart was made for something more.

My early years were not without religious experience. Papa was a strict Catholic of Irish descent, and Mama was a convert. Sunday morning was always a routine of rounding up the family and driving the five miles to church. There was a Catholic grade school attached to the church, and it was here that I began school at the age of six. I remember very little about that first year, but one scene made a deep impression on me. Standing before the class with a crucifix in her hand, Sister described the sufferings of Jesus in the passion and spoke of his great love. I was moved to the point of numbness.

During a retreat while I was in high school, I experienced a sudden crystalization of awareness that I could call conversion. I must admit there was a good deal of fear about the way I received the Lord into my life at that time, but as a result of the experience I began to attend Mass daily, sometimes even at the effort of getting up at five-thirty in the morning. One day I was kneeling in prayer and just looking at the tabernacle. Suddenly I felt a kind of tug inside me that almost took my breath away. It was a mixture of fear and delight, like the times my older brother had tossed me into the air and caught me in his arms. I can say no more except that I knew the experience was from the Lord. I hardly dared to think that it might mean he was calling me to cast all else aside and follow him, but as the days passed, that is what it came to mean. In the spring I announced my intention to enter the Society of Mary.

Maryhurst in Missouri was quite different from the ranch in Texas—colder weather, taller trees, soccer instead of horses, and the dark endless tunnels they called hallways in the motherhouse. It was one of the happiest years of my life. I rejoiced in new-found friends—though I knew how to keep a bit aloof—and the lives of the saints became a passion with me. I was excited by these heroes and I wanted to be like them—then and there.

The next year of novitiate began a curious development in my life. I was taught that the conquest of sanctity is a science and an art, extremely intricate and organized. I'm sure I derived benefit from this organized approach, but it put me on the road of seeking perfection more as a work than as an opening to grace. It reinforced my tendency toward isolation and independence. From then on, through the years of college formation, the experience of Paul was mine. "I advanced beyond many of my own age, so extremely zealous was I for the traditions of my fathers" (Gal. 1:14). I was out to prove to myself, to others, and to God, that I was perfect. Sanctity was a race, and passing up others was so much assurance that I would be first to the goal.

As I recall the days of the seminary in Fribourg, Switzerland, where I was ordained and where I did my doctoral studies, I remember vividly a bike-hike I took through the mountains with four or five of my peers. I recall distinctly the passion I felt to lead the pack, even though one of my brothers was having trouble with his bicycle. I let someone else worry with him. To be first to the foot of the mountain and first on top—that's all that interested me. This scene is symbolic of where I was spiritually, of how important it had become for me to excel rather than to put others first.

I returned to the United States, and after a year of high school teaching, I made a Cursillo. Sitting in the sweltering June heat, I listened to blue-collar workers, some of whom had hardly finished grade school, talk about Jesus as a personal experience in their lives, what a difference Jesus made to them, and how their lives had never since been the same. These men had the kind of personal Christ-wisdom I had studied about, without deeply experiencing. I felt a compelling desire to have that kind of faith.

But a few years later I entered a period of spiritual and emotional exile. The securities which had supported me to this point in my life began to erode. For one thing, the stable church I had known began to fall apart. When Pope John and Vatican II relaxed the tight controls, the repressed adolescence of thousands created household chaos. But more than that, in my own personal life I began to feel the horrible limitations of my own strengths. My aloofness, independence, and self-sufficiency had not brought me oneness with others, and I began to painfully feel my alienations. I noticed how preoccupied I was with my self-image and reputation, and how many tasks I had taken on precisely to prove (to myself, primarily) how good I was—and therefore how worthy of being loved!

In the summer of 1968, still impressed with my ability to do everything, I took on the preaching of six week-long retreats, besides the regular session I was teaching at St. Mary's University. In the middle of July, after a succession of sleepless nights, I went to my doctor, who told me, "Drop everything at once and take a six-week rest." The diagnosis: emotional exhaustion.

The rest brought physical strength, but I knew the deeper root of my problem was still unhealed. I still felt like a spectator at the dance of life—not like one so involved in the dancing as to forget myself. I wasn't even sure life was a dance. The dancers, I suspected, are the phonies. But I wasn't eager to affirm that my spectator position was real either.

At about this time, a few people began to gather

weekly at our Scholasticate residence on St. Mary's campus to pray. I did not attend, but I heard a lot of talk about the Holy Spirit, about tongues and prophecy and such things that made me suspicious about the mental balance of the people who attended. Some of the members of my community went to the meetings, however, and I became impressed with the change I saw come over them. I saw greater love, joy, peace, and patience in them, and these I could identify as the fruits of the Spirit (Gal. 5:22). I was particularly impressed with the spontaneity and even enthusiasm with which they were willing to take up the dull and monotonous chores in the community—doing the dishes, cleaning the house, serving at table —*putting others first!*

I began to see that they had something I lacked, something I needed, something I wanted. I decided to go and find out what turned them on so much. I went to a prayer meeting.

But now the prayer group had grown to a regular attendance of fifty to sixty persons. My first feeling was great discomfort. There was an exuberance and a freedom of outward expression that was alien to my way of praying. There seemed to be a hypnotic preoccupation with praise of the Lord. This bothered me, for I did not feel there was that much in my life to be praising the Lord for—Job's laments seemed to fit my experience better. But these people began with praise, and then they witnessed to the fantastic things the Lord was doing in their lives, and this led to even greater intensity of praise. It was as if the praises sent up were seeding the clouds, and then came the flood of wonders, with more praises resulting. It certainly was different.

I knew I secretly wanted what I saw, but I was scared to death at the price that might be asked. The "baptism in the Holy Spirit" might be just the thing I needed—and feared—the most; the gift of *being given* to the Lord in a new way, a way in which I would let *him* take over the controls.

Whatever moved me, I don't know, but on Christmas Eve, 1970, I stepped forward and asked to be prayed over. As I knelt there, hearing the voices of those praying over me, I began to feel a bubbling inside. It was just there and I didn't know what to do with it.

One of the ways in which I sought to release it was by finishing the last three chapters of a book I was writing—and I did it in less than three days. But the bubbling was still there. On New Year's day, as I drove to the ranch to visit my family, I felt moved just to relax and let the bubbling come out however it would. It came out in a melody without words. Three days later, words came to fit the melody: "The Spirit of the Lord has touched my soul. . . ." Far from being spent by the song, the bubbling was still there. It seemed to go beyond what I could put in either melody or words. Could this be the gift of tongues?

I went to my room, closed my door, knelt down —and let go. I stopped a couple of times as if looking at myself in the mirror, and reflected how stupid this sounded. But then I tried to ignore that. I began to focus on the Lord, and then it was easier to let go. More and more came. And then I began to feel, for the first time in my life perhaps, like the buzzards I had as a child watched gliding in the sky for hours without flapping their wings—they let the wind carry them. (Sorry about mentioning *buzzard* when you were expecting something more esthetic like dove or seagull—but I'm from Texas—and it's the *wind,* not the bird, that gets the credit. In Texas the most repulsive bird is the most graceful flier—and it's all because he lets the wind do the work!) So that's tongues! Praising God by letting the Spirit do it in you, for you, and with you!

Since then, my life has been so different, so rich, so full of inexplicable events. I have witnessed physical healing. I have witnessed the powerful inner healings of soul and Spirit—the healing of marriages and families, the healing of long-festering hatreds. But my greatest witness to the Lord's deep healing is myself. I have found a new strength and vitality, a greater willingness to risk for the Lord, a greater ability to cope with stress and chaos. I have been able to say "praise God" for the whole of my own past. Especially, the Lord has shown me how to love even myself, with less and less need for the kinds of reassurance I used to seek.

The reality of my healing is matched only by the realization of how far I have yet to go. The Lord has given me to see that life is not a race to be first to the mountain but a daily yielding to his Spirit, wherever and however he leads. It is not a question of beating my wings but of learning how to lend them to the Wind.

An Interview with Heribert Mühlen, Theologian of the Holy Spirit

By Ralph Martin

... "for 15 years I have only reflected on the Holy Spirit—but now I have come to know him with my heart too, and wish the same joy for you."

At the first International Leaders Conference of the Catholic charismatic renewal, held in Rome in October of 1973, Ralph Martin interviewed Fr. Heribert Mühlen, also a participant at the conference. Fr. Mühlen is regarded by many as the leading theologian on the Holy Spirit in the Catholic Church today.

Q: Can you introduce yourself by giving some of your background?

A: As a young man I began my theological studies at the University of Bonn, in order to become a priest. I received my doctorate in philosophy from the University of Freiberg in 1951, and my doctorate in theology from the University of Munster in 1962. Moreover I studied at Rome, Innsbruck, and Mun-

An Interview with Heribert Mühlen

ich. I am currently Professor of Dogmatic Theology at the University of Paderborn, with my special area of interest being the theology of the Holy Spirit. I've published a number of works, the more important being *How is the Holy Spirit a Person?*, *One Mystical Person,* and *Desacralization.*

Q: How have you come to be involved in the charismatic renewal?

A: In January of 1971, a priest from Taiwan who was involved in the charismatic renewal was visiting Germany. He came to me and said: "You have written many books about the Holy Spirit, and I'd like to talk to you about him and what is happening in the world today." After we talked for a while he said, "Now, let's pray," and proceeded to pray personally and out loud, which simply flabbergasted me. It is very unusual for us theologicans to pray with people we're having a theological conversation with.

This stirred in me a question I had had for 15 years: How can the teaching of the Holy Spirit be pastorally effective and how could the whole Church open herself more to the working of the Holy Spirit. Then a Jesuit from Fordham who did his dissertation on my books visited and said: "You have the theory of the Holy Spirit, but we in America have the practice, the experience of him in the charismatic renewal; we must get the two together." As I looked into the charismatic renewal I was amazed to see many of my theological observations about the Holy Spirit happening in the daily lives of people. I was overjoyed.

My first real contact with the renewal came in Zurich at one of the sessions of the Vatican-Pentecostal dialogue, with some of the Protestant pentecostals involved in the dialogue. Shortly after that I saw the film that a German television crew had made on the charismatic community in Ann Arbor, and the next morning I started a prayer meeting at our university. This group is gradually growing until now about 40-50 people are coming each week.

Q: What changes have you noticed in your life since becoming personally involved?

A: For me, baptism in the Spirit has been a gradual process over a period of six to eight months. I am praying more now and reading Scripture, not just with a scientific interest but to personally respond to the Lord who speaks to us in Scripture. I also find myself drawn to the prayer meetings, and a growing joy in being with other Christians simply as a fellow Christian and not just in my identity as professor of dogmatic theology.

One experience which happened recently illustrates the change. A group of students and I were driving from Paderborn to Munich for a lecture, a trip that took over five hours, and we prayed and sang together almost the entire time. This would have been unthinkable. impossible, in the past. I have no doubt that the Holy Spirit himself is acting with power in the charismatic renewal, and that this will have profound implications for the lives of many individuals like myself, and for the church as a whole.

Q: What are some of the implications you see

the charismatic renewal having for the Church as a whole?

A: Three major changes come to mind immediately. The first is, we must simply admit that most Christians and many priests too do not pray any more today. The root of this is most often a dificiency of faith or a worried uncertainty in faith. I am of the opinion that the charismatic renewal gives and renews a real conscientious faith and brings with it a deep renewal of prayer life and missionary witness.

The second implication is that in the charismatic renewal I see the roles of priests and bishops changing without conflict, political manipulation or pressure. The strengthening and support of their spiritual lives are also needed by the priests and bishops of the Christian community. When they pray together with other Christians in a personal and witness-giving manner, then the problem of authority appears in a rather different light. In the charismatic renewal I see a more biblical, New Testament pattern of church life emerging by the power of the Spirit, and I see it coming peacefully.

The third thing is that I see more clearly that theology has to be reflection on real experience, and not just a purely intellectual exercise or invention. I see theology being profoundly changed by the charismatic renewal. If theology is truly to be life-giving and in touch with reality, it needs to begin with an experience of God, not with philosophical reflection on absolute being. Theology in the future, as it did in the New Testament, must begin with the experience of the indwelling of the Holy Spirit in the Christian community. The doctrine and person of the Holy Spirit is not one doctrine among others, but a fundamental doctrine and reality in the Church. A renewal in the life of the Spirit as we are beginning to experience will affect not just one sector of church life or theology, but the whole.

Q: Would you elaborate some on the new pattern of church life you see emerging from the charismatic renewal?

A: Surely. I think the charismatic renewal is God's response to what was called for in Vatican II as regards a more collegial, brotherly, communal way of making decisions and exercising authority in the Church. In many ways the style of ecclesiastical organization the Church has today is more based on the structures of Old Testament monotheism and imperial Roman lines of organization, than on a more distinctively New Testament, Trinitarian model. When you see God simply as one (and not also as three), it is easier to feel that therefore it is necessary to have one bishop, one emperor, one way of doing things. When you see God as a community of persons, a community-oriented way of doing things is seen as more fitting. When church structure was being formed in the early second century, the great Trinitarian insights were not yet articulated. By the time they were, in the fourth century, it was too late to influence an already fixed style of doing things.

As time has gone on, this lack of community emphasis in our basic doctrine of God and its subsequent reflection in church organization and style, has resulted in a popular Catholicism which views the church as being mainly the pope, bishop and the priest, and only dimly the average person. We must thank God that in so many ways we see God acting to correct this tragic development and to bring the whole people of God alive by the power of the Holy Spirit.

The Holy Spirit is not simply a "he," but a "we": the Father and Son coming to us, the dialogue of the Father and Son. I think of the Holy Spirit as the divine "we," so intensely does the Spirit make present to us the Father and Jesus, and so transparent is he in himself. He is the "we" that makes us the people of God, one with the Father and Son. The Holy Spirit is also the ecclesial "we." When we say "we" Christians, or "we" the people of God, it is the Spirit within us that enables us to say "we." He is one person in many persons in the Church, one person in two other persons in the Trinity.

We are in the midst of an epochal change in the Church. We are experiencing something of the results of more fully appropriating the changed situation that is ours by passing from the Old to the New Covenant. In the Old Testament, God dwelt in a temple made by hands. In the New Testament God dwelt in Jesus, the new temple, and as we become joined to Jesus, God dwells in us: we are the new temple of God on earth. That's why it's so important that we know that God is not primarily present in church buildings, but in us, the people of God. That is why even comparatively minor things like the growing acceptance in the universal Church of the faithful receiving communion in the hand, rather than from just the anointed hands of the priest is symbolically important, in changing from an Old Testament style to a New Testament style of Church life. The fact that for the past 1000 years only priests could give communion and the faithful couldn't touch the communion host, and now in 26 countries communion in the hand is approved by the pope, is in some respects trivial, but in other respects very significant. It reveals a change in mentality.

What I am saying basically is that the rediscovery of the full doctrine of God, the Trinity, including the full and profound role of the Holy Spirit has profound implications for the Church. In traditional dogmatic textbooks the Trinity is only an intellectual doctrine without consequences for piety or church structure or style of life.

Even today the Trinity doesn't really function in many aspects of the Church as more than a theory. For example, the Trinity isn't the foundation of St. Thomas Aquinas' theology. For him the fact of one God, monotheism, is the base, and this has its influence in all of Catholic life. I am not saying that we need a democratization of the Church, but rather a pneumatization, a Spirit inflowing of the Church. In all the world, a new epoch is dawning. In the secular realm, the age of kings and emperors is over; in the Church too, a new age is dawning, an age of the Spirit, which has already unsurpassably begun with Jesus, and in post-biblical times must be continually adapted anew.

Q: We've spoken mainly about the Catholic Church so far in this interview; do you have any reflections on the implications of the charismatic renewal for Christian unity?

A: Yes. I think the charismatic renewal has

An Interview with Heribert Mühlen

great promise from God for carrying on his work of reuniting Christians. In fact, I am coming out with a new book called "Tomorrow Will Be Unity," which talks about the coming great council of all Christians. I think that a passage familiar in the charismatic renewal has real light to shed on the ecumenical situation: I Corinthians 12. The cited relationship of the charisms to one another can also be applied to the divided church. Each church has its own gift, but often it's been exaggerated and absolutized. Each church has to ask: What is our unique spiritual gift? What can we bring to the coming union of Christians? How do we absolutize or exaggerate this gift? How can we correct this exaggeration? Each church has to build up the other churches with their gift and receive the gifts of the other churches. No church, including the Catholic Church, has experienced all the gifts fully. In each Church only certain gifts are alive and the Church needs the gifts of the other Christian churches. (cf. Decree on Ecumenism, Vatican Council II, article 4.)

Q: Would you like to say some closing words to our readers?

A: I would like simply to say that for 15 years I have known the Holy Spirit with my head, but now I also know him with my heart, and wish the same joy for you. The Holy Spirit is real, and is being sent by the Father and Son to bring the human race to a knowledge of the mystery of the Trinity. I longed for this knowledge but it was merely in my head and an unfilled desire. But now it is in my heart and has transformed my life. Praise the Lord.

The Baptism in the Holy Spirit: Theological and Pastoral Questions

By Fr. Salvador Carrillo Alday, M.Sp.S.

An essential element of the charismatic renewal is, undoubtedly, the "baptism in the Holy Spirit."

From the beginning, people who are active in the charismatic renewal have made the bold claim that God is pouring out his Holy Spirit as he did in the early Church after Pentecost. "Jesus is baptizing us in the Holy Spirit."

This claim isn't unfounded, but is based on the fruit of the Spirit that is observed in the lives of these people.

The object of this article is to explore the nature and significance of what we call "the baptism in the Holy Spirit."

Pentecost: Baptism in the Holy Spirit

The best way to understand Pentecost is to examine a passage from the beginning of the Acts of the Apostles: *When he had been at table with them, he had told them not to leave Jerusalem, but to wait there for what the Father had promised. It is, he had said, what you have heard me speak about: "John baptized with water but you, not many days from*

Theological and Pastoral Questions 183

now, will be baptized in the Holy Spirit" (Acts 1:4-5). Jesus' command is clear. The Apostles must not leave Jerusalem; they must remain there until they receive the Father's promise.

What is this promise? Jesus expresses it clearly: *"John baptized with water, but you will be baptized in the Holy Spirit, not many days from now."* This is the culmination of Jesus' teaching: the disciples will be baptized in the Holy Spirit.

But what can this baptism mean? Jesus' answer is the key. In Acts 1:8 he tells the Apostles, *"You will receive the power of the Holy Spirit that will come on you and then you will be my witnesses. . . ."*

Obeying the order Jesus gave them, they remained in Jerusalem. Luke carefully lists all the Apostles who were present in the upper room and adds, *"All these joined in continuous prayer, together with several women, including Mary the mother of Jesus, and with his brothers"* (Acts 1:14). This list is important because this is the small community that will receive the baptism of the Holy Spirit in a few days. The reference to Mary is important because just as the Holy Spirit descended on her and covered her with his shadow so she could conceive Jesus (cf. Luke 1:35), so now the power of the Holy Spirit will descend on this small nucleus to give life to the growing Church. Mary had an essential role to play in the birth of Jesus and it is fitting that she also assist in her role as mother at what Pope Paul VI has called "the historical birth of the Church."

Luke clearly feels that the phenomenon of Pentecost is the fulfillment of Jesus' promise of a baptism in the Holy Spirit. As we read the account of Pentecost in Acts 2:1-4, there is no doubt that Jesus was pouring the power of the Holy Spirit into their hearts, to transform them interiorly and to make them effective witnesses who would take his name to the ends of the earth.

We know the results. The Apostles *"began to speak foreign languages as the Spirit gave them the gift of speech,"* and people from many nations heard the Apostles proclaiming the greatness of God in their own languages.

Later, Peter stood up before a large crowd and with the anointing of the Holy Spirit gave an authentic interpretation of that morning's events and his first testimony about Jesus.

Peter starts his testimony by giving Jesus the title of "Jesus of Nazareth" to emphasize his human condition and to present Jesus as our brother. His testimony is a small "catechism" that contains the basic elements of the early *kerygma.* There are four principal points in this proclamation:

1. Jesus of Nazareth was a man shown to us by God through miracles, marvels and signs. He was charismatic prophet.
2. This Jesus was given up to a death on a cross that was carried out at the hands of lawless men. But in the last analysis, Jesus died on the cross due to a *"deliberate plan and foreknowledge of God"* (Acts 2:23).
3. This Jesus, a descendant from David, was resurrected by God and delivered from death.
4. Finally, once resurrected, Jesus was exalted by God's sovereign power: *"Now raised to the heights by God's right hand, he has received from*

Theological and Pastoral Questions 185

the Father the Holy Spirit, who was promised, and what you see and hear is the outpouring of that Spirit" (Acts 2:33).

This last point is the culmination of the message, the substance of the mystery of Pentecost. As a supreme gift of his glorification, Jesus received from the Father the gift of the Holy Spirit. Glorified, Jesus in turn poured it out so that the Church could begin its life, the new People of God be born, the ancient prophecies fulfilled and the New Covenant sealed forever and written in all its fullness in the hearts of men (cf. Jer. 31:31-33; Ez. 36:27). The mission of Jesus-Messiah reached its fullness. Peter ends his testimony with a solemn declaration of faith: *"Therefore, the whole House of Israel can be certain that God has made this Jesus whom you crucified both Lord and Messiah"* (Acts 2:36).

God has made Jesus *"Lord."* He has made him to be his royal heir and Lord of all humanity and the entire universe. He has declared him Victor over all his enemies, Victor over the devil and over every evil power that opposes the establishment of the Kingdom of God. The title of "Lord," given only to God in the Old Testament, affirms that Jesus is above all other created beings, and boldly proclaims his divine character.

God has made Jesus *"Messiah."* When the Father resurrected and glorified Jesus, giving him the fullness of the Spirit, he made him Messiah in all his perfection. Jesus, the giver of the Holy Spirit, is the person announced in the Scriptures, the Son of David, the Restorer of the people, the Servant of Yahweh, the King anointed by the Holy Spirit, the Son of man who came with the clouds from heaven.

As a result of Peter's testimony on that day, three thousand souls joined the Church that was being born.

The Baptism in the Holy Spirit within the Charismatic Renewal

The expression *"baptism in the Holy Spirit,"* which is so important in the charismatic renewal, comes from the text in Acts 1:5: *"John baptized with water, but you, not many days from now, will be baptized in the Holy Spirit."*

The baptism in the Holy Spirit usually occurs in the context of a prayer in which a Christian community asks Jesus glorified to pour out his Spirit in a new way and in greater abundance upon the person who is asking for it, so that this person will be his witness everywhere, even to the ends of the earth.

The one who baptizes in the Spirit isn't one brother or another, but the same glorified Jesus because he alone can baptize in the Spirit according to the Gospel: *"The man on whom you see the Spirit come down and rest is the one who is going to baptize in the Holy Spirit"* (John 1:33).

The baptism in the Spirit is neither the sacrament of baptism not of confirmation; it is another outpouring, a new effusion of the Holy Spirit that activates the rich potential of grace that God has given every Christian according to his vocation and to the charism of his state of life (cf. 1 Cor. 7:7). In some it will activate what they received in baptism and confirmation, in others it will also activate the graces that God has given through penance and the Eucharist. In married couples, it will renew the graces of matrimony. In priests, it will renew their priestly charism. In some it will fully kindle the call to simply live a single life. In others, it will carry to perfection the gift of consecrated virginity.

This new outpouring of the Spirit of God, with all the richness of its grace, produces a radical inner conversion and a deep transformation of a person's life. It helps him to better understand the mystery of God. It helps him to make a new personal commitment to Christ and to open himself entirely to the work of the Holy Spirit. It gives him the gifts necessary to accomplish his personal mission in building the Body of Christ. It confers on him God's strength to testify to Jesus everywhere and in different circumstances.

It's useful to emphasize that receiving the baptism in the Holy Spirit is not the same as making a consecration to the Holy Spirit. In the consecration to the Holy Spirit, an active attitude predominates: the person gives himself, offers himself, delivers himself, "consecrates" himself to the Holy Spirit so that he will carry out the plans God has for him. In the baptism in the Spirit, a receptive attitude prevails: Jesus glorified is asked to pour out his Spirit and his abundant gifts upon the person who is "baptized in the Holy Spirit." This receptive attitude is similar to Mary's when she answered to the will of God, as spoken by the angel Gabriel: *"Behold, I am the handmaid of the Lord; let what you have said be done to me"* (Luke 1:38).

The baptism in the Holy Spirit does not cover all the riches of the charismatic renewal. For the Apostles, the baptism in the Spirit was only the start of a new life, in the new covenant, in the new people of God. In the charismatic renewal, the baptism in the Holy Spirit is only the start of a new life, of a new way to walk in the Spirit and to live the Christian life in greater fullness.

The Relations Between the Baptism in the Holy Spirit and the Sacraments

The baptism in the Holy Spirit, as experienced in the Catholic Charismatic Renewal, does not deny the sacraments of Christian initiation: baptism and confirmation. Rather, it assumes them. But neither is it a duplicate of these sacraments.

As we have said, in the baptism in the Holy Spirit, the Holy Spirit is given in a new way that sets in motion and augments the potential of grace that each one has received in his lifetime. In this sense, with the baptism in the Holy Spirit the graces of baptism and confirmation are revived, and the graces and charisms of the state of life to which God has called each person are revitalized. This is why this spiritual rebirth is referred to as a "renewal."

The sacrament of confirmation, certainly, has its roots in the events of Pentecost day. Nevertheless, this sacrament does not exhaust the total contents of that pneumatic experience. Pentecost has such a richness that it can't be confined solely to confirmation. The Gift of the Holy Spirit is received in the sacrament of confirmation, but by no means does confirmation exclude further outpouring of the Holy Spirit, sacramental or extrasacramental.

Two experiences in Scripture are related to the sacrament of confirmation but are not the sacrament of confirmation. They are the narratives about Samarians baptized by Philip in Acts 8:14-17 and John's disciples at Ephesus in Acts 19:1-7. Acknowledging the exegetic difficulties of these passages, we can make this reflection after a simple reading: while our sacrament of confirmation is essentially situated in the line of sanctifying grace and of the inner gift of the Spirit, these two accounts present a marked charismatic orientation.

The special case of Cornelius and his household, without any connection to the sacrament of confirmation, is also a good example of an extrasacramental outpouring of the Holy Spirit similar to the baptism in the Holy Spirit. While Peter was telling them about Jesus Christ, the Holy Spirit was poured out upon these gentiles and they began to speak in tongues, much to the surprise of the Jews. Peter then gave orders that they also be baptized in the name of Jesus Christ. Later, when the Jerusalem community reproached Peter for having entered the house of a gentile, Peter told them what had happened: *I had scarcely begun to speak when the Holy Spirit came down on them in the same way as it came on us at the beginning, and I remembered that the Lord had said: "John baptized with water, but you will be baptized with the Holy Spirit." I realized then that God was giving them the identical thing he gave to us when we believed in the Lord Jesus Christ. . . .* (Acts 11:15-17)

The Baptism in the Holy Spirit: Is It for All?

We must clearly affirm that God never rushes the wills of men and that he carries out his salvific work in many different ways. The teachings of the Church have always shown us the safe road and the adequate means to arrive at our salvation.

Nevertheless, it is right to say that "the baptism in the Holy Spirit" in its profound reality, though not necessarily in its outward forms nor in its sensitive manifestations, can be an invitation to all since it is nothing but another outpouring of the Holy Spirit, who deeply renews the inner being of the Christian and sets in motion and enriches all its wealth of graces.

The book of Acts of the Apostles, as the rest of Scripture, is for all Christians. In Acts 2:39 we find Peter's word about the charismatic gift of Pentecost: *"For to you is the promise and to your children and to all who are far off even to all whom the Lord our God calls to himself."*

All of this goes along with wishes of Pope Paul VI in connection with the Holy Year. He said: "We must all place ourselves windward of the mysterious, but now in a certain way, identifiable breath of the Holy Spirit. It is significant that precisely on the joyous day of Pentecost . . . the Holy Year unfurls its sails in each one of the local Churches, so that a new navigation, *we mean a new movement, truly pneumatic, that is charismatic,* may drive believing humanity in the direction and in harmonious emulation towards the new goals of Christian history, towards its eschatological port."

The Baptism in the Holy Spirit, a Problem in Terminology

"The baptism in the Holy Spirit" is an expression that frequently raises problems. It surprises some, disturbs others. In some it causes confusion, in others, it provokes distrust.

It seems that these problems arise when people

first hear about or have their first contact with the charismatic renewal and its terminology, or when they remain aloof or hostile to this renewal.

Many people, after a serious and adequate explanation of the charismatic renewal and the baptism in the Holy Spirit, join it with true personal commitment and self-giving, and do not suffer from uncertainty. The name "baptism in the Holy Spirit" condenses and synthesizes for them a double experience; the inner renewal (conversion or metanoia) that has taken place within them and the new outpouring of the Gift of the Spirit that has set in motion their spiritual energies and has uncovered new horizons and higher dimensions for their life.

It is noteworthy that in the Catholic Church the expression "baptism in the Holy Spirit" has never been used in a common and ordinary way to designate either the sacrament of baptism or of confirmation. Moreover, the recent liturgical documents on these sacraments do not make use of this title. Therefore, the expression "baptism in the Spirit" is not necessarily tied to one sacrament or another.

In view of this, my opinion is—always subject to the judgment of the teaching of the Church—that it would be convenient to retain the expression "baptism in the Holy Spirit," which comes directly from the Bible and proclaims in an admirable manner the new commitment that the believer wants to make with Christ and the decided will with which he wishes to open himself up to the work of the Holy Spirit.

The Baptism in the Holy Spirit and Christian Tradition

The experience of Pentecost has been known to Christians throughout history. Traditional Christian spiritual writing often indicates a familiarity with that outpouring of the Holy Spirit which we in the charismatic renewal have come to call the baptism in the Holy Spirit. Although circumstances and terminology may change from age to age, the experience of the presence and power of God itself remains substantially the same.

It becomes important, then, to examine Christian tradition for what it can clarify and explain about the baptism in the Holy Spirit. The following two articles have just such a purpose: the writings of the twelfth century abbot, Aelred of Rievaulx, and of Thomas Aquinas in the thirteenth century not only help us better understand the nature and the effects of the pentecostal experience, but also contribute towards establishing a sense of continuity and a broader perspective.

I. By Fr. Basil Pennington

The term "baptism in the Spirit" seeks to express an event, very real and very beautiful, which takes place in a Christian when he freely and fully opens himself to the Holy Spirit and allows Christ's promised Comforter to enter into his life to guide him into a life of love, praise, and joyous service. In a word, when he gives the Spirit a blank check and lets him write on it what he will. This tremendous new impulse of life can find no better analogue than that mysterious event which first makes us divinized sons of God, living members of Christ, men capable of knowing and loving God as he knows and loves himself: Baptism into Christ Jesus.

This idea that there is a moment in the ordinary spiritual growth of the Christian when the Holy Spirit of love comes in a very special way into his life is not new to Catholic tradition. One witness to that tradition is the twelfth-century English saint and mystic, Aelred of Rievaulx. A disciple of Bernard of Clairvaux, the towering spiritual leader of that century, Aelred served God's people in Great Britain in his own more modest way as the "Bernard of the North." For over eight centuries now, Christians have drawn guidance and nourishment from the spiritual writings of this Cistercian abbot.

In his *Second Sermon for the Feast of Pentecost,* Aelred traces out the normal stages of spiritual growth for a Christian. He draws his model from three successive events in Christ's life: his baptism, his transfiguration, and his glorification.

> *Take these three stages to represent three stages in the soul's progress: purification, probation, and rewarding. Christ's baptism represents our purification, his transfiguration our probation, and his glorification our rewarding. We are*

> *purified by confession, we are proved by temptation, and we are rewarded by the fullness of charity.*

Aelred expands upon each of the three stages, but his description of the third one especially concerns us, since we are joyfully seeing it develop in our own lives and the lives of our communities. In this stage, sorrow gives way to joy, toil to rest, and fear to the certitude that nothing will separate us from the love of God. "Here one tastes how good and how pleasant it is for brothers to live in unity," Aelred continues. "Here we are made truly disciples of Christ, 'together in the same place.'" This can only come about because the love of God has flooded our hearts through the Holy Spirit. Although the Holy Spirit is certainly given to us at the "Jordan" (the first stage—spiritual growth or conversion) and on "the mountain" (the second stage—being proven), Aelred maintains that the fullness of the Spirit comes in the third stage:

> *In these places some part, if I may so express it, of the Spirit is given. But in the cenacle, "in the same place," the very plenitude of the Spirit is conceived. . . . Such great fullness of the Spirit is therefore given at this stage that in comparison it may be said neither to be given nor to be possessed at the others.* "For the Spirit had not been given previously because Jesus had not yet been glorified" (John 7:39).

I think Aelred expresses very well here the reality of the experience of many good traditional Christians who have been "baptized in the Spirit." The Holy Spirit has been present and active in their lives since their Baptism and conversion, and he has continued to abide with them and strengthen them all along the way. But there was that time when they were brought into "the cenacle" and received such a plentitude of the Spirit into their lives that it was like a wholly new beginning; they were "baptized in the Spirit." Aelred does not use our terminology, but he certainly expresses our experience. It is noteworthy, too, that he connects this baptism or special outpouring of the Spirit with the glorification of Christ. In fact a mark of "baptism in the Spirit" is the desire and ability to praise and glorify Christ. Most Christians will attest that before being baptized in the Spirit their prayer was one of asking, repenting, and some thanking, but little or no praise. With the baptism in the Spirit, however, Christ was glorified in their lives, and now they cannot cease praising and glorifying him in the Holy Spirit.

One final reflection: Aelred has placed the "baptism in the Spirit" on the summit of perfection. But the Lord is limited by no scale of perfection or human calculation of merits. Another twelfth-century Cistercian, William of St. Thierry, expressed this view in his work, *On the Nature and Dignity of Love:*

> *It must be remembered, however, that the stages of love are not like the rungs of a ladder. The soul does not leave the lesser loves behind it as it moves onward to the more perfect love. All the degrees of love work together as one, and for this reason another soul's experience of the*

stages of growth may well follow an order which differs from the one described.

Praise the Lord who pours out the Holy Spirit upon his people in a variety of ways. Praise him for his love and compassion: *". . . when the Lord wants to show mercy, he does . . . "* (Rom. 9:18). Praise him!

II. By Fr. Francis Sullivan

If we are going to look for light on the question of baptism in the Spirit from the writings of the traditional Catholic theologians, we should look to see what they have to say about the "giving" and the "sending" of the Holy Spirit. St. Thomas Aquinas treats this question in the first part of his *Summa Theologiae* (question 43).

St. Thomas points out that we can speak of the Holy Spirit's being sent to us and given to us when we begin to have a new relationship with him, as to a person intimately present to us through the love which he pours into our hearts. This must involve a new way of our knowing him—not a merely speculative knowledge, but a kind of experiential knowledge. While this does not involve a real change in God, it does involve a radical change in us. It is a new creation. It is a new life: *"It is no longer I that live, but Christ who lives in me"* (Gal. 2:20). St. Thomas uses two key words to express what happens in this experience: the Holy Spirit comes to dwell in us *("inhabitatio")* and does so in such a way as to make us new *("innovatio")*. In Catholic teaching this takes place *initially* at the moment when we become

Christians, when we are *"born anew of water and the Spirit"* (John 3:5).

A crucial question now arises: can there be more than one sending of the Holy Spirit to the same person? Obviously there can be only one *initial* sending. But, while he is dwelling in that soul, does it make any sense to speak of another sending of the Spirit to the same person?

It is helpful here to look at traditional Catholic belief about what happens when a person receives the sacraments of Confirmation and Holy Orders. In Catholic tradition, these are "sacraments of the living" (i.e., to be received by persons in whom the Spirit is already indwelling), and they are understood to involve a new coming of the Holy Spirit, with new gifts which the person did not have before. St. Thomas explains that there is a sending of the Spirit not only in the initial gift of grace, but also with respect to an advance in virtue or an increase in grace:

Such an invisible sending is especially to be seen in that kind of grace whereby a person moves forward into some new act or some new state of grace: as, for example, when a person moves forward into the grace of working miracles, or of prophecy, or out of the burning love of God offers his life as a martyr, or renounces all his possessions, or undertakes some other such heroic act. (Summa I, q.43).

St. Thomas speaks of a "new sending" of the Spirit where it is a question of a decisively new work of grace in a person's life. What I found surprising here is that when St. Thomas comes to give examples of such "new acts or states of grace," he does not speak of the effects of Confirmation or Holy Orders. Rather, he speaks of "going forward" into the grace of working miracles, or of prophecy, or of martyrdom, or a total renunciation of worldly goods. All of these fall under the heading of "charismatic," rather than "sacramental" graces.

How might this teaching of St. Thomas help us to interpret the pentecostal experience in terms of Catholic theology? This experience can be described as a "religious experience which initiates a decisively new sense of the powerful presence and working of God in one's life, which working usually involves one or more of the charismatic gifts." Can we not say that this is just the sort of thing that St. Thomas was talking about when he gave his examples of a "sending of the divine Person for an increase of grace"? The fact that, in giving his examples, Thomas spoke of charismatic rather than of sacramentally conferred gifts suggests that a Catholic need not try to interpret the pentecostal experience merely in relation to Baptism and Confirmation, as an "actuation," "release," "manifestation" or "reviviscence" of gifts already received in those sacraments.

A Statement of the Theological Basis of the Catholic Charismatic Renewal

The following statement was drawn up during the International Conference in Rome at the suggestion of Cardinal Suenens. Fr. Kilian McDonnell was asked to prepare the preliminary draft. A small group of theologians discussed the text with Fr. McDonnell and aided in its revision. The final draft was presented to conference participants, but was not publically discussed or voted upon. It should be viewed as a statement of the theological basis of the Catholic charismatic renewal, and not as an official pronouncement of the conference. Working with Father McDonnell were Frs. Salvador Carrillo from Mexico, Albert de Monléon from France, Francis Martin from Canada, Donatien Mollat from Rome, Heribert Mühlen from Germany, and Francis Sullivan from Rome.

The author of this statement intends to describe in brief form the theological basis of the Catholic charismatic renewal. It is directed to those outside of the renewal who seek to understand it.

Those involved in the renewal have as their purpose the proclamation of the Gospel and the promised restoration of all men in Christ which "has already begun in Christ, is carried forward in the mission of the Holy Spirit, and through him continues in the Church" *(Lumen Gentium,* art. 48).

The Catholic charismatic renewal has as its basis the Gospel of Jesus Christ. Without reservation those in the renewal wish to embrace the full mystery hidden from all ages in the Father, revealed in the Son, and demonstrated in the Holy Spirit. There is no other Gospel than that of Jesus Christ, crucified and risen.

Without wishing to absolutize the Acts of the Apostles, many see the central theological intuition of the renewal described in Acts. Jesus, crucified and risen, sends the Spirit. *"Being therefore exalted at the right hand of God, and having received from the Father the Promise of the Holy Spirit, he has poured out this which you see and hear"* (Acts 2:33). Jesus both receives and sends the Spirit. The outpouring of the Spirit results in baptism (Acts 2:38), and the birth of Christian communities (Acts 2:41). These communities are built up by the teaching of the apostles, fellowship *(koinonia),* eucharistic celebration and common prayer. *"And they devoted themselves to the apostles' teaching and fellowship, to the breaking of bread and the prayers"* (Acts 2:42). Charisms appear among the apostolic community for the upbuilding of the Church. *"Many signs and wonders were done through the apostles"* (Acts 2:43). The experience of the Spirit's presence and power is directed specifically to witness and mission, and is related to the Lordship of Jesus. *"You shall receive power when the Holy Spirit has come upon you; and you shall be my witnesses in Jerusalem and*

Theological Basis of Renewal

in all Judea and Samaria and to the ends of the earth" (Acts 1:8).

Those in the renewal do not seek to isolate certain New Testament doctrines, practices, or charisms in order to attribute to them a greater role than they have in the New Testament witness. The Gospel in its New Testament expression did not isolate the Spirit and the coming to visibility of the Spirit in the charisms from the Lordship of Jesus, and the full proclamation of the Kingdom. Both the Spirit and the full spectrum of his charisms are integral to the Gospel of Jesus and were accepted by the New Testament communities as belonging to the meaning of a Christian and to ecclesial life.

Our hearing of the Gospel takes place within a tradition and history which has formed us and of which we are a part. This tradition joins us to the Gospel while this history separates us in time from the Gospel as it was preached and experienced in the early Church.

The Church preaches the same Gospel which was preached by the Apostles. But the renewal asks whether the history out of which we come has the same kind of awareness and the same expectations as the early Church had and preached. Many Catholic charismatics point out how contemporary awareness and expectations differ from that of the early Christians. If our awareness of what it means to be "in Christ" and "to walk in the Spirit" differs from that of the early Church, and if we have more limited expectations than they did of how the Spirit comes to visibility in the charisms for the service of the Church and the world, then would this not have a profound effect upon worship, evangelization, and engagement in the life of the world? Those within the charismatic renewal make no claim to a special spiritual endowment or to a special grace which distinguishes those involved in the renewal from others not so involved. If they differ at all they differ in awareness and expectations and therefore in experience. The purpose of the renewal is not to bring to the Church something she does not have, but to bring local churches and the Church universal to Jesus Christ, and to widen the expectations of how the Spirit comes to visibility in the charisms within the life of the Church.

Persons within the renewal wish to point to aspects of the Gospel without attributing an undue importance to them. In particular they wish to call attention to the manner in which the Holy Spirit and the charisms are related to the Lordship of Jesus, the glory of the Father, the service of the Church and world.

If Catholic charismatics were asked in more specific terms to describe the theological basis of the renewal, they would have to say that theological research and reflection have not been sufficient to permit a final answer. There is a further difficulty which those in the renewal, as also those not involved, have in assessing the work of the Spirit. The very nature of the Holy Spirit, who is Breath, involves a difficulty of a different kind from that present when speaking of Jesus, who is Word. However, an attempt will be made to give some explanation of the theological foundations of the renewal. Without prejudice to other explanations the author gives a theological-sacramental formulation which represents the most widely accepted view within the renewal.

Theological Basis of Renewal 203

As one reads the literature coming out of the renewal it becomes obvious that those who write from within the renewal wish to be Catholic and wish to situate the renewal within the Catholic theological tradition. This is an expression, one of many, of the fidelity of the renewal to the Church.

The Spirit and the charisms through which the Spirit comes to visibility belong to the nature of the Church, which is the body of Christ. The Spirit and his charisms are constitutive of the Church and are not added to an already existing body of Christ. Without the Spirit and his charisms there is no Church. Therefore there is no group or no movement within the Church which can claim the Spirit and his charisms in any exclusive way. If the Spirit and his charisms belong to the nature of the Church they also belong to the nature of the Christian life in its communitarian and individual expression.

St. Paul defines the Christian in terms of both Christ and the Spirit. *"Anyone who does not have the Spirit of Christ does not belong to him"* (Rom. 8:9). In the Gospels, that which distinguishes the messianic role of Jesus from the role of John the Baptist is that Jesus baptizes in the Holy Spirit. In particular, by the sacrament of baptism one becomes a member of the Body of Christ because in baptism one receives the Spirit. *"For by one Spirit we were all baptized into one body—Jews or Greeks, slaves or free—and all were made to drink of the one Spirit"* (1 Cor. 12-13). The New Testament describes in various ways the process by which one becomes a Christian: it is a process under the aegis of faith. The anointing of faith (1 John 2:20,27) precedes and accompanies conversion, which is a *"turning to God from idols to serve the living and true God and to await his Son from heaven, whom he raised from the dead"* (1 Thess. 1:9-10). Conversion leads to baptism, the forgiveness of sins, and the receiving of the Holy Spirit, this faith process is admirably summed up in the conclusion of St. Peter's speech at Pentecost itself: *"When they heard these things, they were cut to the heart* (faith—cf. Acts 15:9) *and said to Peter and the other apostles, 'What shall we do, brothers?' and Peter said to them: 'Be converted, and let each one of you be baptized in the name of Jesus Christ for the remission of your sins, and you will receive the gift of the Holy Spirit'"* (Acts 2:37,38).

Around these steps of initiation, and the subsequent *"walking in the Spirit"* (Gal. 5:16), we can group many of the other New Testament expressions that refer to the process of becoming a Christian: baptism (Rom. 6), illumination (Heb. 6:4), baptized in the Holy Spirit (Acts 1:5), to become a new creature (Gal. 6:15), to be filled with the Holy Spirit (Acts 2:4), to receive the Spirit (Gal. 3:2), receiving the gifts and call of God (Rom. 11:29), entrance into the new covenant (Heb. 8:6; 12:24), new birth (1 Pet. 1:23; John 3:3), being born of water and the Spirit (John 3:5).

The decisive Christian-constituting coming of the Spirit is related to the celebration of the Christian initiation (baptism, confirmation, Eucharist). Christian initiation is the effective sign of the Spirit's bestowal. The early Christian communities not only received the Spirit during the celebration of initiation, but expected that the Spirit would demonstrate his power by the transformation he would effect in their lives. To receive the Spirit was to change. Further, they expected that the Spirit would come to visibility along the full spectrum of his charisms in the community, which included, but by no means were limited to, such charisms as helping, administration, prophecy, and tongues (1 Cor. 12:28; cf. Rom. 12:6-8).

The charisms of the Spirit are without number and they constitute the means by which each member of the Church ministers to the whole body. Charisms are essentially ministerial functions directed outward for the building up of the body and the service of the world rather than exclusively inward toward the edification of the individual. The Spirit comes to visibility in a service ministerial function in each Christian. No Christian is without a ministry in and for the Church and world.

One of the things which distinguishes the local and universal Church today from a community in the early Church is that the contemporary Church is not aware of some of the charisms of the Spirit as real possibilities for its life. The contemporary Church has more limited expectations as to how the Spirit comes to visibility. One of the reasons for the restricted expectations is the tendency to describe the assistance of the Holy Spirit primarily in terms of the hierarchical ministry.

Persons in the renewal make no distinction between the essential content of initiation celebrated in the communities of the early Church and that celebrated in the Church today. In both the Spirit is and was received. Today, however, Christians generally have a more limited expectation, awareness, and openness as to how the Spirit comes to visibility in the life of the community. If the expectation is limited, so will be the experience of the Spirit in the Church's life. The modality of the Church's life in the Spirit is affected by the Church's expectations. People within the renewal wish to widen the expectations of the local churches and the Church universal so that the full spectrum of the charisms become real possibilities for the total life of the Church. In no way do those involved in the renewal wish to restrict the Church's theological and pastoral attention to the more prophetic charisms. Those in the renewal recognize that an excessive attention to the charisms of the Spirit results in a basic distortion of the Gospel. The charisms are not ends in themselves. But they contribute to that fullness of life in Christ and the Holy Spirit to which the Church is called.

The charismatic renewal, therefore, has its theological foundations in the celebration of initiation and calls for a renewal of baptismal consciousness broadly conceived, that is, *"That we might understand the gifts bestowed on us"* (1 Cor. 2:12). Those in the renewal urge that the Church open itself to that life received in Christian initiation so that it may attain its fullest expression.

The charismatic renewal is based on the assumption that the Holy Spirit is sovereign and free. He blows when, where, and how he wills. Though the Spirit takes persons and local churches where they are, the Spirit in no radical way is dependent on the subjective dispositions of persons or communities. The Holy Spirit has and retains the initiative at every moment of the community's life.

Some attention should be paid to aspects of the renewal which raise questions in the minds of those who are not participants. Reference was made to the more limited expectations of many in the contemporary Church in comparison to the wider expectations of the early Church. The kind of repristination which renewals represent turns their attention with a kind of inevitability to the life of the New Testament churches. However commendable this return to the New Testament witness is, it should not be forgotten that in the course of the Church's history the Holy Spirit and his charisms were not absent. The Holy Spirit manifested himself in a multiplicity of ways in various epochs of the Church. One could mention the lay monastic movements, the founding of religious orders, the prayer gifts in the Church's mystical tradition, the social awareness as manifested in the papal encyclicals, the movements of political and social engagement. Though the modality in which the Spirit is manifesting himself today appears to take a new form, one cannot suggest that the charismatic manifestations began with what is called the Catholic charismatic renewal.

Many of the charisms present no problems to persons not involved in the charismatic renewal. However, the charism of tongues does present a problem. It is also clear that the Catholic renewal is not characterized by an insistence that praying in tongues is in any necessary way tied to the spiritual realities received in initiation. Many outside of the renewal attribute a centrality to tongues which is not reflected in most sectors of the renewal. On the other hand persons involved in the renewal rightly point out that this charism was quite common in the New Testament communities. Those who stand outside the renewal attempting to evaluate the charism of tongues will fail if it is not understood in the framework of prayer. It is essentially a prayer gift enabling many using it to pray at a deeper level. If those within the movement esteem this charism it is because they want to pray better and the charism of tongues helps them to do that. For a sizeable number of persons who pray in tongues, this is only one of a number of forms of prayer. They also engaged in liturgical prayer, eucharistic celebrations, and in other forms of public and private devotion. This charism, whose existence in the New Testament communities and in early post-apostolic times is well attested, should neither be given undue attention nor despised. Since it is the lowest of the charisms, it should not be a matter of surprise that it is so common.

Another feature of the renewal which causes confusion is the use of the phrase "baptism in the Holy Spirit." For historical reasons, many Catholics in the renewal have adopted this phrase, already current among classical Pentecostals, to describe the experience through which they came into a new awareness of the presence and power of the Spirit in their lives.

But there is a problem in the use of the phrase, as it could be taken to mean that only those who have had a particular kind of experience of the Spirit have really been baptized in the Spirit. This is not the case, since every valid and fruitful Christian initiation confers *"the gift of the Holy Spirit"* (Acts 2:38), and "to be baptized in the Holy Spirit" is simply another scriptural way of saying "to receive the Holy Spirit."

Hence, many prefer to use other expressions to describe what is happening in the charismatic renew-

Theological Basis of Renewal

al. Among the alternatives which have been proposed are: "release of the Spirit," "renewal of the sacraments of initiation," "a release of the power to witness to the faith," "actualization of gifts already receive in potency," "manifestation of baptism whereby the hidden grace given in baptism breaks through into conscious experience," "reviviscence of the sacraments of initiation." These are all ways of saying that the power of the Holy Spirit, given in Christian initiation, but hitherto unexperienced, becomes a matter of personal conscious experience.

The emergence of the graces of Christian initiation into conscious experience can happen without any emotional elevation. Experience should not be equated with feelings even though feelings of joy, peace, and love may be present. Further, experience can occur in a growth pattern. That is to say that the emergence of the graces of initiation into conscious experience can be a gradual process, without any peak experiences or without what are called "mountaintop experiences." There is no given moment which one could name as that moment in which the emergence into consciousness took place. There is only the gradual growth extending over months and even years.

Besides this growth pattern of experience, there is what might be called a crisis pattern. This occurs when one can date with some precision the moment when the graces of initiation emerged into conscious experience. The crisis pattern is less familiar to Catholic theological cultures, but is in fact the manner in which many Catholics within the renewal (and outside it) experience the emergence of baptismal grace into consciousness. Both the growth pattern and the crisis pattern should be looked upon as authentic ways of realizing the graces of initiation at the conscious level.

There are many objective elements in the renewal as in the whole Catholic tradition: the celebration of initiation, obedience to the teaching magisterium of the Church and to its discipline, eucharistic celebration, the sacrament of penance, and the sacred Scriptures. One of the more subjective elements is this affirmation of the commitment made at initiation. The persons involved in the renewal emphasize the necessity of personal commitment. As an adult one cannot be a Christian by proxy. One can only be a Christian by personal commitment. Each adult must say *yes* to the baptism received as an infant. This move toward personal decision and personal commitment is in keeping with the more personal and explicit adherence to faith taught by *Gaudium et Spes,* art. 7. The constitution speaks of "a more critical ability to distinguish religion from a magical view of the world and from the superstitions which still circulate." This more critical ability "purifies religion and exacts day by day a more personal and explicit adherence to faith. As a result, many persons are achieving a more vivid sense of God."

If one were to point to the strengths of the renewal, one would mention the genuine conversion experience which leads to a living faith, a profound love of prayer, a love of the Eucharist, a new appreciation for the sacrament of penance, healing of interpersonal relationships, moral transformation, renewed sense of discipleship, awareness of the necessity of firm doctrinal basis, fidelity to the bishops and to the Pope. In some places, especially in Mexico and

South America, involvement in the charismatic renewal has meant a new level of engagement in social and political programs. Pervading all these areas is the sense of the presence of the person of Christ, the power of the Spirit, and the glory of the Father. The response to presence is most characteristically praise.

The strengths of the renewal may be instruments for the transformation of the interior life of the Church. Many people, in fact, need a new assurance of faith and a renewed life of prayer. It is well known that many have ceased to pray. This is true even of priests.

The strengths of the renewal can lead to social and political action based not on class hatred, but love of the oppressors and prayer for them. Prayer for the oppressors in no way lessens the struggle against them and against the structures of poverty and violence. It only means a more radically Christian style of social and political action.

There are also problem areas. There is some uncritical acceptance of prophecy and tongues without sufficient discernment as to what comes from the Holy Spirit and what comes from the human psyche. Discernment of spirits is one of the major ongoing problems of the renewal. It should be remembered that the final judgment as to the authenticity of charisms "belongs to those who preside over the Church and to whose special competence it belongs not indeed to extinguish the Spirit, but to test all things and hold fast to that which is good" *(Lumen Gentium,* art. 12).

There is also present in some quarters an exaggerated supernaturalism with regard to the charisms, together with an undue preoccupation with them. Sometimes one meets persons in the renewal who attribute too quickly to demonic influence a manifestation which is judged not to be of God. Occasionally views are expressed which would indicate that when one has the Gospel one does not need the Church. At the sacramental level there are some who oppose the subjective experience of salvation to the celebration of the sacraments. Insufficient attention is sometimes paid to the theological training of persons whom the various communities judge to be called to specific ministries. Some place in false opposition the necessity of the transforming power of the Spirit and the necessity of theological training. There is reluctance among some leaders to listen carefully to criticism which emerges both from within the renewal and outside it. Finally, some within the renewal have not drawn the inevitable social implications of life in Christ and the Spirit. In some cases there is real social engagement, but the involvement is superficial in that it does not touch the structures of oppression and injustice.

An attempt has been made to formulate the most widely accepted view of the theological-sacramental basis of the renewal, that is in relation to the celebration of initiation. Something has been said about the strengths of the renewal and about the specific problem areas. A final word should be said about the relation of the Catholic charismatic renewal to other renewals. Those involved in the Catholic renewal recognize that there are other renewals within other ecclesial communities and churches, as well as outside of them, which give quite different theological explanations for the same spiritual realities.

Even though the theological formulations vary, and even though the understanding of Christian revelation differs in important ways, those within the renewal recognize the presence of the Spirit in those who proclaim the Lordship of Jesus to the glory of the Father. That presence in all streams of the renewal is the bond of their unity.

Restoring the Full Spectrum of the Charisms

In May of 1974 an international team of theologians and lay leaders were invited to Malines, Belgium, by Cardinal Leo Suenens to draft a document that would attempt to answer the great number of questions that were being raised about the charismatic renewal. They produced a document entitled "Theological and Pastoral Orientations on the Catholic Charismatic Renewal." The following article excerpts from sections of the 64-page text.

The decisive coming of the Spirit by virtue of which one becomes a Christian is related to the celebration of Christian initiation (Baptism, Confirmation, Eucharist). Christian initiation is the effective sign of the Spirit's bestowal. By receiving the Spirit in initiation, one becomes a member of Christ's body, is introduced into the people of God, and is joined to a worshiping community. There is evidence that in many of the early Christian communities, persons not only asked for and received the spirit during the celebration of initiation, but they expected that the Spirit would demonstrate his power by the transformation he would effect in their lives. To receive the Spirit was to receive power. To receive the Spirit was to change. It was not possible to be joined to Christ and to receive the Spirit without a reorientation of one's life. If one did not change, if there were no *metanoia,* one was not yet a Christian.

Further, the early Christian churches expected that the power of the Spirit would come to visibility along the full spectrum of his charisms in the community, which included, but by no means was limited to, such charisms as helping, administration, prophecy, and tongues (1 Cor. 12:28: cf., Rom. 12:6-8). The manifestation of the Spirit in charisms was related more immediately to the life of the community than to the life of the individual Christian.

Though the charisms are principles of order and mission in the Church, the Church today is not sufficiently aware that some of the charisms are real possibilities for the life of the Christian community.

However, there are differences between a community of Christians in the early Church and a community of Christians in the contemporary Church. In the first place, this difference is to be found in a difference of awareness, expectation, and openness. By way of example, imagine for the moment that the full spectrum of how the Spirit comes to visibility in a charism extends from A to Z. This example has a built-in limitation. By saying that the Spirit will come to visibility along a spectrum which extends from A to Z, one has already limited the Spirit. Obviously what the Spirit has to offer is the unlimited expanse of his life and the unlimited possibilities of ministries and services. This weakness of the spectrum analogy is clearly recognized, but the analogy is nonetheless helpful in clarifying how early communities differ from contemporary parishes.

It is here supposed that in the section of the spectrum which extends from A to P are such charisms as generosity in giving alms and other acts of mercy (Rom. 12:8) and teaching activities of various kinds. Obviously the charisms in the A to P section of the spectrum are so numerous and varied as to be beyond the possibility of numbering and naming them. The section of the spectrum which extends from P to Z is supposed here to include such charisms as prophecy, gifts of healing, working of miracles, tongues, interpretation.

It is evident that in the life of the early Church the communities expected that the Spirit would manifest himself in ministries and services which might fall within the spectrum which extends from A to P, but they also expected the Spirit to manifest himself in the other ministries and services within the section of the spectrum which extends from P to Z. They were aware that prophecy, gifts of healing, working of miracles, tongues, and interpretation were real charisms, real possibilities for the life of the Church. The early Christian communities were aware that these gifts were gifts to the Church, they expected that they would be manifested in their communities, they were open to them, and these gifts were in fact operative among them. In this they differ from most contemporary communities. Communities in the Church today are not aware that the charisms in the section of the spectrum which extends from P to Z are possibilities for the life of the Church. These communities do not expect the charisms in this section to be operative and manifest in their midst. To that degree they are not really open to them, and in most communities these charisms are, as a matter of fact, not operative.

For a community to have a limited expectation as to how the Spirit will manifest himself in its midst

Restoring Full Spectrum of Charisms 217

can profoundly affect the life and experience of that community. It can affect its public eucharistic worship, the private prayer of its members, the manner in which it proclaims the Gospel and serves the world. This is obvious when one recalls that charisms are ministries to the Church and the world. And if a community limits how the Spirit manifests himself there is some measure of impoverishment in the total life of that local church.

That awareness, expectancy, and openness can affect the life and experience of a local church should not be strange to Catholic ears. In a modified form, one found that concept in the doctrine of subjective dispositions with regard to the sacraments. It was called *ex opere operantis*. The effect of the sacraments is in some manner affected by the subjective dispositions of the recipient. If one approaches the eucharistic celebration with a thimbleful of openness and generosity, then that is the measure of what one receives, even though God offers the infinity of his life and love. Subjective dispositions affect what one receives in a eucharistic celebration. So subjective dispositions, awareness, expectancy, and openness of a given Christian community can affect both what that community brings to Christian initiation and what that community receives in that celebration.

To be more explicit, if a Christian community, a local church, is not aware that the charisms in the P to Z section of the spectrum even exist as real possibilities for the life of the community, if they do not expect that these gifts will be manifest among them, and if they are therefore not open to such gifts, all of these subjective dispositions will affect the life of the community, will affect what the local church brings to the celebration of initiation, and what the local community receives. It would be highly unlikely that the charisms in the P to Z section of the spectrum will be operative in the life of such a community.

Here a qualification must be made. It is true that ordinarily God takes communities and individuals where they are. If communities come to him with limited awareness and expectations, then ordinarily he deals with them at the level of their limited openness. However, there is a distinct danger in placing too much emphasis on subjective dispositions as determinants of what the local church receives and experiences. Alongside the declaration that subjective dispositions affect what one gives and receives is a companion declaration that in no ultimate sense is the Spirit of God radically dependent on the subjective dispositions of communities or individuals. Though ordinarily the Spirit deals with communities and individuals where they are, he is in no radical sense bound to do so. The Spirit is sovereign and free. He blows when, where, and how he wills. The Spirit can give to communities and individuals gifts of which they are not aware, which they do not expect and are not, in a general sense, open to. The Spirit has and retains the initiative at every moment of the community's life. This principle of the Spirit's ultimate freedom does not cancel out the other valid insight; namely, that ordinarily the Spirit takes communities and individuals at the point where they are, and that subjective dispositions in some sense affect experience, affect what communities and individuals bring to the celebration of initiation and what is there received.

While it is too soon to speak definitively of the

Restoring Full Spectrum of Charisms   219

full fruits of the renewal within the Church, it might be possible to indicate those areas where the experience and theological reflection within the renewal could be of service to the Church both local and universal.

Programs of evangelization have been developed in various countries which present to individuals and societies outside the Christian fold the personal call of the Gospel to believe in and follow Jesus as Lord and Savior.

In various parts of the world, programs of catechesis for those who have already become Christians have been designed. These programs of catechesis, emphasizing both the content of faith and the need for a personal encounter with Jesus who is Lord, often lead to a renewed commitment.

The renewal has called attention to the contrast between Christian initiation as it is practiced in the Church today and the models presented by the churches of the New Testament and the early post-apostolic period. The present pastoral practice of Baptism, Confirmation, and first Eucharist seems to fall short of these models. Some theologies of initiation current today idealize the subject in a way which does not correspond to pastoral practice, more especially does not correspond to the apparent effects among the people. On the other hand, the experience within the renewal indicates that it is not only possible but normal for Catholics to come to a most fruitful encounter with Christ through his Spirit in their celebration of initiation. This encounter itself leads to a mature participation in the worship and mission of the eucharistic community. The contemporary crisis of unbelieving believers and baptized pagans impels the whole Church to act in this important area.

Experience within the renewal has shown how fruitful it is to focus on the reality of the Risen Lord and the life of prayer and service when engaged in liturgical preaching and other forms of sharing of the Word.

One of the most important developments in the renewal is the move towards community. This emphasis upon Christian community, where clergy and laity alike share their lives, stands in contrast to the individualism of today. Such community life is marked by various ministries based on charisms where there is a mutuality of service. The large participatory character of community life and worship is a reflection of the nature of the Church where the charisms are the principle of order and structure. The renewal asks whether the revitalization of the structures of the Church is not to be found in this shared ministry.

The renewal points to these areas and asks those who have pastoral leadership in the Church to evaluate what the Spirit is saying to the Church in the renewal, to confirm what is good, and to move towards its actualization.

The prayer of Pope John XXIII for the success of the Council contained these words: "Renew Thy wonders in this our day, as by a new Pentecost." In the general audience of November 29, 1972, Pope Paul VI said: "The Church needs an eternal Pentecost." One manifestation of this Pentecost is the charismatic renewal. Those in positions of pastoral authority will wish to be open to this and other manifestations of the Spirit's presence and power. Those

Restoring Full Spectrum of Charisms 221

in the renewal invite the bishops and priests to be present at their meetings so that they might see the renewal from within and might have firsthand information on its character. It would be unfortunate if those in pastoral positions had an acquaintance with this renewal only from the outside and by hearsay.

The charismatic renewal is of the Church and in the Church and it is spreading. There is every indication that it will remain a permanent expression of the Church's life. Therefore, one is not dealing with a passing fashion. The renewal sees its theological basis as a renewal of baptismal consciousness (Baptism, Confirmation, Eucharist). Its concern is to renew the whole of Christian life through the power of the Spirit under the Lordship of Jesus.

Were one to look at the fruits of the renewal, one could mention the following. The rather formal relationships with Christ as risen Lord and Savior through his Spirit become deeply personal. There is a realization of the community nature of one's relationship to God. No person goes to God alone, but in community as a member of the body of Christ, the people of God. This is the reason for the deep love of the Church and the oft-repeated assertions of fidelity to its pastors found in the renewal.

The experience of the power of the Spirit leads not only to a realization that Jesus is real and present but also leads to a new kind of hunger: hunger for prayer, most especially the prayer of praise; hunger for the Word of God. There is in the renewal a profound sense of the presence of God which moves those involved toward community and to a new depth of personal relationships. Many have experienced a healing of personal relationships in marriage, in the family, and in professional contacts. The experience of the graces of Baptism at the conscious level has brought many back to a new appreciation not only of Baptism and the Eucharist but of the whole of the sacramental life. The renewal sees in the social teaching of the Church a clear sign that the Spirit calls the Church to be actively present in the promotion of justice and peace for all men. Those already engaged in programs of social reform find that the renewal invites them to a service of others at a more primary level.

There is a new appreciation of the vocation to the priesthood and to religious life. Priests and religious have found a deeper sense of their ministry, new meaning to their calling.

A major strength of the renewal is in the area of evangelization. The reestablishment of a personal (though not individualistic) relation to Jesus through the experience of the power of the Spirit has made those in the renewal aware of that power as the basis for proclaiming the Gospel, arousing faith in others, and prompting that faith to unfold and grow. To receive the Spirit is to change *(metanoia)*. To receive the Spirit is to be moved and to move others to the recognition that Jesus is Lord. To receive the Spirit is to be zealous for that kingdom which Jesus will hand over to the Father.

The renewal, then, makes the same request to the ecclesiastical authorities and to all concerned as that made by Popes John and Paul and repeatedly made in the council, namely that all "Be open to what the Spirit is saying to the churches!" *Lumen Gentium* asks those who preside over the churches "not to extinguish the Spirit, but to test all things and hold fast to that which is good" (Art. 12; cf., 1 Thess. 5:12, 19-21).

In this way the new and eternal Pentecost, for which Popes John and Paul prayed, is the hope of the Church of today.

PART THREE
A Renewed Church

The Charismatic Renewal and Church Renewal

By Bert Ghezzi

This past winter, the planet Venus was visible in the morning sky over the Midwest. I was fascinated by it; hardly able to keep my eyes on the road while driving to work.

It also made quite an impression on my seven-year-old son, Paul. He discovered it one crisp morning when he poked his head out the front door to check on the weather. "Dad! Dad!" he exclaimed, "there's a big star out there! You should see it!" If I had not restrained him, Paul would have awakened the entire household to share the good news. Paul thought he had set his eyes on something no one had ever seen before, and he wanted everyone to share his excitement.

As I reflected on Paul's behavior, it occurred to me that many of us in the charismatic renewal act the same way after being baptized in the Holy Spirit. We discover the Morning Star and we become enchanted with him. Our excitement grows as we come to know Jesus more. We act toward others as though we were the first to have had any spirtual experience. To our new eyes, the church appears somewhat shabby and in need of repair. We want to jump in and renew it.

The Lord does want to use charismatic prayer groups to make some contribution to the life of his church, but it will not be automatic. If we want to build with him we must go with him where he is and grasp as much of his vision as we can. The first step toward this is expanding our understanding of the church and renewal. The more we see how the Lord has been working to build his church and give it new life, the more we will stand back to gaze at it in awe. The more we appreciate the fullness of the church, the better will we be able to shape the charismatic renewal to serve the Lord's plans.

Over the centuries, the Lord has chosen to use movements in the church as one of the ways he generates renewal. The Body of Christ is incarnate in a hostile environment. Movements have helped rally the church in the face of new challenges, bringing new life and new hope. The reform movements of the 11th century—fostered by centers such as Cluny—provided the initial impetus behind papal efforts to rescue the church from the grasp of feudal overlords. The Dominican and Franciscan movements refreshed the 13th-century church by calling townspeople to live the gospel life simply and in deep personal union with God.

Considering the history of earlier movements can help us understand the place of the charismatic renewal. The experience of the early monastic movement is particularly instructive. In the fourth century thousands of Christians in the eastern Roman Empire began to respond to God's call to give up their lives in order to find him. Men and women abandoned their homes and careers to dwell in the solitude of the desert, sometimes as hermits and sometimes in informal or formal communities.

While they conducted no programs of evangelization, they were nonetheless superb evangelists. By the witness of their lives they proclaimed a version of the gospel which brought refreshment to a suffering church. Their lives given to God and to each other persuaded thousands of Christians in the Church that the kingdom of God was within. Members of the Church in the post-Constantinian era needed to rediscover the inner depths of their oneness with the Lord, and the example of the brothers in the desert taught them how to pray. The monastic movement was not a new church. It was a renewal movement which subordinated itself to the Church. Ultimately it ceased to be a movement and was incorporated into the Church's life, providing leadership and spiritual education for thousands.

The experience of the recent liturgical movement also helps to bring the charismatic renewal into focus. The goal of the liturgical movement was the restoration of worship in the Catholic Church, in particular, bringing the Mass to the people. The movement—which began several decades ago among a handful of scholars and pastors—gradually involved thousands of priests, religious, and laymen. Through books, journals, talks, conferences, and remodeled worship services the participants developed concern among Catholics for the restoration of the liturgy. The movement accumulated a vast wisdom on the history and nature of Christian worship and a great deal of pastoral sense about helping groups of all kinds give corporate praise to the Lord. The liturgical movement peaked in the early 1960's. The Second Vatican Council appropriated the fruit of the movement for the entire Church by laying the foundations for a thorough reformation of the liturgy. Since the Church itself assumed the initiative, a movement with a separate identity was no longer needed. The liturgical movement had reached its end—the liturgical renewal of the Catholic Church. This does not say that all the work was done; the work of liturgical renewal, in fact, has just begun. It does say, however, that the need for a separate movement to generate interest in the renewal of worship has passed.

Lessons from Other Movements

Three lessons drawn from the examples of early monasticism and the liturgical movement are useful in determining the role of the charismatic renewal in the renewal of the Church.

1. Movements for Church renewal are not ends in themselves. They come to an end when the Church appropriates for itself their contributions. Realizing this should help participants shed the false sense of importance we sometimes place on the charismatic renewal and begin to understand its real importance. The end of the charismatic renewal is bringing a charismatic renewal to the entire Church. All the valuable things the Lord is doing among us—personal renewal through being baptized in the Spirit, the renewal of charisms such as speaking in tongues, the prayer meeting, the prayer group and other new forms such as households and communities—are for his church's benefit. The Church is already incorporating the fruit of the renewal into its general life. The more this happens, the sooner the charismatic renewal can cease to be as a movement.

2. For a time a movement needs to maintain its

identity as a separate association within the Church. The monks were able to call other Christians to personal renewal by separating themselves from the ordinary environment and building new forms of Christian living in the North African desert. The liturgical movement needed its identity to create a situation in the Church which prepared it for a fullscale reform of Catholic worship. Had there been no liturgical movement, Vatican II would not have been able to restore the liturgy.

For the present the charismatic renewal needs to continue to develop as a movement in the Church. It is still young and has much to learn. There is a great deal of work to be done in building prayer groups, in helping others who want to be baptized in the Holy Spirit, in helping each other along in becoming mature Christians, and much more. If we understand that the renewal is for the church, we will want to remain actively subordinate to the church. But in the interest of relating the charismatic renewal to the church, we should not be too quick to de-emphasize important characteristic elements. In my judgment, for example, we would be mistaken to stop speaking to others about "being baptized in the Spirit" and "speaking in tongues" for the purpose of making the charismatic renewal more accessible to the church. I think to do this may even make the charismatic renewal completely inaccessible by deactivating it. Just as the early monasticism and the liturgical movement did, the charismatic renewal should relate respectfully to the church, while at the same time developing the special features the Lord has given it.

3. Movements successfully foster church renew-

al when they maintain their concern for personal spiritual renewal. The early monks dedicated themselves to living for God daily; helping one another learn to pray, to cope with problems, and to mature as Christians. Even when the movement acquired some organization, it never strayed from the foundational concern of bringing men to dwell in prayerful harmony with God.

Participants in the charismatic renewal should understand that authentic Church renewal is rooted in personal spiritual renewal. The Church lives in its individual members. Its holiness grows as the individual members grow in holiness. If prayer group members want to renew the Church, the place to begin is in our own hearts. If prayer groups want to renew the Church, they ought to become better prayer groups. By their presence in the Church, prayer groups which help us turn to the Lord and live for him already constitute a vital renewal. To say this is not to advise prayer groups to turn in on themselves. Prayer groups are training us in brotherhood and service, which spills over into our normal relationships with the Church. Church renewal is new life and it is new life which charismatic prayer groups have discovered and continue to foster. Building prayer groups with the Lord, then, is building Church renewal.

Renewal of the Church

By Archbishop James Hayes

When, before Vatican II, Pope John began to speak about and pray for a new Pentecost, I think a lot of us misunderstood. Many of us were expecting it to be a rerun of the old Pentecost, but that is not what is happening. What is happening is a new Pentecost, one that will have its own way of gathering people together, its own way of pouring out the Spirit on all men so that they will see visions and dream dreams; but it will not be a return to anything we've known before. It will be a step ahead to something that no one can possibly envisage right now.

I am convinced that the charismatic renewal is part of that new Pentecost Pope John prayed for. Wherever I go in Canada or here in the U.S., I see the things coming to pass that we were talking about as part of the renewal we hoped for back in 1964 and 1965. The liturgical weeks then had themes of Jesus Christ reforming his church and the church building community. That is what is being talked about and what is happening in this renewal. As communities are renewed in prayer and worship, the Bride of Christ will be renewed.

One of the things that has impressed me strongly about the charismatic renewal is the deep love for the church that I've found everywhere. A lot of crit-

Renewal of the Church

ics think of this as something that is out of the main stream of Catholicism or runs away from the church as an institution, but what I've found is the very opposite. There are Roman Catholic charismatics who find it difficult to relate to the institutional church, but this is not, in my experience, characteristic of the movement. What is characteristic is a tone of loving obedience and prayerful desire that the Lord continue to purify and perfect his church in its members. This is a confirmation for me that charismatic Catholics need to be looked to as one of the forces in the renewal of the church, including the structural renewal of the church.

I have become convinced that the pastoral structures of our church will change, have to change. The church that we live in now is highly priest-centered. Traditionally, the church has recognized three different orders: bishop, priest, and deacon, but many of those different functions have been telescoped into the role of the priest. We need to recover the distinction in practice so that we can see the ministry of the church in its full scope. If our focus is on the minister, we can lose sight of the ministry. It is the whole church that ministers, but in our present situation the ministry seems to come from the priest. The church should be a body that ministers, with different ministers officiating at its different functions. The ministry of the church needs to be broadened out to include more people doing different things in the name of the church.

The bishop has a unique role in the Christian community as a sign and center of unity. The bishop gathers a people together and, by the laying on of hands, he takes possession of them and makes them fully members of the Christian community. As the sign and center of unity, when he confirms he says to each individual, "You are now fully plunged into the Paschal mystery and grafted into the vine which is Christ." The priest is authorized only by a bishop to say to a penitent, "What happened to you in confirmation is now renewed and put back in good order again; you are now reconciled and accepted back into this community which is the Body of Christ, and because of that you are considered to be worthy to receive the sacraments and therefore free from any kind of sin that would prevent you from receiving the sacraments." It is God, of course, who forgives, but it is the minister of the sacrament who plays the role of the bishop in absolving the penitent from anything that could separate him from the community, and receiving him again. This sense of the ministry of unity in the church focused in the bishop as sign and center of unity is generally lost in our present priest-centered pastoral structure.

I think that as we move away from our present structure into one in which it is more obvious that the whole church is serving, the church will officially and publicly recognize more orders. As the whole body is seen more clearly as the one who serves, carrying out its functions in different ministers, other things that the body does will be ordered. We are going to see a broadening out of the ministry of the whole church as the administrative and service functions that the priest carries out are shared among more members of the body. In the beginning, as the priest joins the people, becomes part of the group, it will look as though the issue is just getting more confused, but the end result will be a clarification of function and role. The service of the church should be and will be multifaceted, and more people will share in that service. Demands are being made that women be given a "greater share in the ministry," and they will be: not necessarily in the services of the priest as we have known them, but in the fuller ministry of the church of which the priest will be one part. Many different people in many different ways will be sharing in that ministry.

I see some things already beginning to happen within the charismatic renewal. The church has not publicly recognized and ordered any of the various ministries that are being exercised in an unofficial way in the charismatic renewal, but I think we can already see some of the functions which the church as an institution may one day order. There is an obvious function in the communication and proclamation of the Word of God. The Word is being proclaimed in charismatic groups like it is nowhere else. Something like an order of evangelist might be the first such function to be officially recognized. There are people who will be leaders of prayer meetings—not presidents of worship, since that is already provided for in the church's official ministry—but rather those who lead and encourage prayer among Christians. This may be another ministry that will one day be ordered. A third might rise out of the obvious growth of the practice of Christian hospitality, and there may be a recognition of that as a public ministry of the church. This is speculation, but it is based on what I see already happening in the charismatic renewal.

Another area in which I see the charismatic renewal having an impact on the renewal of the church is in the area of community. I found myself in agreement with much that I found in Max Delespesse's book, *The Church Community: Leaven and Life-style* (reviewed in April 1972 issue of *New Covenant*). The parish community as we now know it does not correspond to the sociological situation of many catholics. It does still meet the needs of the vast majority, but for many it does not provide the community atmosphere and relationship they need to live their religious lives. I see new things happening in that regard in the charismatic renewal, and I think what is happening there will be an aid to all of us as we review and revise our concepts in the working out of community.

My contact with the charismatic renewal has given me great hope for the renewal of the church. I see within it some of the elements of the new, wholly new, Pentecost that Pope John announced and prayed for more than a decade ago. I am firmly and strongly convinced that the leaders of the charismatic renewal in the States are really instruments of the Lord in renewing his people here and now. We will see that new Pentecost in the Roman Catholic Church.

A Church Reborn

By Fr. Graham Pulkingham

I became rector at Church of the Redeemer parish in Eastwood, in the east end of Houston, Texas, in the fall of 1963. The neighborhood was a near-poverty situation. Alcoholism, drug addiction, prostitution, and child neglect were a common daily sight. I was convinced the Gospel preached through a caring church could say something life-giving to such conditions. But I found we had nothing very valuable to say. The neighborhood on the other hand had lots to say to us; most of it was expressed with aggression, hostility and anger. Some of the other denomination churches in the neighborhood had already closed their doors and moved to safer ground. Others had been changed into settlement houses with programs for young people, but they were not functioning as worshiping congregations. Churches that were still active had difficulty making ends meet. We had difficulty identifying a stable community called the parish: our membership, our programs, and our life were faltering.

When I arrived, I opened the doors of the church buildings as a friendly gesture to the neighborhood. Within a few months' time, the parish church that I had thought was going to bring about a positive influence in the neighborhood had suffered such destruction that I had to close its doors again. My efforts to save that church for the neighborhood had failed, and my attempt to convey life to my needy neighbors came to a humiliating halt.

A New Vision

That led me to a deep search to find out just what the Christian ministry in that situation was all about. It was then that I began to see from the New Testament and in the meditations of my own prayers what it meant for a parish church to minister the grace of Jesus Christ to people who were desperately in need.

First, I realized that the parish needed men and women totally committed to serve Jesus Christ. I was desperate enough to think that some people—I didn't know who—would be willing to commit themselves one hundred percent to be the servants of Jesus Christ in that difficult situation, where I found myself to be a failure. I realized the Christian ministry must be a corporate endeavor in order to be fully graceful.

It became clear that if I really intended to be the instrument of God's grace to the people in Eastwood, I would have to live a life similar to theirs— not just for a few months at a time or for eight hours a day, but as a full-time occupation. The persons who lived in Eastwood neighborhood in 1963 and 1964 were of the sort I would not have associated with before that time. We were of a different intellectual, economic, educational and cultural background. Nor had I ever heard of another priest of the Episcopal Church who identified his life with such a deprived social environment.

Something inside me said, "No, I can't do that." But it wasn't a very loud no, because during that year of failures at attempting to help my neighbors, God had worked in me a tender concern in love for them. I decided to take on whatever life-style would satisfy my hunger to identify with them.

Shortly afterward, in the summer of 1964, I went to see Dave Wilkerson. He was ministering in the streets of New York City, identifying with somewhat the kind of people I found myself involved with in the east end of Houston; by all reports his situation was far more difficult, and he was successful. In the context of that visit, I received a baptism in the Spirit. At that time, baptism in the Spirit meant to me an acceptance in a conclusive and dramatic way the things God had been preparing me for all of my life—especially the things I had been learning the previous year. Until then, I had never suspected that Graham Pulkingham might be the instrument of God's grace for a plain miracle. But somehow, after Dave Wilkerson prayed for me I knew my ministry would be filled with healing and miracles and other powerful gifts of the Spirit—not because I was special but because that's what God had shown me was a ministry that could do a grace-filled job for him.

A Hard Choice

When I returned to Houston I began to see charismatic gifts of the Spirit at work in my everyday parish ministry. The poor were having the Gospel preached to them in a very fresh way. God was healing them and setting them free; he was performing all kinds of miracles in their lives. This spectacle of miracles in the east end of Houston lasted from about September to December of 1964, and it attracted the attention and interest of literally hundreds of people all over the Gulf Coast of Texas; they came from every denomination to see what was going on. Eventually, about three or four hundred people became associated with me and my life because of what they saw there.

Many of those from the "middle-America" where I had come from had been following after miracles for years, and rejoiced to see God do a healing once every two or three months, but when they became associated with Redeemer parish they found he was doing them five or six times a day. They saw the implications: "If I really want to see God work that way through my own life and not just be a spectator, I'm going to have to join that character Pulkingham and live the sort of life he does."

About eighty or ninety percent of these people said, "I can't hack it; I'm sorry. I have too many responsibilities elsewhere; I've got my wife and children, I've got debts, I've got my house to pay off, I've got fields and cows and commitments, I can't do it." A few took the leap; 33 of us to be exact. My wife and myself and our then four children and 27 others. As we drew closer to one another for encouragement and fellowship in the Gospel, they too began to see tremendous works of power happening in their own ministry.

The people who were willing to make the necessary changes in their life-style and identify with us, living our life—doctors, lawyers, the very poor and culturally dispossessed, college graduates and their friends—these soon began to move into the neighborhood of the church so we might increase the amount of time spent together. A doctor who lived in a city forty miles away sold his home and possessions and brought his family to live in Eastwood. Shortly after that a lawyer from fifty miles away sold his law practice, his possessions, and his home, and he also brought his family to live in Eastwood. The rest of us supported him and his family for several months while he built up a new practice in Houston. Some of the single people quit their jobs and lived in our houses so they could help with the difficult job of raising children in that kind of environment.

In the midst of it all we made sure we lived a life-style comparable to that of our neighbors, some of whom now lived in our homes with us. Our children were in the same schools as theirs; we shopped in the neighborhood shops and lived like everyone else in Eastwood neighborhood.

Charismatic Community

We were called together into this strange new life-style and we were fully committed to serving one another. Everything we had was given to support one another in love—no matter what the need. We were willing to live together to the fullest degree, and to identify completely with one another's needs. This was the beginning of the charismatic community that formed and grew in Eastwood during 1965. In that context there was a remarkable sharing of the risen life of Jesus Christ: there was a sharing of the Word of God and prayer. All of us came from such different backgrounds. It was really exciting to be involved in such a varied expression of Christ's body.

All this time the parish was dying. It began its

most serious decline during the year 1965, and continued to worsen until 1966. But I really didn't care whether the institutional forms of the parish lived or died. In association with this growing charismatic community I discovered a tremendous ministry of faith, healing, and deliverance. Through it people's lives were being changed by the power of the Gospel. We prayed, we blessed the Lord, we loved each other, we served, we did all the things an alive ecclesiastical community ought to do in its fellowship. The only things we didn't do were baptisms, celebrations of the Eucharist, weddings or burials. These were performed "next door," and were done by me as a functionary of the church. However the rest of our life was lived in a charismatic community of praise in which there were magnificent evidences of the power of God to heal and fulfill his word in everyday life.

At one point in 1966 the charismatic community saw that the institutional structure of the parish church was about to falter. The community members committed seventy percent of their resources to support the church financially. This was done because of their commitment to me. I felt called to the parish as its rector and they agreed that was where God had put me; they really loved me and wouldn't let me fail in my calling for lack of funds. Their commitment carried the church to the end of the year when its financial base became secure once again. By then the church membership had begun to increase.

The charismatic community developed and strengthened—both as a stable community and as a training-ground for ministry. Men and women were being efficiently trained in an "in-service" program of powerful pastoral gifts and ministries. They gained experience and insight that neither ordinary parish nor seminary could offer.

A Parish Reborn

In 1967. those men and women who had been trained in the community began to supply the parish with the leadership it needed to become a strong parish church. By 1968, the parish had itself become a charismatic community and the "renewing" community disappeared. There was now a parish in which the ministering staff, ordained and lay; all of the helping ministries; the worship and music; the youth leadership; the education program; the women's and men's organizations; and all the outreach ministries were under the leadership of community-trained, stable, mature men and women.

When they assumed leadership in the parish programs, they solicited the prayers and help of parish members who had not been trained in the earlier community. Suddenly the parish ministries became a training ground for laymen in the same way that the charismatic community had been. In 1969 the parish had a surplus of leaders—strong, powerful, well-trained, mature ministers of the Gospel who really knew what they were doing. They knew their calling, they were experts in ministering the life and gifts of the Spirit. At that point the parish reached out to serve others: we had to release the power within our midst and make it available to the world beyond Houston's east end. A traveling apostolate had begun.

The informal charismatic community imparted vital Christianity to the dying parish; then when it was no longer needed, the community lost its identity and vanished into the heart of the renewed parish. Because of it, Redeemer parish is now a community which is vitally conscious of its Christian calling, its commitment and power to witness in everything it says and does in the Lord's name. The institutional forms of the parish are not much different than those of the average Episcopal church, but now in its eucharistic life and ministry, in its fellowship and outreach—all of which are renewed—God's power and love are active in ever-fresh and unique ways.

Marriage, Community, Service: Interview with Fr. Graham Pulkingham

Q: What is the overall perspective with which you view marriage in today's society?

A: I think it is becoming increasingly clear that the institution of marriage in our society is failing in almost every respect. The growing number of divorces and multiple marriages, the rejection of family life by a growing number of young people, and the general unhappiness and unresolved tensions in many "good" marriages all bear witness to this. And yet for many, marriage has become the last desperate hope for a dependable relationship. It then becomes a kind of hiding place for people, and is presented as the ideal love relationship. In most cases marriage doesn't measure up to these expectations. It becomes a sad knot of periodic pleasure which holds things together, a possessive relationship which produces jealousy, exclusiveness, and hostile and destructive tensions.

Q: What do you see as God's provision for a successful marriage?

A: God's provision for successful marriage is that it be lived under the lordship of Jesus Christ, in the power of the Holy Spirit, in the context of a deeply committed Christian community turned outward in service to the needs of man. In the last 25 years, the major Christian churches have seen a great deal of writing on Christian marriage, but most dealt very incompletely with these four important elements: Christ, the Holy Spirit, committed Christian community life, service orientation.

Most writers tend to treat the family as an isolated unit for all practical purposes, and tend to be unaware of the transforming power of community life on the family. They also tend to ignore the power we have if we take seriously our call to service as a people. This approach—treating the family as an island unto itself—simply expects too much from the family alone, and by and large hasn't worked.

Q: Are you saying that living in a Christian community oriented to service is the key to a marriage finding its most healthy setting?

A: Yes, the key way in which Jesus and his Spirit communicate their healing and unifying power is in the reality called the body of Christ—community in its deepest form. We have lost virtually all feeling for community in the Western world and the Churches share deeply in that malaise. The majority of Christians know nothing but an individualistic, isolated Christian life. Naturally this affects the way they live their marriages and work on its problems.

Q: Will you expand on that for us?

A: I'll try. We in the Western world have for

quite some time been systematically isolating the husband-wife relationship. We add children to it, of course, but even this is changing. We have been isolating that relationship from the rest of society, from the rest of the Church, the body, and holding it up as the epitome of true love and fulfillment. This has been done in such a way as to make the relationship exclusive. Exclusive marriage relationships are a real block to the growth of genuine Christian community. This has grievously harmed the body of Christ; it has also grievously harmed the relationships thus isolated. Children who grow up in family relationships like that at some point must reject them in order to be able to relate freely as persons in relationships of their own. And yet the relationship they start seeking for, from their early teens, is the very kind of relationship that has caused them such problems by its exclusiveness and unresolved tensions and bondages. The whole dating, marriage-happiness pattern that dominates our lives is fundamentally distorted. In the plan of God marriage must be seen in the context of community, not as an island in itself.

Q: In what ways do you see community helping marriage and the family?

A: I think asking the question that way reveals a distortion in perspective that's significant. Everything isn't to be judged by how it helps marriage and the family; having a marriage or family-centered perspective in life is in many ways not to have the full Christian perspective. The thrust of God's plan now is to build a people who are committed to him and to one another, to gather his people around the person of his Son so they live and function as organically and inter-dependently as the human body. They are to be of one mind and heart, loving one another and laying down their lives for one another. The Christian's relationships to one another as brother and sister in Christ is a primary relationship, to be taken seriously. The additional relationships that Christians may have—as friends, as husband and wife, as parents and children, worker and employer, are instances of our fundamental relationship to one another as brothers and sisters in the Lord. The fact that together we form one body, and must experience one another and function effectively together as one body is as important as the order of our particular relationships. Both are essential. The local body of Christ, the church in a particular neighborhood or city, must be one and together in bonds of real love and unity, as well as the particular relationships within that body, if God's plan is to come to pass.

Since this is God's plan, trying to solve problems with a perspective that is exclusively family or marriage-oriented, and not also community and service-oriented, is to take an approach that cannot bear all the fruit that God desires and intends. The family is not intended to bear the burden of all man's needs and problems by itself, but the community as a whole is intended in God's plan to help bear the burdens of finances, of caring for and raising children, of working out problems. The help that God wants to provide in these situations in many cases is meant to flow from other members of the body.

If the distinctive relationships within the body have become walls, have become exclusive, self-centered, and closed, the love and gifts of God's Spirit working in the body can't flow. If Jew and Greek, rich and poor, male and female, married and unmarried, are more those things than they are one in Christ, expressed practically in deep community life, God's plan for the healing of his own people and the spread of his gospel will be significantly blocked. Meditate on John 17:20-26, Acts 2:37-47, and I think you will see what I mean.

Q: How has this worked out at the Church of the Redeemer?

A: It has been difficult for every family to one degree or another. A husband and wife living together by themselves can tolerate a lot of destructive and hostile aspects of their relationship. Pleasurable times together that reaffirm the relationship compensate for many things. They can go for many years without ever dealing with the hostile and negative aspects of their relationship, living with a perennial frustration and deep-down hurt. They don't know how to stop hurting each other. It's only when they are called by the Lord to enter into a community committed to living in perfect love and unity with one another that many of these problems come to the surface and have to be dealt with. It is only in the context of community that many of these problems can be dealt with. The protective, selfish basis of so many relationships is threatened by the Christian community where the warm and open sharing of love and the ideal of service are prominent. Many of the values associated with marriage are intended to be values lived in the whole Christain community. They have been associated with genital sex and the marriage relationship only as true Christian community has disappeared. Being free in our emotional responses, relating with freedom, warmth and tenderness, loving all men and one another genuinely and completely, are *characteristic* of genuine Christianity. But in most of our minds these values are associated exclusively with the marriage relationship, and this quite simply isn't God's plan.

I don't think that the Lord ever intended for complete self-sufficient community to exist just between two people. I don't mean by this that two people can't establish a very wholesome community, they can; but it seems that the purpose of this kind of relationship between two people is to include others. And yet in our society the marriage community has become turned in on itself and isolated. This is causing problems; problems so deep that many couples don't want to face them.

The fact that must be faced by many couples is that their marriage is based on something other than Christian love. Unfulfilled and unhappy people looking to marriage for fulfillment and happiness oftentimes just pool their problems; incapable of authentic, unselfish, love relationships as brothers and sisters with others in the community, they find themselves equally incapable as the added dimension of sexual love is added. Unfree and bound by fears and resentments, marriage oftentimes becomes simply another forum for these bondages to be manifested. Many marriages need to be reconstituted in the healing love and light of Christian community. It can be a very painful process but one well worth going through.

Q: If many of the values associated in our culture with sexual love in marriage such as warmth, openness, expression of affection and tenderness, are intended to be characteristic of the relationships as a whole in the Christian community, what would you see as the unique characteristic of the marriage relationship?

A: I see marriage as having the potential to be in some ways the most perfect expression of community possible, a true sign here and now of Christ's union with his bride, the church. I see it as allowing those called to married life to share in the creative life of God as well as his redemptive life. God goes on creating new life, as well as restoring it through the cross of Christ, and marriage is a unique opportunity to share in the fulness of the Fatherhood of God by participating in the whole process of creation and redemption. The added dimension of sexual love allows a unique union to be formed and allows God to express his Fatherhood in bringing forth children.

I think it important to add that I don't think that you have to get married to be fulfilled. When the Church, the local Christian community, is providing wholesome, loving, stable Christian relationships as a fundamental characteristic of community life, a person becomes perhaps for the first time truly *free* to marry or not. Most people now are not free. Because of the generally rare experience of genuine Christian community life, marriage appears as the only option, the last, desperate hope of finding meaningful personal relationships in life. People in this situation, not being really free and capable of mature relationships, rarely find marriage to be their salvation. Only Jesus, present to us in his Body, is that.

Q: Do you think that the Lord is calling other established families to enter into a deep community life oriented to service as families at Church of the Redeemer have done?

A: I would say that the Lord would take anything that any family would give him for the advancement of his kingdom here on earth. That's the way I would answer your question. The call of Christians to serve in this world provides me with what I think is an essential perspective for so many decisions we as Christians have to make. It seems to me that in a world in which there are so many desperate and hungry people, who are literally perishing for lack of the experience of God's love in the Christian community, anything we would do to cause the family to close in on itself, to become an exclusive, self-protecting society, is a serious threat to the body of Christ and its call to ministry or mission.

Of course, I'm not saying that the family does not have to be strong in Christ's love and love of one another in order to serve in this way. I am saying that the family is to become strong and enter into fuller community life, in order to serve, in order to give of itself, so others may have life. It may take a period of time for a couple, a family to work out its problems, to be healed, to become capable of fuller community life and service, but they should praise and thank

God every step of the way. Deep communal life and service is a vision that I believe the Spirit is giving to many of his people in this critical time of his action on this earth.

A Bishop, a Diocese, and the Charismatic Renewal

By Dr. Bill Burnett

In the last 16 years my main concern has been simply to be a bishop. This is especially hard in a land where the Church, and indeed the whole of society, is cruelly fragmented. The bishop, in our understanding of him, is the center of unity, the shepherd of the sheep; if the family is fragmented he finds himself in an impossible situation. Where black and white are alienated and kept separate not only by custom but by a law, a kind of divide cuts right through the bishop. How does one hold people together who are being separated by force and also by sins of avarice, pride, and fear?

I always believed in the unity of the Church of Jesus Christ, but I had not really heard much about the charismatic movement. (Once somebody asked me about it, and I gave her five good reasons why nobody was ever expected to speak in tongues.) Besides reading a bit of Edward O'Connor's book, *The Pentecostal Movement in the Catholic Church*, my only other contact was with the Assemblies of God in my own city. They were attracting our best members, and that made me pretty mad, because it was evident they had a power I did not have.

It was not, however, out of despair that I came into this experience of the Spirit. At an annual clergy retreat in my diocese I had been enabled by God to lay some things at his feet—particularly the need to witness in the Church politically and socially on matters of unity. It had been a time of great blessing for me, and I had been able to say, "Lord, I will do whatever you ask me."

One Sunday after that retreat, I celebrated the Eucharist in the chapel at St. Andrew's College and settled down with the newspaper. But about twenty minutes before lunch, I was somehow drawn to my chapel to pray. I have not in the past been a very good prayer; I have said my office, celebrated the Eucharist, and made my meditations dutifully; but I never found it easy and I certainly did not generally go to my chapel at unusual times. Somehow it seemed appropriate on this occasion, and so I went.

I simply offered God silence in the faith that he could use silence because he is God. And presently he seemed to say, "I want you to offer your body to me." I couldn't think of all the parts of my body because I'm not very well educated in these things, but I mentioned all those I could think of. That silly prayer was obviously what the Lord wanted because before I'd gone through the catalogue, the Holy Spirit simply fell on me.

I can only speak of it in terms of a mighty rushing wind. I did not really know what was happening then because I wasn't expecting anything very much. But there was a wonderful tingling and a sense of the love of God, and an overpowering sense of his presence. I found myself being pressed to the ground and simply submitting to him in joy, saying the one word "yes" and not able to say another word.

Later that afternoon I again found myself in chapel, and once again the Lord anointed me in a very deep and loving way. With incredible joy, I found myself repeating, "I am your son, I am your son": God had not just accepted me as a person, but had created me anew as his own son.

Eventually I had no words left. The last word I could say with any authenticity was "God," and I just said it very lovingly. When I found myself without any words, I began to make some rather strange noises! I didn't know what they were at the time, but 10 days later one of the archdeacons in my diocese— a person who had been a charismatic for some time —came and explained what God had done in my life.

I rejoice because the Lord has done great things for me. This has involved first of all submission to the Lord, sonship, praise, the fruits of the Spirit being given instead of striven after, and a wonderful sense of victory. The Lord has just taken away sins that I have been battling for years.

How has all this affected the diocese? In some ways it has been difficult; although I wanted everybody to become charismatic overnight, I could not really expect that. My wife and a few friends advised me to go around and speak to all the priests and tell them what the Lord had done, lest they should learn about it by hearsay.

When I did that, I found my priests rather perplexed, but they were open and generous in their attitude and have given me wonderful support even when they have not been able to come all the way with me. We cannot agree about all the theology,

Bishop, Diocese, Charismatic Renewal 257

but we are nonetheless being made one in the Spirit. Even those who have not been baptized in the Spirit have been able to testify to what they describe as "fringe benefits."

There have been remarkable signs of the presence and power of God. One of the humbling things I had found as a bishop was that I never could give the priests in my care adequate spiritual encouragement and nourishment. But now by the grace of God, I can. I have the freedom to do it in the Spirit and so now when I visit the parishes I pray and have bible study with my priests.

Another perplexing question for me had been how to deal with the two alcoholic priests in my diocese: I had been able to do absolutely nothing except send them to clinics for treatment. But praise God, who made it possible to help them. I invited the priests in turn to come to my home, and we prayed together. One has since then received manifest blessings from the Spirit and is really living a victorious life. The other was baptized in the Spirit quite wonderfully. One morning while we were reading our offices together in my chapel, it seemed appropriate to praise God for delivering this priest. As I prayed in thanksgiving, the Holy Spirit filled him with praise and wonder and delight. He was totally changed and went back to minister in his pastoral charge.

Another development was the beginning of little group meetings of prayer and bible study. Since I do not have a parish (I am not unemployed! I only have a seat in my cathedral), I invited half a dozen people to pray in my home. Without any advertising at all, the group grew steadily to 60 people, and then by stages to 120. We now meet each week for bible study and prayer and we pray with those who wish to be baptized in the Spirit.

Wonderful things are happening throughout the diocese. In one school, there has been a remarkable movement of revival: about 120 boys meet for bible study every week, and some 35 of them have been baptized in the Spirit. The same kind of thing is happening in the university, which is a ten-minute walk from my home. But it is also now penetrating other parts of the diocese.

One example of this involves the Community of the Resurrection, an indigenous women's community. They asked me to give their retreat in January, and as I tried to minister to those sisters, I found that they were not really free to respond to one another. I also discovered, to my great astonishment, their need to know and experience the love of God. The sisters obviously longed for the power of the Holy Spirit, and to my very great joy the reverend mother and the assistant superior and later about 15 of the sisters all were baptized in the Spirit. In what was a dying community, there is now a movement of new life. The sisters are sharing in prayer and bible study, they are finding new ways of relating to one another.

The most unusual thing for a bishop is to find synods and diocesan councils changing. A diocesan council is one of the power structures of the church where the senior clergy and laymen get together and discuss how money is to be used. The last thing they normally talk about is the mission of the church or evangelism. But we have had a wonderful transformation there too.

Our diocesan council decided one day that they had to work our priorities for the next year. They discussed the matter, and to our astonishment and excitement they made it very clear that the priority was renewal of the church in the Holy Spirit. I said nothing about prayer and bible study, but when I started the next meeting someone said, "Where's the prayer and bible study?" We arranged it that evening in my home and we spent two and a half hours in prayer and bible study. That has made an astonishing difference.

The final aspect I want to discuss concerns a mission—a series of evangelistic meetings—that we had in East London, a city in my diocese. I had conducted other parish missions before this time, but this turned out to be something quite different.

For me the tremendous experience in that mission was its ecumenicity. I had been working in the ecumenical movement to devise formulae for reunion until I was blue in the face, and nothing much happened. When you get theologians together it is like putting porcupines together. But this was a wonderful sight to behold—the church full every night and the numbers becoming more and more ecumenical. There were Baptists and other extraordinarily un-Anglican people among us. There were even Pentecostals of the Assemblies of God who had come to be blessed in an Anglican church. (In fact, I know one Assemblies of God woman who received the baptism in the Spirit in that mission.) Here, people already united in heart were being joined to one another in the Spirit, irrevocably linked.

By the end of the mission it was obvious that everybody wanted to break bread together. It became quite impossible for me to say no to a Eucharist together, so I decided to use my episcopal prerogative and declare this an ecumenical occasion. We had a glorious and greatly blessed Eucharist together on the Sunday morning.

It is a thing of incredible joy to many of us that God is so greatly blessing the diocese of Grahamstown. Although this is just a stumbling beginning, we are expecting revival and renewal and we believe that God will honor our prayer and our expectations. We know that God is going to change our country and our church.

The First Pentecostal Abbey

By Mary Ann Jahr

In 1969 Our Lady of Guadalupe Benedictine Abbey lay wounded under the hot New Mexico sun. Financial disaster loomed like the mountains surrounding the 1,100-acre retreat center. Few people were interested in attending retreats and the abbey was about to fizzle into history. Today about 10,000 people each year attend the retreats, which are booked nearly a year in advance. "We've refused hundreds of retreats because we can't handle them," emphasized Fr. David Geraets, the abbot.

Not only are retreats flourishing, but the abbey's community of about 30 people now also runs a publishing house, sponsors a coffee house, teaches classes, organizes prayer groups, and operates a credit union.

The adobe buildings are the same, the life of poverty is still there, New Mexico's climate hasn't changed, but the monastery has changed dramatically. 'Pentecostal community' is the key, according to Fr. Geraets.

Although most abbeys have "a couple of monks who are pentecostal," he said, "this monastery is the first and only pentecostal abbey in the world."

In 1969 Fr. Geraets, then living in Benet Lake, Wisconsin, visited the monastery and discovered it was "falling apart" as a retreat center. A few months later he received permission to establish a pentecostal community at the monastery. Twelve Benedictines in solemn vows transferred from other monasteries to form the core community.

As time went by both men and women began committing themselves to the abbey for periods of three months to three years. The women form a "satellite community" he said.

"What's happening in our day is community," Fr. Geraets stated. Religious life was experiencing a "tremendous loss of people," he emphasized, but now he's observed a renewal of religious life. "We're a general witness to how God is renewing the Church charismatically."

Fr. Geraets believes monasteries must open up to spiritual renewal if they are going to survive. "It's renewal or eventual death," he stressed.

The crowds of people who fill the abbey's rooms each weekend testify to the renewed life that has replaced the dismal days of 1969. Between 50 and 90 people attend retreats each weekend of the year and about 120 people stream into the abbey each week.

During his time at the abbey, Fr. Geraets has noticed a "significant progression" in the retreats. At first the emphasis was on introduction to the charismatic renewal, he said, but now most of the people who come to the monastery aren't people newly baptized in the Spirit. They are seeking deeper teaching. The emphasis has shifted from marriage and the family to pentecostal renewal and Scripture.

People from all around the country attend the

The First Pentecostal Abbey

retreats, while two or three priests from the abbey travel nationwide conducting retreats. About 80 percent of the people attending the retreats are Catholic.

Fr. Geraets, who travels once or twice a month to different parts of the country, has noticed a "tremendous change" in people. "People are no longer satisfied with materialism. They are seeking new meaning to life . . . the Spirit wants to enter and transform the world and people are open to it," he said. He added that every major metropolitan area now has several prayer groups.

The monastery, a former dude ranch and later a farm run by Trappists, is located in the mountains of northern New Mexico near Pecos, a town of 1,500 people who are predominantly Spanish. About 80 percent of its people are on welfare, Fr. Geraets noted.

"We're very concerned about people financially and spiritually, Fr. Geraets emphasized. Two priests from the monastery live in Pecos and run a coffee house. "Many people believe pentecostals are turned inward," the abbot smiled, "but the monastery is reaching out to the young, families, everybody."

As the monastery has become stronger, new activities have emerged. A credit union among the poor has been established, catechism classes are taught, and between 10 and 15 prayer groups within a 50-mile radius of the abbey have sprung up with the help of the monks.

Last summer two priests branched out to Mexico City to aid poor families and orphans in the city slums and nearby villages. They hope to set up a permanent monastery similar to the one near Pecos.

Geraets, who formerly played trumpet in a jazz band, now plays guitar at prayer meetings and masses. His experience with the baptism in the Spirit was a gradual one beginning when he was six years old when he first "heard the voice of the Lord." It's been a gradual outflowing and unfolding, he said, with "many, many fantastic things" including miracles and healings.

People on retreats and at prayer meetings have been healed of broken bones, "incurable" schizophrenia, blindness, deafness and many other ailments, he said. "But the most beautiful are the conversion experiences," he believes.

Weekdays at the monastery begin at 6 a.m. with morning prayers and breakfast. Each member of the community spends the day working on maintenance, retreats, counseling or Dove publications, which produces charismatic literature. Prayers at 5 p.m. are followed by dinner, a recreation period and an evening prayer meeting and Eucharist. Recreation includes riding horses and hiking in the nearby national forest.

The monastery, which received independence as an abbey in March of last year, is financed by the retreats and Dove publications, which publishes pamphlets, booklets, tapes and a monthly newsletter with a circulation of 15,000. A bookstore and mail-order house which stocks about 500 titles are also part of the abbey. Dove's first book, *Man: the Divine Icon* by Fr. George Maloney, S.J., will soon be released. About 50,000 copies of Dove's bestseller, *Baptized in the Spirit* are sold every year, Fr. Geraets said.

The abbot believes the charismatic renewal

"will end up being the greatest outpouring of the Spirit since Pentecost. It's going faster than any other (movement) has. It took the liturgical movement 100 years or more." He is optimistic about the future of the renewal because of the many bishops involved and an increasing number of cardinals and priests.

"The renewal," he said, "is having a tremendous effect on the Catholic Church." He sees it as a renewal of the sacraments of healing, of penance as inner healing, confirmation and baptism as a commitment to Jesus and a renewal of prayer life and the faith of people.

"There will come a day when you can go into parishes and prophecy will be manifested, healing will be manifested, all the gifts will be manifested."

The Ultimate Test

By Mary Ann Jahr

Raymond McMahon worked hard to get away from the rows of shabby tenements of his childhood on Smith Hill. He made it. But at Christmastime he moved back.

Jack and Pixie Pendergast and their six children left a large, comfortable home in the highest-income area in the city for a three-story tenement in the lowest-income area—Smith Hill.

The Sam Drivers sold a $60,000 home on the safe, exclusive East Side, moved to Smith Hill and now have prostitutes and pushers as neighbors.

Smith Hill, tucked under the shadow of the Capitol building in Providence, Rhode Island, had gradually slipped into the quicksand of urban decay. Residents were fleeing to the suburbs. An interstate expressway sliced its way through the middle, forcing hundreds of families to move. Housing projects begun 12 years ago lay half-finished. The gray stone St. Patrick's Catholic Church towering over the neighborhood had lost 700 members in five years. The neighborhood seemed to be groaning its way into the heap of inner-city casualties.

But to many of Smith Hill's newest residents, the neighborhood isn't a casualty at all. In fact, it's on its way to becoming "a light on the mountain,"

The Ultimate Test

they agree. Since the summer of 1972 when Jim and Mary Ackroyd sold their suburban home and bought a multiple on Smith Hill, about 30 upper and middle-class families have purchased and remodeled run-down tenements and moved into the dying area. And it is giving hope to their neighbors.

These new residents are part of the Word of God Community at St. Patrick's. "It is important to realize that the *Lord* has called us to move here," emphasized Pixie Pendergast. Involved for years in social action, the Pendergasts found that social action can produce little and even bitter fruit if the Lord is not leading.

"When the Lord leads you to make a big change, if you're in his will, things go well," stated Pendergast, a partner in a large law firm.

And the Pendergast home at 21 Violet Street, which had no heat, bad wiring, holes in the walls, now is a "beautiful house," smiled the dark-haired community leader. In fact, five neighbors, encouraged by the new look of the Pendergast home, have begun painting their houses.

Many of the community houses have become Christian households with single men and women joining the families in an extended family situation.

The vision for Smith Hill began to change in July of 1971 when Fathers Raymond Kelly and John Randall arrived at the door of St. Patrick's Church. Plagued by a declining membership, financial crisis, and the closing of St. Patrick's elementary school, few church members experienced hope for the parish. "Many thought we had come to bury the parish," said the 45-year-old Randall.

Along with the two priests arrived a 500-

member charismatic prayer group, which Fr. Randall had been leading at a neighboring parish. Rumors began circulating among the "old-guard" parishioners that Holy Rollers were meeting in the church. For months the Word of God Community had little other impact on the ailing parish. Few parishioners attended the prayer meetings.

"I didn't understand what this group was about," exclaimed Marty McDonald, a 60-year member of St. Patrick's. "I waited more than a year, and when I saw the good they were doing, I became involved. We're gradually making a dent in the older people," he said.

"The good they were doing," was expressed concretely when the community announced they were going to reopen the school which had closed in 1971 because of the financial crisis. "For the first time people in the parish realized that perhaps this prayer community could offer something besides a weekly prayer meeting with all its emotionalism, excitement, and crowds," said the enthusiastic McDonald.

Earlier the church had considered selling the empty school to pay off bills. As the community prayed regularly for guidance for what to do with the school, the priests discovered that more than a dozen community members had degrees in education and would teach for little or no pay.

In September of 1972 the school, freshly painted and repaired by community volunteers, became the first Catholic pentecostal school in the nation.

"The focus of the school is the education of the total family," said Sister Patricia Considine, one of a team of three principals in the school. The 200 children are from homes where one or two parents are involved in the charismatic renewal and in the ongoing Christian education of themselves and their children. The teaching staff includes a total of 50 persons, 12 full-time and 38 part-time volunteers. The school pays only $31,000 a year in salaries.

At a time when traditional parish elementary schools are in a state of crisis, St. Patrick's school operates in the black and hasn't any debts. The money is "prayed in" every month to keep the school going.

During the summer of 1972, St. Patrick's parishioners experienced a setback when they learned that the church building was structurally unsound. "When the building was condemned," noted the white-haired McDonald, "we were afraid it was the end of St. Pat's. But then we realized that a church is a people and not a building." Since then the church has been meeting in the yellow brick parish school.

Community members have been affecting the neighborhood in many ways. At Thanksgiving and Christmas, they drive around in cars picking up the poor and lonely wandering the streets and invite them to join the several hundred community members for a joyful dinner and celebration at St. Patrick's auditorium.

Across the street from the school in a new high-rise apartment building for the elderly, Word of God Community members sponsor parties, dinners, and concerts for the residents, and the priests conduct a special Mass each week in the apartment house.

In the Earthen Vessel, the community's used-clothing store, Robert Fitzgerald, who gave up a lucrative salesman's job, "spreads the Word of the Lord" as he sells items from the stacks of clothes.

An observer of the community, the Rev. Thomas D. Twitchell of the nearby United Presbyterian Church, credits the community with "the most effective work I've seen on the drug problem." The community's drug program is the love of Jesus Christ.

People on Smith Hill are beginning to ask "Can these people (the charismatic community) save this dying parish? This neighborhood?"

"That is the ultimate test of the charismatic renewal," declared Fr. Randall, "Can the charismatic renewal renew a parish?"

Gradually, as more "regular" parishioners are becoming involved in the Word of God Community, the parish and community are merging.

"We are a parish that has come alive through the charismatic renewal, giving hope to parishes that it can be done, not by men, not even by the joint efforts of men, but by God who gives the growth in all circumstances. Unless the Lord builds the city, they labor in vain who build it."

Renewal and an American Mission

By Fr. Richard Jones

The charismatic renewal has invaded Sioux Indian land!

I should begin our story with a brief description of the setting. St. Francis is one of 21 Indian communities on the Rosebud Reservation in south central South Dakota. Except for a small number of white faculty at the St. Francis Mission School, which borders the southern edge of the town, St. Francis is composed entirely of full-blood and mixed-blood Indians. The Indian language is still very common, especially among the older people. The average annual family income is about $2,000. The tribal police and federal and state welfare agencies consider St. Francis the most violent town on the reservation. It reminds me of the setting of *The Cross and the Switchblade,* though it does not have the heavy dope. It is under these conditions that the charismatic renewal is taking place.

As is common in many other situations, the charismatic renewal began with a number of people coming together on a regular basis to share prayer and seek the Lord together. The prayer group was started at the Mission itself and led by a Jesuit scholastic, Dennis Linn. It consisted of a small number of priests, sisters, and lay volunteers; it was not charismatic.

This was just the beginning of the Lord's work of renewal. In August of 1970 Gene and Donna Loverich of The Word of God in Ann Arbor came to St. Francis Mission School as volunteer coach and nurse. This couple, working with Dennis, managed through the grace of our Lord to pray with 10 people for the baptism in the Holy Spirit—one sister, three lay volunteers, one woman from the Indian community of St. Francis, and five high-school seniors. At this time the charismatic element began to appear in the prayer group.

In May of 1971 Gene and Dennis explained the charismatic movement to the Jesuit community and asked for assistance. I knew that there was a prayer group among the faculty and had heard something about "strange tongues," but like Martha I was "busy about many things." Though I had tried many projects in my apostolate among my Indian parishioners, I seemed to be getting nowhere until I volunteered to help the "charismatics."

The next month, a number of the people who had received the baptism in the Holy Spirit went to the Notre Dame Conference and also to Ann Arbor. This was their first experience of a fully charismatic prayer meeting and a prayer community; they returned home most enthusiastic.

The summer of 1971 was fruitful for me as well. I spent much time praying, thinking, and reading about the charismatic renewal. I was "converted," and in September received the baptism in the Holy Spirit. This renewal in my own life brought me a greater love for prayer and Scripture. I wanted to

Renewal and an American Mission

pass this renewal and love on to my Indian people.

At this time, though the Mission charismatic prayer group was growing in the gifts of the Spirit, it was not fully charismatic. Quite a few people had the gift of praying in tongues, but the gifts of speaking out in tongues at the prayer meeting, interpretation, and prophecy were not frequently used. This group was predominantly white, not Indian. It seemed to me that the traditional Catholic background of these white people held many back from praying out spontaneously, being perfectly relaxed and open at the prayer meeting, and committing themselves entirely to the prayer community.

In the fall of 1971, the Mission charismatic prayer group moved their meetings to my parish house in St. Francis. We hoped to attract more of the Indian people to the prayer group through this move. Though a number of priests, sisters, and lay volunteers, and a few Indian people made a renewed commitment to the Lord, this move downtown did not attract our Indian people as we had hoped.

For the sake of those who find themselves in a similar situation I will go into a bit of detail on this point. Let me say, first of all, that the Indian people traditionally hold much respect for God—they have always lived close to him in nature. Their native "Yuwipi" religion is also rather similar to a prayer group meeting in form—there is much spontaneous praying, singing, sharing. Yet in spite of these positive points the charismatic prayer group had little appeal.

I can now see some of the difficulties that prevented more Indian people from participating. The religious in the group, while committed to their own religious community, could not see their part in the formation of the Indian community. The lay volunteers were more involved in the school than in the village. There was a lack of leadership—no one could really keep the prayer meeting moving along. The Indian people had been brought up in the traditional services of the Catholic Church and had a deep respect for the clergy; thus they came with a great deal of reserve and submissiveness. The fact that the group was predominantly white and "intellectual" only added to the complication. A number of the Indian people had never finished grade school, let alone high school, and could not speak or understand English very well; many times they did not understand much of what was being said in the meeting. The Life in the Spirit Seminar was adequate for the religious and lay volunteers; our Indian people needed something much more simple and basic.

In order to get past some of these difficulties, I decided to start a Bible-study prayer group, basically for the Indian people. We moved from home to home each Wednesday evening, while the Mission charismatic prayer group continued to meet in the parish house on Tuesdays. The focus of the meeting was mostly singing, in English and in Indian, which the people enjoy very much, and simple teaching. Our objective in the teaching was to present the Lord to our people right out of the Gospels. The meetings would end with Mass and a light lunch and just being together. There was little spontaneous prayer. The people would write out Mass intentions and we would read these before Mass. (Poor as many of the people are, their prayers almost never asked for material things—a job, money, a car—but for spiritual

Renewal and an American Mission 275

things—greater unity in the community, more people to come to our prayer meetings, a drinking or family problem, love of one another. Some of the kids would ask for success in their school work or a basketball victory.) While we emphasized the role of the Holy Spirit in our prayer meetings and in life, we did not stress the charismatic gifts or the baptism in the Holy Spirit. But it did not take long for rumors to spread along the "moccasin trail": we had started a new religion! we had become "Yuwipis"! we had to be baptized again!

I am also pastor of the Indian community of Spring Creek only 10 miles from St. Francis. Prayer meetings began here on Thursday evenings and followed much the same pattern as those in St. Francis. Once a month we would have a combined prayer meeting for the people of St. Francis and Spring Creek in the parish house basement. The people looked forward to these monthly meetings.

To coordinate the renewal work of the two Bible-study prayer groups and the Mission charismatic group, we decided to set up a pastoral team: Gene Loverich, myself, and an Indian woman whom the Lord has used much to get the prayer groups started. We met each week to discuss the direction in which the Lord seemed to be leading us in the three prayer groups. One team member felt that the Mission charismatic group should be the one to grow and simply absorb the St. Francis Indian group—it was in the Mission group that the gifts were manifested and potential leadership lay. I guess we as white people always seem to think we "have it in the bag," and it is just a matter of time until everyone will grow enough to accept it. Another team member thought that we should concentrate on the Spring Creek group where growth to a well-functioning Christian community seemed most natural and possible. The last viewpoint and seemingly the most illogical and impossible was that the St. Francis Bible group would become charismatic and eventually the basis of our Christian community.

By June, 1972, all of us were frustrated and at a complete loss as to the direction the Lord was leading us. During the summer the Mission charismatic group was discontinued since many of the staff left for new assignments or summer school. The St. Francis group was poorly attended as a result of destructive gossip and factions inside and outside the group. The Spring Creek group was faltering as well. We combined the St. Francis and Spring Creek groups for the summer.

I guess the Lord figured we had suffered enough. He led us to the formation of a "parish team" and to deep, spiritual growth. My parish team consisted of Gene and Donna Loverich, Sister Bernard O.S.E., Kathy Kowalski, and myself. All have been prayed with for the baptism in the Holy Spirit. While I carried the major pastoral responsibilities, my team carried out much of the pastoral work: visiting homes, planning and setting up for prayer meetings, teaching CCD. Besides our pastoral work we had daily Mass and prayer together as a team, a weekly shared meal, and recreation. As homes are very close together, we frequently visit and discuss our apostolate. One of the purposes of the team was the formation of a nucleus about which a Christian community could develop and grow.

Things began to happen. We decided not to

Renewal and an American Mission 277

start up the Mission charismatic prayer group again, but leave it open for other leadership. We visited all homes and among other things quietly explained our prayer group to the Indian people. Within a month many misunderstandings were broken down.

We also made some changes in the format of our prayer meetings, in order to draw more participation from the people. At the beginning of the prayer meeting each person would write his name on a piece of paper; these names were then distributed at random: you would pray for the person whose name you drew during that prayer meeting and throughout the week. The people also wrote out their prayers of praise, thanksgiving, and petition on slips of paper; three or four of the Indian men would read these prayers aloud just before Mass. People were encouraged to participate by requesting songs that they would like the song leader to start. If a person found a psalm or a passage from Scripture that was meaningful for him, he or someone else could read it aloud or he could have all of us read it together. People were encouraged to come prepared with something to share—a passage, some reading, an experience, an exhortation. We did not give so much teaching. Within a month after the home visitations by the parish team and the changes in the format of the prayer meetings we had to move our meeting from the homes to the parish house basement. More Indian men began to attend. Our St. Francis prayer group increased from 20 to over 50.

Fr. Chris Keeler, S.J., from the White River Indian community, outlined a seven-week seminar leading to the baptism in the Holy Spirit, which we gave before the regular prayer meeting. They were simple and direct, with talks on: Jesus loves me (our Indian people are a defeated race and have a deep feeling of inferiority); I turn from sin to Jesus; Who Jesus is; We learn about our Lord through personal prayer and Scripture; the Holy Spirit is a Person who helps us by his gifts and power; The baptism itself; How to live this giving of myself completely to the Lord.

After the third talk of the seminar a parish team member visited each person taking the seminar each week to review, discuss, and clarify the teaching. Such visits helped surmount educational and language difficulties. Finally, we asked each person whether he wanted to give himself entirely to the Lord with the help of the Holy Spirit. All those making the seminar said yes; 16 received the baptism in the Holy Spirit. The evening of the baptism was undoubtedly the most exciting and moving experience we had witnessed since we began our prayer groups. Each person was deeply and tangibly touched by the Holy Spirit and his love.

Our next step was to form growth groups of four or five among those who received the baptism. We meet once a week for an hour in the home of one of the members. We share with each other our prayer life, Scripture reading, our successes and failures in the spiritual life. Personal and shared prayer play an important role in the growth group. We also discuss cassette tapes. (A group in Ft. Lauderdale sent us 50 free tapes on prayer, the Holy Spirit, and so on, which we loan to our people, who find them a great help.)

Besides the growth groups, we set up a Growth in the Spirit Seminar before each prayer meeting for those who have received the baptism in the Holy Spirit, at the same time as a seminar preparing others for the baptism. We have a monthly day of recollection; 65 attended the first. We are now praying for a house of prayer where we can take our growth groups and others for retreats. We also look forward to the day when St. Francis and Spring Creek will become true Christian communities.

The Lord has worked with us in a way we did not understand. He chose the people who would be least expected to open up and grow in him. It wasn't the white people who always seem to have the answers; it wasn't even the most "suitable" Indian community. It was the Indian community most torn apart by factions, gossip, fighting, and drinking in which he chose to begin his work. It was many of the lowliest, those with the greatest difficulties, that the Lord has called first in St. Francis.

The charismatic renewal is now spreading to other communities on the Rosebud Reservation. It is the "little ones" of St. Francis who are most zealous in spreading the Good News to the other Indian communities. Praise the Lord!

The Church: A Charismatic Community

By Rev. Ken Pagard

Ten years ago I heard Billy Graham say that for the next decade the focus of theological study would be on the Holy Spirit. Ten years ago Pope Paul prayed, "Renew your wonders in our time, as though for a new Pentecost." How accurate has that forecast proved to be: how wonderfully has the Lord answered that prayer.

This past decade has proved to be the decade of the Holy Spirit. Who, in 1962, with even the wildest imagination, could have pictured the conditions in the Church today? Thousands attending a Roman Catholic pentecostal conference at Notre Dame; thousands of Lutherans meeting in Minneapolis for their charismatic conference; hundreds of pastors and thousands of laymen in every major denomination baptized in the Holy Spirit! Yes, the sixties saw a wonderful moving of the Holy Spirit "upon all flesh," a moving that has only just begun.

What about the next decade—what does the Lord have in store? I'm convinced that over the next ten years the focus will be on ecclesiology—the Church. This is only to be expected. We have seen a renewed coming of the Holy Spirit in power: the

The Church: A Charismatic Community 281

primary mission of the Holy Spirit is to create community, to form the "Body of Christ." We have already seen the first stirrings of this work.

In 1962 the Lord Jesus baptized me in the Holy Spirit. For a long time I had been perplexed with the glaring contrast between the life evidenced in the early Church, particularly as described in the book of Acts, and the life of the Church around me—if indeed it could be called life. As a Baptist, I had been indoctrinated with the ideal of patterning out faith and practice after that of the early Church, but something was missing. After several years in the pastorate, frustrated, grappling with these inconsistencies, my hopes were stirred by the witness of a fellow pastor as to how his life and ministry had been transformed through an experience of being "filled with the Spirit."

I quickly saw how this fit into the scriptural pattern, but I did not know how to appropriate it for myself. I spent two or three weeks of earnest searching, finally just surrendering to the Spirit as I simply asked Jesus to "baptize" me. What joy; what peace; what love! What a sense of God's presence; what power! This was the kind of Christianity the New Testament spoke about. It was alive, dynamic, something you wanted to share with others! The Bible itself seemed to come alive and become contemporary.

Right from the start, I was intuitively aware that this was not just for personal enjoyment, but related to the total life of the Church. I know that there are many who think of the "baptism of the Holy Spirit" as primarily something to deepen the individual's spiritual life, expressed in two different ways. The "tolerant" attitude of many is that "it's okay for those who feel they need it." Some in the charismatic renewal become very independent—they have their private pipeline to the Spirit so need no one else. They flit from group to group, to meeting after meeting to have their ears tickled by one amazing speaker after another. How tragically both miss what it is all about.

The Scripture is clear that the purpose of Jesus and the mission of the Holy Spirit is to create community. The effect of sin is disintegration. God's work is love, *"which binds everything together in perfect harmony"* (Col. 3:14). His work on earth is to undo the divisive work of Satan, to bring people back into a perfect unity in his Body, the Church. His concern is not just with "saving" individuals, but also with fitting them into the Church.

A year and a half after I was baptized in the Spirit, the Lord called me to become pastor of the First Baptist Church of Chula Vista, with a sense that the Lord was about to do something special in that church: a kind of pilot program of what he was about to do throughout his Church. We had no idea what this would involve, but our desire was to follow the Lord no matter where he would lead us, to take the Scripture at face value and to be willing to change anything the Lord wanted changed. At the same time, we resolved not to "push" anything, to avoid getting ahead of the Lord.

A handful of people in the church had already been baptized in the Spirit before I came. I hardly mentioned anything about it the first ten or eleven months, except as individuals asked me. Gradually, the number of those entering into this life grew.

The Church: A Charismatic Community 283

Then the whole church wanted to know what was happening. I shared openly in a series of sermons, and the open-hearted response overwhelmed me. Over the next six months, half of the deacons and scores of the members were filled with the Spirit. We knew that the Lord wanted us to be a "Spirit-filled church," but, at this point, our only concept was a church in which everyone was baptized in the Holy Spirit: we still were limited to individualistic thinking. More and more of our people came into this life in the Spirit, until almost all were included. Then we noticed that our whole life was gradually being changed on a far more profound level.

The most obvious changes were in our services. First our prayer meetings really began to come alive. Then our Sunday worship services began to have a sense of vitality while still retaining the traditional format. There would come a testimony of God's grace, a word of prophecy, a tongue and interpretation. At first I was a bit anxious as to the reactions of visitors, but the Lord took care of it and we never had any negative reactions. The spontaneous "additions" became more numerous until we finally stopped having a printed order of worship. There has now developed a type of worship service which is a beautiful blending of order and spontaneity, peace and joy, praise and worship. Communion also became more meaningful until, instead of observing it once a month, we celebrate it every day.

Then, the structure of the church began to evolve. The elected board of deacons, which functioned more or less as the board of directors of a corporation, started to become more spiritually sensitive. The people of the church began to recognize a few men as spiritual leaders and started to call them elders. The board of deacons gradually faded out, and the elders became established. They are not elected, serve no limited term of office, but are recognized by the church body. Their authority (something quite foreign to Baptists) is accepted by the people of the church. They meet at least twice a week, growing together into a real unity of spirit. As they meet, much time is spent worshiping, praying, listening to the Lord, with no action taken unless all feel this to be the Lord's direction.

The church is now ministry-oriented. Over the centuries, Christianity developed into a "spectator sport," with a few paid professional "ministers," and a lot of committees. We have come to see that the function of the various leaders in the church is to *"equip the saints for the work of the ministry"* (Eph. 4:12), not to *do* the ministering. The "saints," all the members of the church, are to be the "ministers." Consequently, in our church, every Christian is expected to have some area of service. The gifts of the Spirit are meant primarily as tools for service, and as we are involved in ministry and come face to face with great needs, we find that all God's resources are available to us. A wide variety of ministries has developed: prison ministry, hospitals, street evangelism, singing, dance, drama, arts and crafts, teaching, custodial and rescue mission ministry, to name a few. Each of these has a leader, responsible to the elders. The various ministries meet weekly for a time of prayer, preparation, and ministering to one another.

Actually, we have found that it is the church body itself that is the minister, more than any indi-

The Church: A Charismatic Community 285

vidual members. We have come to see the church as the people of God coming together as a people, each giving all that he is as a resource material for this ministry. Our sense of fellowship, of oneness with each other, began to grow. People started staying longer after the services, enjoying each other, seeing a lot of each other during the week. Christian commitment is not just a vertical commitment to Christ, but also on a horizontal commitment to each other. The division between our "church life" and "private life" has disappeared as we find our entire lives intertwined with each other. This has grown to the point where, at present, about one-fourth of our people live together in community.

It all began simply enough, almost four years ago. There was a girl from Seattle, pregnant, living in an apartment by herself, going to pieces. We invited her home with us. Then an incorrigible boy from the school where my wife teaches was sent to Juvenile Hall. We felt nine years old was too young for that, so we asked the authorities if we could have him. My brother, a missionary in Africa, asked to leave his two teen-age children with us to finish high school. Then an alcoholic whom I had tried to help for years was invited to join us, then a man just out of prison and a divorcee with two children.

Other families in the church were also doing the same. We would get together to help each other, compare notes and pray together. Gradually, the sharing became broader and deeper. People who had come needing ministry were healed, and wanted to stay on as part of the ministry. Others from the church joined in to strengthen the ministry. This was given increased impetus through contacts with the community at Church of the Redeemer in Houston, Texas, a couple of years later. The households ministering to broken people began to come together into a single entity sharing with each other while remaining geographically separate. Over the following two years, this group of families caring for needy individuals gradually developed into a real ministering community.

The name explains what it is. It is a "community"—people sharing together. More and more it has come to the point of sharing all things in common, as in the early Church (Acts 2 and 4). This involves sharing of material possessions—those who work contribute their total income to the community households. If one household is short and another has extra, there is sharing from one house to another. However, the sharing is more than material, it is the sharing of a whole *life.* It is a matter of living together with real love for each other, learning what it is to consider each other, adjust to each other, give in to each other. It is a matter of *"in love being subject to one another,"* surrendering something of our independence so that we can become one body serving the Lord. This means a growing in being open with each other, and being freed from many bondages.

There are at present about a dozen households, each consisting of about ten to twenty-five people. We have regular meetings of the heads of households, to work out our common problems and directions, and to grow together into a total unity. Each house consists of a core community, committed to the Lord, each other, and to ministry. Around this core are others who have real needs for ministry, and

The Church: A Charismatic Community 287

have come for healing. As these are made whole they very often continue in the community, becoming a part of the core community.

This brings out the second part of the name—"ministering." The purpose of the community is for ministry. In our society there are overwhelming numbers of people who are broken in spirit—with emotional problems, weakened by drugs, not knowing what love is. Even after accepting Christ, there is often the need for "tender loving care" on a twenty-four-hour basis, the need to live in a community of love and support. One of the primary areas of ministry is with these right in the household. There have been remarkable healings, for which we praise the Lord. Many who would have undoubtedly "gone down the tubes" have been caused to stand on their feet and come into "the glorious liberty of the sons of God."

Living in community has been a tremendous environment for all of us to grow spiritually. We have found that with conventional living, with casual contacts with people, we can function fairly adequately with a very shallow kind of Christian life. Living and ministering together on a twenty-four-hour basis involved a much deeper kind of relationship, and necessitates taking the new Testament very seriously, dying to self, and really learning to walk in the Spirit. It is the only way in which this kind of a life can work. We have found it a very cleansing experience—cleansing from ourselves, from materialism, from pettiness. It brings us face-to-face with the realization that the Christian life is a total involvement. The cross becomes a crucial part of our experience. The grace of Jesus becomes our constant resource, and the fruit and power of the Spirit an essential ingredient.

In Jesus' great prayer before his death, he asked *"that they may all be one, that the world may believe that thou hast sent me"* (John 17:21). Before that he had said: *"By this shall all men know you are my disciples, by the love that you have for one another."* We have found that the most effective means of evangelism is just Christians loving each other, sharing together the life of Jesus. Hundreds of people have been accepting the Lord each year through the ministry of the church.

The Lord has also used our church as a witness in denominational circles. We have felt all along that the Lord wanted us to remain faithful right where we were, in the American Baptist Convention. In the early days, denominational leaders looked very much askance at the charismatic. There were many fears, suspicions, prejudices—we were treated as lepers. Now fellow pastors and denominational leaders at all levels have become aware that something worthwhile is happening in Chula Vista. At our national convention last year we were asked to make a presentation on "The Charismatic Church"—and the sessions were packed. A few years ago we helped start "The American Baptist Charismatic Fellowship," which now has six or seven hundred pastors on the mailing list. What has happened here has helped to alleviate the fears of others, and they have been emboldened to press forward in the Lord.

A verse of Scripture that has become very meaningful is from the Phillips's translation of Romans 8:19: *"The whole creation is on tiptoe to see the wonderful sight of the sons of God coming into their own."* For a long time Christians have not realized their rightful heritage, they have been living in poverty, in fear, molded by the world around them. Today we see at least the beginning of the fulfillment of this verse. The sons of God are beginning to come into their own, and the world is sitting up to take notice: and many are glad!

The Lord, the Spirit and the Church

By Kevin Ranaghan

Just five and a half years ago, small groups of Catholics around the country began to pray for a renewal in the Holy Spirit that would bring to new life the graces of baptism and confirmation. Who knows how many hundreds, or better yet thousands of these prayer meetings have sprung up and matured in the last five years? How can one sum up the Catholic charismatic renewal except to say that Jesus is Lord of his People—in the broad strokes and in the fine detail, the hand of God is seen to move clearly and surely, renewing us in every conceivable aspect of life and work. In a little over five years, the Lord Jesus has released and nurtured this charismatic renewal as a strong, powerfully fruitful, and remarkably effective movement of his Spirit for the reformation and renewal of the Catholic Church.

This Jesus is Lord of all his People. He is a King who establishes his Kingdom from close at hand by being clearly and concretely the head of the members of his Body. He is a King who began his reign by mounting the throne of the cross and who continues to rule his People by pouring out his life upon us. Everywhere that his followers call on his name, he is molding his Body in his own image. Everywhere that Christians cry out in faith for a fresh outpouring of his Spirit, that breath of God is reviving his People, giving them Christ's own power for the salvation of the world.

We subjects of this King are Catholics, Episcopalians, Presbyterians, Lutherans, Baptists, Methodists, Mennonites, Pentecostals, and others. As a rule our families have not always loved or trusted each other very well. But Jesus is determined to be Lord of all his People and he is pouring out his lifegiving Spirit upon us all. No matter what church background we come from, no matter what feelings we may have had about each other, no matter what serious theological difficulties may still lie between us—Jesus is teaching us that we are basically and fundamentally called to be one People, one holy nation, one royal priesthood, a new humanity led by the New Adam. Regardless of our different denominations, we do know and accept Jesus of Nazareth as our Lord and Savior, we are together plunged into the mystery of his death and resurrection, and in his Spirit we share one life together which is the very life of God. It is no empty slogan that we are one in the Spirit but it is a profound reality which, praise God, is being revealed to us in these days.

I am not suggesting in the least that we pretend that serious differences do not exist among Christians. Nor am I suggesting that we abandon the discipline of the Church in ecumenical matters. Rather, we can honor what God is doing among all Christians by renouncing wrong attitudes of superiority, inferiority, or even attitudes of indifference.

First, we can accept all Christians as fully our brothers and sisters with all the possibilities for holiness, spiritual gifts, and effective life-giving service that we expect among ourselves. Secondly, we must renounce any attitude that does not recognize that all Christians are basically and fundamentally one in that by accepting Jesus as our Lord and Savior, we all share in his life with the Father and his empowering with the Holy Spirit. Thirdly, we have to accept the call to suffer the pain of separation when we long to be one, so that our fidelity in our churches may be a ringing prophecy and sign to all Christianity that we must become really one according to Jesus' will. And fourthly, we have to be willing to work hard in our own Church and to encourage our brothers and sisters in other churches to work hard, prayerfully and lovingly, to create concrete situations on the local level and on national levels where we can actually have more officially approved unity in our worship, doctrine, and ministry. But we are here today to talk about the charismatic renewal in the Catholic Church.

What is the Catholic Church in which this charismatic renewal is growing? There are over 600 million Roman Catholics in the world, over 47 million in the United States. We live in hundreds of dioceses with hundreds of bishops supported by thousands of priests, with great numbers of nuns and brothers in schools, colleges, universities, hospitals, nursing homes, inner-city teams, and social-service centers. Somehow we are all tied in with the United States Catholic Conference and the National Conference of Catholic Bishops. We are influenced by a host of national organizations, some as old as the Confraternity of Christian Doctrine and some as new as last week's big issue.

Most Roman Catholics live in a geographically defined parish with a church and a school that we or our parents worked long and hard to pay for. Our church life is under the direction of a pastor and his assistants, or perhaps a pastoral team. In this setting Catholics in fact hear God's Word proclaimed and explained; within those walls Catholics worship God in the liturgy and meet him in the sacraments. This is not the Church of theory, nor is it the Church of seminary hopes or university debates. But it is the Church as it exists among her people. It is the Church in which most of us have grown up, which we mostly love but sometimes find infuriating, which we strive to support but which we sometimes despair of.

Now we come to a very important point. This American Roman Catholic Church is in the Body of Christ. All the millions of men and women who are members of this Church are in fact members of the Body of Christ; they do belong to the People of God, and Jesus is their Lord. It is the continual and clear teaching of our Lord through the Church that when a person is baptized he becomes a member of Christ and is given the gift of the Holy Spirit. Therefore, we in the charismatic renewal, who are so conscious of what this means and so anxious to respond in faith to it, are not members of a small separate Body of Christ, but we are a small fraction of a much larger, Spirit-endowed Body of Christ: the Church at large.

There are many people in the Church who are not fully aware of who they are in Christ and of what gift they have been given. Their Christian life is minimal, perhaps just a cultural or ethnic expression having little to do with how they live and where their hearts lie. It is not my purpose to analyze the pastoral and personal causes of this situation. I simply want to point out that inasmuch as they are baptized they do belong to Christ, they belong to us, and that we share the responsibility for their hearing the Word of God in an effective way and for their awakening to the life of grace that lies dormant within them.

There are many others who are aware of who they are in Christ and of the gift they have received. The Holy Spirit moves powerfully within them and they serve God and us well in all sorts of ways. They are not involved in the charismatic renewal. They may not understand it or even have a bad opinion of it for one reason or another, yet they are fully our brothers and sisters in the Lord, united to us in the Body of the Holy Spirit. It is for us both to acknowledge the powerful working of the Lord in them and through them and also to witness in love and humility to what the Lord is doing among us, for we are one Body and members of one another.

This charismatic renewal has not happened in a vacuum. It has not been created by God out of nothing; it has happened within the Body of Christ as part of the life of the Body of Christ. It began and has developed in Catholicism chiefly among Catholics who were or have become anxious for a fuller Catholic life and for the renewal of the whole Church. It is little wonder that the Lord has had Spirit-filled Catholics all over the world simultaneously see the Catholic identity of what he is doing among us; that he is doing it within the Church, not outside or alongside the Church.

The Lord, the Spirit and the Church

This leads us to what I believe is the major principle which Jesus as Lord of all his People wants to teach us at this conference: the charismatic renewal in the Catholic Church is the expression or embodiment of a movement on the part of Almighty God for the purpose of charismatically renewing the Church—that is for the renewal on every level of Catholic life of the fullness of the gift of the Holy Spirit with everything that that means, especially in the areas of lively faith in Jesus, worship, and the gifts and ministries of the Holy Spirit. The charismatic renewal is not an end in itself, nor can it have an existence separate from that of the Church. Rather the charismatic renewal is part of the Church and exists for the renewal of the Church. Thus the resources, spiritual energies, and very lives of individuals and communities who are in the Catholic charismatic renewal are to be laid down in service for the well-being of the whole Church.

Put another way, the success of the charismatic renewal, the success of the Lord's plan for the Catholic Church depends upon our loyalty to the Church, our love of the Church, our work for the Church, our forgiveness toward the Church, and our hard and consistent effort to integrate all the good fruit of the charismatic renewal with the life of the whole Church. This includes the injection of everything we are experiencing that is truly from the Holy Spirit into all areas of Catholic life. It also includes our careful effort to weed out any elements which may have arisen in the charismatic renewal which are not truly of God nor upbuilding for the Church as a whole.

Let us look together at some of the good fruit of

the charismatic renewal, not the work of human hands alone, but fruit nurtured by the Lord Jesus himself for the good of all his People, which the charismatic renewal must integrate into the whole Church on every level, in every structure, in every institution, office, "function," and life that is Catholic.

Above all else, is the realization of and the emphasis upon the Lordship of Jesus Christ. From top to bottom and around the world every Catholic is called upon by Jesus to affirm anew that he alone is Lord of our lives. It is his plan that all come to know him personally as Lord of our corporate and individual lives, as Savior and liberator from the kingdom of darkness. With this goes the realization that the person and work of the Holy Spirit are absolutely real and essential components of authentic Christianity; that the Holy Spirit is truly present among us and that he can be counted upon day-in and day-out to supply the power and the grace for every challenge faced by every Christian. All of this must be taken and given in the context of our realization that God does have a plan for his People, a strategy for the salvation of the world, a design for our individual lives as members of him, and that we can enter into that plan of God's by becoming immersed in his Word.

Another good fruit of the charismatic renewal that can permeate the whole Church is the rediscovery with the Lord of the role of community in normal Christian life. We have discovered, and the whole Church needs to *experience,* that we are not meant to be saved as isolated individuals, but as brothers and sisters who belong to each other in Christ in types of concrete, real associations where

The Lord, the Spirit and the Church 297

we can serve the Lord together, and serve each other, growing together in holiness and in service to mankind as small microcosms of the Body of Christ. In this, we have also come to see that there is real diversity of ministry in the Church. That is to say there are different gifts, or abilities, or services in the Body of Christ that are all equally from the Holy Spirit and that are all necessary for the Church to function well. Ministry is not limited to bishops, priests, and deacons, though these are the major ministries of the Church. All are called to minister in the Church, not just in a vague sense but with concrete gifts of service appointed by the Spirit.

In that life of ministry together we have seen that Jesus is the source of all authority in his Body and his authority is radically different from models of authority in the world. The models being offered of monarchy, democracy, or anarchy as Church lifestyles are worldly, not Scriptural. What we have been learning is that the only authority in the Body is that of its Head who is Jesus Christ. Now Jesus entered into his authority and became fully Lord precisely by laying down his life for us; thus his authority is characterized by life-giving service. The whole Church should be encouraged to find leaders who will use authority or headship not to dominate others as in the world, but who show a willingness to serve, to lay down and empty their lives for the well-being of the Body of Christ. We have also learned that there are many other ministries and services in the Church which are not ministries of authority or leadership but ministries of subordinate service and support. In the world men rebel at being submissive to other men, but in Christ we can rejoice in being submissive to one another according to the gifts, ministries, and offices that we have been given by the Holy Spirit, according to the part of the Body we are.

Ultimately, we have seen and the whole Church must see that the Church as a whole, and each community in the Church, and each individual in each community shares in a commission from the Lord Jesus to convert the world to him, to bring the world out of the kingdom of darkness and into the kingdom of light, to proclaim the word dynamically.

Having pointed out all these wonderful things that the Lord is teaching us and that he wants to make part of his charismatically renewed Church, we must turn our attention seriously to the fact that there are some peripheral elements popping up in conjunction with the charismatic renewal that are obstacles to integration with the Church and which need either to be weeded out or corrected from within the movement itself.

The principal problem which we must work to overcome is that of any attitude or action which makes the charismatic renewal and its participants look like a special "in group," the elect of God, or the select few who have the whole truth. An example of this would be cultivating our own language or religious vocabulary to the point where other Catholics could not readily understand us. Now it is clear that we have to develop vocabulary to express the truly new things that the Lord has been doing among us, and that for ecumenical understanding the language of classical and neo-pentecostalism is often helpful. But I think we must take care, inasmuch as we can, always to express what is happening among

The Lord, the Spirit and the Church 299

us in language that is both scriptural and familiar to Catholic ears.

Also, we have to avoid an attitude that in any way looks upon non-charismatic Catholics as non-Christians or unsaved or second class. This attitude, in my experience, is very very rare, but where it exists it is so divisive and insidious that it is worth mentioning and condemning.

Similarly we must renounce any attitude that regards the prayer group or community as the true spiritual Church existing within or alongside of a "carnal" parish or diocese. Again, such a separatist point of view is small, but it is extremely dangerous. We must correct any Catholic group which might think of itself as a truer Body of Christ than the parish it is within; and we must correct in love especially any Catholics in interdenominational groups whose members attend no church but make the prayer meeting a substitute for full church life.

Finally, we must avoid any attitude which tends to reject teaching and preaching and counsel from non-charismatic Christians. We must acknowledge that the Lord speaks indeed in the whole Church, can speak through all her members, and does indeed speak through the official teaching and pastoral offices of the Church. We must be ready to use gifts of discernment and understanding so that we can recognize the Lord's true voice when he does speak through others.

Now all of these tendencies, although small, are dangerous because they are symptoms of a recurring pattern in Church history which may be called come-out-ism. Come-out-ism is a movement or tendency for pious groups of enthusiastic Christians to separate themselves from their parent church because (1) they could not or would not integrate their valid insights with the Church; (2) because they could not or would not endure misunderstanding and even persecution; and (3) because they began to believe that they were the true church and that the parent church was false, carnal, unspiritual, and had to be come out of. It is not in the will of Jesus Christ that the charismatic renewal result in more factionalism, division, and alienation within the Catholic Church; it is not the Lord's will to create from the Catholic charismatic renewal another new denomination or church; but it is the Lord's will that we make every effort in the Spirit to be one with the Catholic Church which has been his Body since the day of Pentecost!

To avoid these dangers and to correct any misdirected efforts, what can we do? We can proclaim the great and common bond of baptism which unites us to all Christians and unites us especially as members of the Catholic Church; we can realize on ever deeper levels that we are all together plunged into the death and resurrection of Christ, that thus we belong to him and to each other, and that there can be no basic division among us. Along with this, Jesus calls upon us to proclaim that we have all received the gift of the Holy Spirit. Then we have to get to work in our home communities to help our fellow Catholics realize the full potential of the gift that they have, and be baptized in the Holy Spirit. It will take hard work, long prayer, and much gentleness and lovingkindness to bring the graces of the charismatic renewal to all Catholics in a way that can be both understood and received.

Then too we have to realize that our bishops, vicars, pastors, priests, and deacons are all meant to have the spiritual gifts for doing their jobs. We must humbly but earnestly support them, encourage them, and urge them to open up to the specific ministry gifts they have been given by God, but which they may not know how to use. Beyond this we have to cooperate with our bishops and pastors, being fully open in love with them about what the Lord is doing in this renewal. We must accept their correction and advice, trusting the Holy Spirit to work through them. But, and here I stress this lovingly, we must also remind them that they have the obligation and grace from God to judge, approve, confirm, and bless the authentic movement of the Lord among his People. Let us pray incessantly for our bishops, for upon them rests the heavy responsibility which they must exercise now of recognizing the voice of the Lord among us and leading the whole church to respond to him in faithfulness.

Also, we can work to form our prayer groups and communities as integral parts of parochial and diocesan life. For this work there can be as yet no one model. There are a variety of styles of charismatic prayer groups and communities and there are a variety of styles of regular church life with which they may be able to integrate. For some of the charismatic renewal may in fact become *the* pastoral strategy for the renewal of the parish; for others the prayer group may be able to exist as an approved activity within the parish. In some cities large charismatic associations or covenant communities drawing people from many parishes will need to have a liaison with the bishop and his diocesan staff to stay fully one with the Church. In some cities the community may develop looking like a new religious congregation, in others like a new diocesan-wide confraternity.

I want to make it very clear that I am not calling upon the charismatic renewal to revive or provide personnel for every dying parish or diocesan activity. We must face up to the problem of new wine in old wine-skins and realize that many church projects of the past and even of the present are not the answer to Church renewal. In fact what we should do is to work within parish and diocese to improve and define precisely the strategy for pastoral renewal that the Lord is revealing in the charismatic movement—so that the Lord's plan for personal conversion, and spiritual power for holiness and service in the context of new, authentic Christian communities can become the pastoral plan of the whole Church. What is important is our inner attitude of fidelity to the Church in this, and our commitment to live and act in the best interests of the Church. We must be in harmony with the bishop and the pastor, wherever possible, cooperating with them in their pastoral plan, supporting them with our prayer, but also sharing with them our discernment and vision of the Lord's plan for the renewal of the Church.

In all things, we have to realize that the charismatic renewal is not the Church, not an end in itself, not a substitute for the Church, but truly a tool for renewal of the Church, which is the primary source of the full sacramental life of worship in Christ; it is the Church and not the charismatic renewal by *itself* that is the source of the full and authentic teaching of Christ.

Finally, we must insist among ourselves and to

the whole Church that being baptized in the Holy Spirit and the exercise of the spiritual gifts are not just another "something" going on in the Church today that has to be tolerated along with everything else. The Lord does not want his Spirit tolerated; the Lord wants his Spirit accepted, and embodied by all his People. The charismatic renewal, in its best fruit, in its most faithful representation of the Lord, is meant for everyone, for all of his People. We must not sell the Lord short. We must not be bought off into complacent isolation by tolerance; but rather we must lay down our lives for the total acceptance and participation by every Catholic in the Lord's spiritually renewed Church.

God Is Shaking the Churches

By Rev. Charles Simpson

In the eight years since I have been baptized in the Spirit, the Lord has been consistently dealing with a few themes in my life and ministry, and I would like to share them with my Roman Catholic brothers and sisters, because I think what he has been teaching me is a word he is speaking to all his church.

In 1964, I had been pastor at Bayview Heights Baptist Church for seven years. I had been born and raised in the Southern Baptist tradition, and this was a typical, progressive Southern Baptist church in the suburbs of Memphis, Tennessee. We had grown numerically, and had all the signs of success that Baptists had learned in the 1950s, but I knew something was wrong. What we had basically done was import a segment of society into our church, without changing it very much. It did not take very long before I realized that the problem was not in my denomination or in the congregation, but in me. As I began to study the Bible more deeply, I saw that there was a wide gap between New Testament Christianity and the contemporary Christianity that I was preaching and living. Confronted by this defectiveness in my ministry, I began to cry out to the Lord, and he began to arrange things—people I met, books I read

—to the point that one day as I was praying, he baptized me in his Spirit.

Though I didn't know anything at all about the charismatic movement before this process started and I still didn't fully grasp what was happening, suddenly there was a spiritual explosion in my church. I didn't preach on healing or tongues or any of those sorts of things, mostly because I did not myself fully understand the implications of what had happened to me; I just began preaching about primitive Christianity and the power of the Spirit, and people began to come in in record-breaking numbers. There was a real repentance going on and real spiritual encounter being experienced by the members of my congregation. None of us were joining a movement; we were just coming to know our God more fully. Six or eight months later, the pentecostal implications of what was happening began to become clear to all of us. Some drew back, some left the church, but we realized then that what we had witnessed was the spiritual renewal of a congregation. We knew too that God was calling us deeper. We knew that we were not just involved in a Baptist renewal, that God's purpose was not simply to make us better Baptists. He was bringing us face to face with the Christ of the New Testament; not simply calling us to a rededication of something we knew in the past, but leading us into a new way. We knew he was calling, but we did not know the way, and we decided as a congregation to step back and let him show us. We dismantled our church structure, all our deacons resigned, I offered my resignation—and we began to restructure the church. Everything was resubmitted to the will of God, and in that setting he began to restructure the church. Everything was resubmitted to the will of God, and in that setting he here is that that is where God began to teach me about some patterns of discipleship and pastoring I will take up later in this article.

Many of you are probably wondering how the Baptist denomination took all these developments. Well, there were problems, but not the ones most people would expect. Too many people are talking about restructuring the church for the Southern Baptist Convention or the local Baptist association to come down on anyone for the kind of restructuring we were doing. Also, there isn't a theological problem with gifts of the Spirit, because our Constitution recognizes their validity and uses I Cor. 12:8-10 as the supporting passage. The radical Baptist principle of individual church autonomy meant they couldn't interfere or direct what was happening; the only option would be exclusion, if there was some basis for it. Every year for seven years, the question has been raised. We have told them that we are not breaking fellowship with them, we love them and want to be with them; but each year the question has been raised, though as yet nothing has been done definitively.

It's interesting that the basis of the question has been the practice of speaking in tongues. In a way it is instructive. No revival is ever going to sneak up on any Baptist unawares. Revival has been too much a part of our recent history, and we have lately become too image-conscious for that to happen. We Baptists know that people expect Baptists to be prone to emotional religion, and we don't want that image any more. This is just one of the ways in which the last revival is the greatest hindrance to the next one; the backwash of the last wave on the shore breaks the power of the next one coming in. The charismatic renewal is going through the churches that haven't experienced a revival recently like fire through a hayfield, but among us the renewal is running up against "Tradition."

It seems a little strange to talk about "Tradition" in a Baptist church, but that is the word that gets used. Tradition is a good thing: it gives us a common language with which to communicate to one another what is happening with us, and it keeps us in touch with the Scripture and the great teachers of the church's past, protecting us from repeating old spiritual errors. The tradition we ran into was more like crystallized custom. When God teaches how to do something for one time and place and we find out that it works, it is just our natural tendency to assume that this is his final word on the subject. When, at some later date, he tries to lead us into a way better suited to the situation we are in, his greatest obstacle is often the last thing he taught us. Practices crystallize into principles, customs become part of the "Tradition," and God's work is bound. In our case, tongues was a practice that was not part of the Baptist "Tradition," i.e. custom, and therefore was questionable. That church's involvement in the Southern Baptist Convention is still in jeopardy today because the process of crystallization in the Baptist church does not allow for God's further developments. The same is true in many other churches in other ways: this was just the point at which the Lord began to teach us about crystallization as idolatry.

As all this was developing in my church, the Lord began to lead me personally into an extension of my ministry. Starting around 1967, when I began to be invited to speak in different places around the country and in other countries, an itinerant teaching mission started alongside my institutional pastoral ministry. More and more I began to feel that this was my calling, to disciple more broadly. I had met brothers Prince, Mumford, and Basham, and our association had developed. We were at a conference together in 1970, in Florida, and as we shared the Lord led us to realize that, in our independence, we were in a real sense unprotected (the condition of many ministers). Because we were not submitted to any oversight, we and our ministries were vulnerable to real spiritual dangers. We needed to be covered and protected, and we came into a mutual submission to one another. We didn't lose our individual identity, we aren't being coerced, yet we have become bound to one another spiritually; it has been a powerful thing for all of us.

For a variety of reasons it was becoming clear that I could not maintain the double role of pastor and itinerant teacher, and that the Lord wanted me to take teaching as my full ministry. In the early part of 1972, I and my family moved to Hollywood, Florida, near Fort Lauderdale, to become part of the body in service there.

A lot of people have heard of The Holy Spirit Teaching Mission in Fort Lauderdale. What is happening now has grown out of that. The Mission was involved in a lot of different ministries, like Fresh Bread national tape library, *New Wine* magazine, a developing videotape ministry, lecture tours, Bible teaching by cassette. They were all good things, but they were the source of a real difficulty and the beginning of a real struggle as we came to terms with what was happening. Our very real and very good ministry was leading us into becoming something like a denominational structure. We saw that The Mission was becoming a spiritual octopus, relating a lot of things to itself. That wasn't our original purpose. What we wanted to do was bless what God was doing, be a resource that he could use for renewing his people; we wanted to minister to the Body of Christ, rather than build a separate structure. The Mission was brought into submission to and under the oversight of the elders in the Fort Lauderdale area. We realized further that our work was not to teach about the Holy Spirit—he doesn't come to testify about himself but to help Christians mature. We settled on a new name, and with it a new vision: Christian Growth Ministries.

One of the contrasts we've noticed in our contacts with Catholics in the charismatic renewal is an emphasis lacking in most Protestant circles. Catholics generally emphasize the whole process of salvation, whereas Protestants, at least my kind, tend to emphasize the initial new birth. The two truths, which have been kept isolated so long, need to be taken together. If we see all of Christianity as being wrapped up in the new birth, we miss (I'll use a word we don't use often) the sacramental aspects of the fellowship of the Church. If we don't get the starting point, we might think we can grow in the Church without ever getting plugged in spiritually. Both truths are needed for the Church to be what it needs to be. The Catholic tradition tends to produce a few spiritual giants, the evangelical tradition produces a lot of spiritual babies. We need babies, a lot of them, if the Church is to grow, but those babies need to grow up and reproduce themselves if the Church is going to be real. We have to take the two truths together, and that is what we are trying to do at Christian Growth Ministries. It is God's work to mature Christians, and we are trying to bless and support that work.

We are a body that expresses itself in service in many different ways: tapes, books, etc., always to support and bless the work that God is doing locally in many different places. We are available to serve wherever local elders see a need for our resources. We are not at work to establish Christian Growth Ministries or to promote our organization. We want to feed the Body of Christ, not define it in relation to us. It is not an easy thing to do, Church History shows us, but we must do it. What God has been showing us is that he is already at work in all areas. He doesn't want us sending out colonies to every city, to build our own kingdom, but rather to go and join him wherever he is working to go build his own Kingdom.

This leads me into the first point that God has been teaching me. He began to teach it at Bayview Heights, when I was pastor there, and he has continued to teach it as Christian Growth Ministries develops. The principle is contained in John 12: *"Except a grain of wheat fall into the ground and die, it will not bear fruit."* I had always understood this in personal terms, but he began to show me that it also applies to our structures and our ministry.

As Bayview Heights began to become a successful New Testament community, others began to want to see the same thing happen in their own neighborhood. The temptation was to send out colonies, to export Bayview Heights Baptist Church. I found God resisting me, not the work I was doing, but me. He said, "I do not want you to try to make Bayview Heights Baptist Church the Kingdom of God. If others have to come to me through you, I will break you. Your church is not big enough to be my Church in Mobile and I will not let you even try to get a monopoly on my work. If people in Mobile have to join Bayview Heights to have the experience of a New Testament church, I will resist you all the way." He even showed me that I would have to give up my position as pastor of an institutional church in order to go into a teaching ministry. If I preached what God was teaching about New Testament church life, people would want to come to my church rather than doing it in their own churches. He showed me that I had to bury my ministry back in the whole Body if it was to bear fruit for his Kingdom. He continues to teach the same thing in our co-operation in Christian Growth Ministries.

Related to that is something else the Lord has been dealing with me on for a while. One of the greatest temptations we face is to organize. God is ordering his Church; what we need to do is recognize the order he's putting in. No one would ever think of trying to organize a tree, which has its own principle of growth and order; the same holds for God's Church.

The Lord began to show this to me back to the beginning in Bayview Heights. When my Bible study began to show me that God's order involved shepherds, I set out to get a group of people together that I could put into positions of shepherd in the church. The Lord stopped me; he said that he was already raising up shepherds. If I opened my eyes I would see them. Our work in the renewal of God's Church is not to organize, but to recognize and bless his order, which he is bringing forth. The form in the Church will always follow the function, and the functioning of the parts of the body is under the direction of God. God's order will emerge; it will not be organized.

The Lord has also been teaching me something about instrumentality. He has given us instruments to use in his ministry, and he wants to use us as instruments, and what he has been showing me is related to both of them. It is easier to see in the area of using instruments, so it is best to start there.

One of the things that The Holy Spirit Teaching Mission became known for was the ministry of deliverance. What we sort of knew to start with was that deliverance is not a one-time cure-all, and our experience has borne this out. It can and does have very real and very dramatic results many times, but has to be integrated into the ministry of the body rather than an itinerant ministry. Now what we do is help the local elders see its place in the body and help them integrate it into the body's ministry. An itinerant minister cannot do follow-up, and that is vital. Follow-up is the work of a body, and deliverance is just one of its tools.

One thing we've noticed with deliverance is the process by which we learn to use tools. God is equipping us with a complete tool box for our work as his Church, but we need to learn how to use them. Most

God Is Shaking the Churches

of the time we get wrapped up in the tool. It is as if God gave you a screwdriver, and first thing you know you are trying to fix everything with a screwdriver. It is a wrecking bar, you use the handle as a hammer, you use it as a chisel. You use that one tool to try to fix everything, until finally you run up against something that will not respond to anything you can do with a screwdriver. Then God gives you a pair of pliers, and shows you how to use them. Then you say, "Praise God, that screwdriver was nothing, you ought to see these pliers," and off you go again with the pliers. What we really need is an appreciation of the tools as tools, with limited functions and uses, rather than cure-alls.

The same sort of thing has to be learned in terms of God using us as instruments. Being instruments means that there comes a time when we have to just be laid aside, put back in the box—not as persons but as instruments. The human tendency is to glorify the instrument, to make an idol of it. Every instrument of God tends to become an idol; every means tends to become an end. I preached once on "The greatest movement that ever failed." John the Baptist had to be one of the greatest, if not the greatest, prophet that ever was, and yet his movement was a failure. It is no reflection on him, but on his followers. He had the calling to be the forerunner, the announcer of the Messiah. He could have gotten away with announcing himself as the Messiah—he had the Levitical pedigree, he had the message, he had the preaching power—but he did not. He pointed and said, "Behold the Lamb of God, follow him." He did his work well, and he was a great instrument of God. But a movement grew up around the instrument, and people began to compare Jesus and John. Now God has a problem, his instrument has become his obstacle. Years later, in Ephesus, there would be people still following John and not Jesus. John was himself becoming an idol, and he had to be gotten out of the way. It is not God's way to build great personalities so that cults can form around them, but to build a body. Every instrument of God has to be ready to stand aside when it begins to get in God's way, or God will have to push it out of the way.

The same applies to everything in the Church. Everything is going to be brought under God's headship, and his tools are going to be tools and not idols. God promised in Hebrews 12 that he would be shaking the whole earth so that only that which is unshakeable would remain standing. This is what we are seeing now; it is what God always does. Everything that can be shaken will be shaken, and only what is unshakeable will last. God is doing this work in his Church; ministries, individuals, structures are being and will be shaken. There will remain no idols, no obstacles to God's work in his Kingdom. A lot of things we see now will be shaken away. It is for us to rejoice, for what remains standing will be unshakeable, and nothing will be able to stand up against it.

The Power in Penance: Confession and the Holy Spirit

By Fr. Michael Scanlan

The following is an excerpt from The Power in Penance: Confession and the Holy Spirit, *reprinted by permission of Ave Maria Press. The booklet outlines a specific, practical approach to renewal of the sacrament of penance, an approach which is based on the priest's prayer that God will bestow spiritual gifts of discernment, deliverance, and healing in the sacrament. Elsewhere in the booklet, Fr. Scanlan describes the fruits of this approach:*

The Eucharist and penance are primary sources of reconciliation in the Christian life. Since the Second Vatican Council, the Church has deepened its awareness and appreciation of the Holy Eucharist. A series of changes in the rite emphasized the power of the Eucharist to unite the individual with the Body of Christ and indeed with the Holy Trinity. Correspondingly, however, the sacrament of penance has fallen into more and more disuse and its importance has been generally deemphasized by both clergy and laity.

The purpose of this booklet is to advance a view

with regard to the proper place of confession and the special powers of grace and healing which are available through this sacrament.

It is difficult to generalize concerning the experience of confession. Certainly many people still find regular confession vital and fruitful. Yet, a less favorable experience is the growing trend today. Priests and laity are frustrated by the seemingly limited effectiveness of the practice of regular confession. The penitent repeats the same list of sins and receives approximately the same penance and general admonition. The penitent grows to expect that his list will not change from week to week or month to month and that indeed his utilization of the sacrament of penance is apparently a holding action which at best prevents a worsening of his condition. The priest quickly exhausts his insights into the particular habitual offenses of the penitent and he feels a sense of helplessness when he hears the list time and time again. Frequently the priest resorts to encouraging the penitent, saying that the confession was good and that he must trust in God and go to the sacraments. The penitent often is dissatisfied because he believes there should be changes in his life in those areas where he feels genuine repentance. This stalemate continues over a period of time and usually results in the penitent's adopting a mechanical approach to the sacrament, or ceasing to utilize the sacrament except on special occasions.

Many penitents further believe that a social dimension of sin affecting their fellowmen is ignored in their confessional experience. They believe that neither the effects of personal sin in disrupting and wounding community nor the power of the sacra-

Confession and the Holy Spirit

ment to heal and strengthen community ties is sufficiently paid attention to in confession.

Finally, many penitents and priests are dissatisfied with traditional forms of the examination of conscience. The categorized sins do not meet the realities of the sinfulness of their lives. The traditional understanding of sexual sins, in particular, does not fit the conscious belief of the penitent as to where lies the wrong in sexual immorality. There is a sense, therefore, of communicating trivialities while ignoring, or not sufficiently emphasizing, the most sinful failures.

A number of format changes can be introduced to alleviate some of these problems. Alternate approaches to the traditional examination of conscience will be included in a later chapter. Communal penance services can aid the expression of the social and ecclesial dimensions. The priest can be more sensitive to the needs of the penitent. He may become more competent in selective spiritual direction. The general confession can be encouraged at crucial times in the penitent's life. But these changes will not resolve the difficulties unless they are coupled with a basic change in attitude regarding the power available through the sacrament. There has been too little emphasis on the power of the Holy Spirit to show both penitent and priest what should be at the heart of the confession. This failure to turn to the Holy Spirit for guidance seems to be coupled with the failure to believe the Holy Spirit will enable the penitent to change his conduct.

Underlying the dissatisfactions of both priest and penitent is the belief that there should be a vital reconciliation through the sacrament of penance. A dynamic of change in those lives needing a fundamental conversion should be evident over a series of confessions. The approach recommended in this booklet contends that the expectation of reconciliation would be better fulfilled if both priest and penitent approached confession with a definite anticipation of results and with reliance on the power of the Holy Spirit to change the life of the penitent. Explicitly, the priest and the penitent should expect genuine repentence to lead to a deeper union with God and fellowmen through the power of the Holy Spirit to heal wounds, to deliver from the forces of evil, and to strengthen the ability to do good and resist evil. They should also expect, however, times following a fundamental conversion when the penitent contends only with incidental habitual failures.

Those involved in the charismatic renewal have witnessed the power of God to heal, deliver, and strengthen. They have found these powers available through prayer, and they are inclined to expect them to be at least as present through the sacrament of penance. Such Catholics believe that the Lord wants to forgive them and to transform them so that they will be free and loving Christians unchained by habitual sins. They believe that the Lord took on these sins and made full satisfaction for them through the shedding of his blood. They believe that forgiveness and healing are already given through the power of Jesus Christ.

Covenant Communities: A New Sign of Hope

By Fr. John O'Connor, C.S.C.

For those weary of listening to the "bad news" of so many self-appointed critics of God's household, it is a source of joy and strength to hear again the "good news" of what God is doing for his people. Jesus promised that he would not leave us orphans in this world—as true in the twentieth century as in the first. We are witnesses to the activity of the Holy Spirit to change men's hearts, to God's renewal of his people through an extraordinary outpouring of his Spirit. Daily occurrences in our communities all over the country testify to the great wisdom and goodness of our God.

Those who have persevered by the grace of God through the initial uneasiness with the restoration to the Church of things lost for centuries can only agree with the word of God spoken by the prophet: *"For my thoughts are not your thoughts, nor are your ways my ways, says the Lord. As high as the heavens are above the earth, so high are my ways above your ways and my thoughts above your thoughts"* (Is. 55:8-9). The ways that the Lord has in renewing his Church are certainly not man's ways. Man resists any of God's attempts to change his life, but praise the Lord for his faithfulness and persistence.

The many noticeable effects of charismatic renewal within the Catholic Church during the past few years include: a rediscovery of the importance of the "spiritual gifts" (tongues, prophecy, healing and wisdom) for the upbuilding of the Body of Christ; deeper faith; recovery of the prayer of praise; renewed interest in personal prayer and spiritual growth. We all can testify to a deeper personal relationship with Jesus as a result of being baptized in the Spirit. Yet, it appears that one of the most significant surprises that God has for us in the fresh outpouring of his Spirit is the appearance of a new form of Christian community. Across the country members of more mature prayer groups are finding the Holy Spirit leading them to make a more serious and definite commitment to one another and to the Lord than is possible in the rather loose association or fellowship that characterizes a weekly prayer meeting. People are eating, living and praying together; families are grouping together to purchase food; acknowledged leaders and pastoral teams are emerging. Stable bonds in the form of clear and definite agreements are taking shape, and are being spelled out in public commitments or "covenants," forming the basis of a new kind of relationship, the covenant community.

The formation of charismatic covenant communities is a manifestation of a maturing process occurring within the Catholic pentecostal movement insuring a deep and lasting impact of charismatic renewal on the Church in this country and abroad. It is my own conviction that covenant community is God's answer to a need felt among Catholics for some kind of day-to-day Christian community, God's way of calling us back to the essentially communitarian witness that characterized the early Church. But to appreciate the importance of this new work of God's Spirit it is necessary to examine the nature and theological justification of charismatic covenant communities and, as well, to view them within the context of the pastoral needs of the Church today, one of the most crucial being the need for base Christian communities to supplement the pastoral care provided by existing parishes.

What Are Charismatic Covenant Communities?

Covenant communities are groups of Christians whom the Lord has led to bind themselves to him and to one another in the form of a public commitment. Membership cuts across the normally accepted divisions of God's people, including clergy, religious, and lay people. Each is small enough so that it can be a body of Christians who know and serve one another, while large enough to provide effective pastoral leadership.

The key to covenant communities is divine initiative. Since they involve a partnership between God and a specific group of Christians, their formation depends on his invitation. In some way the Lord's words, "I will be your God if you will be my people," are heard, calling for a collective response from a definite body of Christians. If the group accepts the invitation to form a public covenant among themselves and with the Lord, and this is accepted by him, they attain a new identity before God. The covenant becomes the basis of their relationship with one another and with God.

Covenant communities generally involve some form of shared living. This may take many forms, but simply living together as Christians totally devoted to the Lord is most important. The witness of the common life is one of the most powerful testimonies to the effect of the Holy Spirit on their lives, for without his constant presence they could no longer continue to exist. Community living affords numerous opportunities each day to encourage and strengthen one another in a common resolution to lead a life more pleasing to God, allowing the Lord to work in men's lives in ways which would not be possible if each were attempting to follow the Lord on his own.

The Catholic pentecostal community in Ann Arbor, Michigan, named "The Word of God" has become the prototype or model of what the Lord seems to be doing with prayer groups in many places in the country. Most members of The Word of God live in what the community calls "households." This term covers a wide variety of living situations. It includes couples who live near one another and come together on a regular basis for meals and prayer. It includes small groups of single people who share a house or an apartment. A single family might be considered a household, as might a group of students in a dorm. The important thing about households is not the kind of living situation, but the pattern according to which people share their lives. Households are formed according to Old and New Testament principles of Common living. These principles include some kind of daily shared prayer and a common meal, weekly meetings to confront personal difficulties and to share how the Lord has been working in each member's life, and some kind of supervision or "headship." Households, once established, generally form covenants.

The Ann Arbor community exists as a covenant community because that is what the Lord has called it to be. He invited the members to make a covenant through prophecy and prepared their hearts to enable them to make this commitment. He gave them the name "The Word of God." He continues to guide the community in fulfilling his own special purpose for them. He uses the community as a powerful witness of his love to the many he brings to the community as guests.[1]

Many have thought that the kind of community which the Lord is building in Ann Arbor is more appropriate to a college campus than to prayer groups which are predominantly made up of married couples. They see secular occupations and family commitments as obstacles to community living. However, living arrangements may differ greatly according to individual circumstances. It is also clear that the Lord is calling families as well as single people into covenant communities in Ann Arbor and elsewhere. In the last year a rapidly growing number of non-university people, older, and often with families, have become part of the Ann Arbor community. Christian community in the Lord's plan is not a luxury, but a necessity. We have to admit that certain features of American family life and our existing pattern of work present obstacles to the Lord's plan for our lives. We must establish priorities which allow us to share greater amounts of our time and our lives with other Christians for the building up of the Body of Christ in our city or town.

Theological Justification of Covenant Communities

Strictly speaking, the first Christian covenant community was the "local Church" at Jerusalem. It is described in Acts 2:42-47 as follows:

> *These remained faithful to the teaching of the apostles, to the brotherhood, to the breaking of the bread and to prayers.*
>
> *The many miracles and signs worked through the apostles made a deep impression on everyone.*
>
> *The faithful all lived together and owned everything in common; they sold their goods and possessions and shared out the proceeds among themselves according to what each one needed.*
>
> *They went as a body to the Temple every day but met in their houses for the breaking of bread; they shared their food gladly and generously; they praised God and were looked up to by everyone. Day by day the Lord added to their community those destined to be saved.*

In the early Church there were five steps to becoming a Christian. Christian initiation presupposed repentance through the confession of sin and the turning to God; faith through the confession of Jesus Christ as personal Lord and Savior; baptism by water; prayer to receive the gift of the Holy Spirit, often accompanied by the "laying on of hands"; and incorporation into a living body of Christ by becoming part of a Christian community.

Christians would not have considered living their Christian lives outside daily contact with other Christians, since their manner of living was characteristically different from other members of Jewish and Roman society. Two of their more noticeable traits were generosity toward the poor of the community and hospitality to strangers and guests from other Christian communities.

The home was the normal center for worship, fellowship, and evangelism in the early Church. We know that St. Paul often found someone to stay with when he entered a new town. This home would become the center of his apostolic activity. It was common practice for someone's home to be used as the meeting place of a local Christian community in each town. This explains, for example, the reference to the "church" which meets in the house of Prisca and Aquila (Rom. 16:5), the church in the house of Nympha (Col. 4:15), and the one in the house of Philemon (Philem. 2). Acts 28:30-31 describes how Paul used his house in Rome for purposes of evangelism: *"Paul spent the whole of the two years in his own rented lodging. He welcomed all who came to visit him, proclaiming the kingdom of God and teaching the truth about the Lord Jesus Christ with complete freedom and without hindrance from anyone."*

The first Christians assembled in one another's homes for prayer, for the Eucharist, for common meals, for preaching, and for giving testimony to the mighty works of God in the life of the community or in neighboring communities. In this way they would give praise to God and "upbuild" one another in love. In quality, their relationships with one another were noticeably different from those experienced by their non-Christian neighbors. The "fruits of the Spirit" (Gal. 5:22-23) could be seen in their manner of living. Their community witness of mutual love was the proof of their discipleship to Jesus.

Community and the Church

Christianity is essentially communal. In community, God deals with men as a people. God saves man by making him part of a Christian community. The explicit acknowledgment of Jesus Christ as Lord is the basis for personal relationships. Within Christian community man experiences the first fruits of a new social and cosmic order established through the passion, death, resurrection, and exaltation of Jesus Christ. Christian community provides a space for the Spirit of God within a world hostile to his reign.

The Second Vatican Council emphasized the fact that the Church is the people of God. This is true both of the "universal" and the "local" Church. Each is fully the Body of Christ. Each member has a part to play within the body; no one is without significance or importance. It is the complementarity of ministries and mutual services that characterizes a true Christian community, for in this way Christians as a body become more and more like Christ.

> *And his gifts were that some should be apostles, some prophets, some evangelists, some pastors and teachers, for the equipment of the saints, for the work of ministry, for building up the body of Christ, until we all attain to the unity of faith and of the knowledge of the Son of God,*

> *to mature manhood, to the measure of the stature of the fullness of Christ* (Eph. 4:11-13).

In the mind of St. Paul, Christian maturity is impossible without some kind of daily contact with a living Christian community. Christians are called to holiness not as isolated individuals, but as a people—a community of faith, hope and love, which bears witness to Jesus Christ in the world.

This is why covenant communities are formed, especially in today's world where few parishes are capable of being the kind of community described by the New Testament. Most parishes are simply unable to provide the kind of deeper community necessary for a mature life in the Spirit. The need for basic Christian communities, however, can best be understood in the light of the pastoral realities of many areas of the world today. When we view the emergence of charismatic covenant communities in the context of the general pastoral situation in Europe, Latin America, and the United States, the importance of what God has begun in just a few places is apparent.

De-Christianization in Europe

Northern and central Europe particularly are undergoing what some have called a process of "de-Christianization" due to widespread urbanization and industrialization during the past century. While in most European countries the customs, laws, and traditional values give evidence of a past when Church and society were bound closely together, fewer and fewer people manifest a living, personal faith in Jesus Christ as Lord. Tradition dictates that people continue to be baptized, married, and buried in the Church, but they have failed to appropriate the Christian faith in their day-to-day lives. The working class particularly has been the special cause of concern for the Church; the practice of the faith is least evident among them.

In 1943, Catholics were shocked by the publication of Abbé Godin's *La France, Pays de Mission?* (France, a Mission Land?). Godin's main thesis was that de-Christianization had become so extensive in France that it was appropriate to consider it a mission country in need of re-evangelization. Several pastoral initiatives grew out of the recognition of this new situation. In Belgium, Canon Cardijn began the Young Christian Worker movement out of which the principles of Catholic Action were formulated. The liturgical renewal was increasingly promoted and efforts centered on revitalizing the parish. G. Michonneau is among the most famous of the parish reformers of France. His emphasis was on creating parish communities.[2] Attempts were made in the priest-worker movement to bridge the gap between clergy and laymen. Many of the fruits of this period of renewal within the Church can be seen in the documents of the Second Vatican Council.

Today the situation of the Church in Europe has changed. The process of de-Christianization has continued in spite of the best efforts of committed Christians to remedy the situation. German theologian Karl Rahner now speaks of the Church of the "diaspora." By this expression he means that in the future Christians will be in the minority.[3] Joseph Comblain, a Belgian theologian currently working in Latin America, believes that the parish structure is one of the chief obstacles to an effective presence of the Church in Europe. The parish responds to the rural environment of a village but has never adapted itself well as an institution to an urban setting. He calls for a return to the traditional concept of the "local Church" to replace or supplement the territorial parish.[4] Others speak about the formation of "basic Christian communities," groups small enough so that everyone will know one another personally.[5] Only in this way can evangelism be more effectively carried out than in the large city parish, in which 90 percent of the parishioners are unknown to the pastor.

The charismatic covenant community appears to be an important answer to the need for the formation of basic Christian communities in Europe. Effective means of initiation into the community through instruction in the essentials of the Christian faith can counteract the environment where most remain only nominally Christian. The covenant and the common commitment to doing the Lord's work provide the common identity necessary to sustain a small group of Christians. The charismatic covenant community also provides a means of arriving at effective leadership in countries lacking pastors and priests. Although certain expressions of the charismatic renewal may be more appropriate to the American culture and mentality, the fundamental principles of Christian life discovered through this renewal seem applicable to the European scene where many are searching for viable options to the parish.

Sacramentalization
in Latin America

The pastoral situation in Latin America is dramatically different from that in Western Europe and the United States. The Christianity that characterizes Latin America came predominantly from Spain. People now say that Latin Americans were sacramentalized without ever being effectively evangelized. Pastoral practice dictated that people be baptized whether or not they understood and personally accepted the fundamentals of the Christian faith. In Latin America almost everyone is baptized and many seek Christian marriage and burial, but the Church is identified primarily with the clergy and the nuns and is viewed basically as the guardian of culture and public morals.

Widespread ignorance of the basic content of the faith is common. Generally there is indifference and apathy among the masses to the practice of the faith within the existing ecclesial institutions, especially the urban parish. In recent years this trend has been compounded by the predominance of foreign missionaries who serve as local priests. With a high school and college education required for admission to the priesthood, few from the working class, only a small minority of whom have completed grade school, have become priests. Moreover, the Church's theology and liturgy reflect a Western European culture and are often unintelligible to the common man.

Many members of the upper class and upper middle class have been educated in Catholic schools. These persons may have received a good catechesis but have lacked a family environment conducive to the development of a mature Christian life. The Spanish mentality has led many to divorce the Christian faith from its social consequences as delineated in recent papal encyclicals. In recent years the priests and religious in Latin America have become increasingly identified with the social concerns of the poor and oppressed. The involvement of priests and bishops in the social issues of poverty, hunger, unemployment, and illiteracy has been a source of irritation to some of the upper-class Catholics. Moreover, renewal within the Church following the Second Vatican Council has caused even greater polarization among Latin Catholics.

Evangelical and pentecostal Protestants, however, have been very successful in Latin America. For example, in Chile, a country of 8.5 million people, there are currently 300,000 members of various pentecostal denominations. They are rather aggressive in their street-corner evangelism and want to win converts among those who are nominally Christian. They have a strict moral code and have tended to create a good deal of antipathy among the more lax Catholics for their condemnation of the Catholic Church and the way of life common among most of the poor. But their great success in winning converts comes in large part from their strong communitarian witness. They call one another "brother" and "sister" and support one another in time of need. They have also been able to train pastors from among the people on the street rather than in the seminary. Hence they have some very able leaders and evangelists who have come from among the people themselves.[6]

Basic Communities

In 1968, the Latin American bishops, gathered at Medellín, Colombia, spoke of the need for fundamental evangelization in their countries. They recognized that it is misleading to view Latin America as a Catholic continent. As Bishop Samuel Ruiz of Chiapas, Mexico, put it bluntly, "We should put an end to the myth that Latin America is a Catholic continent. If the Church is a community of faith, hope and charity, then this concept simply does not apply to Latin America."

The bishops at Medellín also spoke about the need to form *communidades de base* (base communities) to replace or supplement the existing parish institutions, where effective pastoral care is increasingly difficult. (There may be from 8,000 to 10,000 baptized Catholics for each priest in a typical parish.) A pastoral synod in Santiago, Chile, following the Second Vatican Council, spoke about the need to find alternatives to the present system of parishes and seminaries. The bishops of Bolivia have adopted an experimental plan to train candidates for the priesthood while they remain at home. (Most of the poor need the support of any family members who can work.) Great emphasis is being put at present on the training of married deacons, though there are few places with a sufficiently developed community to support and encourage these men once they are ordained.

In Latin America, the formation of charismatic covenant communities may be the Lord's way of dealing with an environment hostile to the cultivation of a deep life in the Spirit. When preceded by real repentance and total commitment to the Lord Jesus, the baptism in the Spirit will provide the basis for such communities. With a group of people striving to lead the full life of the Spirit, it will become more apparent which men the Lord is anointing for

Covenant Communities

leadership and the service of the ministry without the need to take such men out of their own environment for lengthy periods of formal training. With the baptism in the Spirit people will be open to the understanding and wisdom that accompany the communication of the Gospel message. Once more it will become manifest that Christianity is not simply for an educated elite, but for all mankind. With the baptism in the Spirit the special love that the Lord has for the poor will become more apparent through healing and guidance. The Lord does not leave his children without food or clothing. Charismatic covenant communities will be a strong communitarian witness of the real effects in people's lives when they devote themselves totally to the Lord.

The charismatic covenant community is not something that can be imposed as a pastoral concept on the Latin American Church from their North American neighbors. It is more a case of simply opening to all that God has for us in our own present situation within his plan of salvation.

Pastoral Renewal in the United States

In comparison to other peoples, Americans tend to form stronger parish loyalties, particularly among ethnic groups. We have built churches and schools at a great financial sacrifice; our investment in places of worship and Christian instruction makes a dispassionate evaluation of our own pastoral reality difficult. People still fill our churches on Sunday so that certainly we would want to recognize that the Christian faith is operative in their lives in some sense. On the other hand, pastors frequently complain that it is difficult to take people beyond a certain minimal commitment to living the Christian life. Few ardently desire and pursue the holiness which the New Testament tells us should characterize the life of every Christian.

Pastoral renewal in this country has been synonomous with religious education for children and adults and the creation of "parish communities" through renewed liturgies and lay involvement in the parish in such things as parish councils. Some experimentation has been attempted with so-called "floating parishes," liturgies in the home, team ministries, and the amalgamation of certain pastoral tasks. But by and large, most of our pastoral care is centered on the individual and his needs.

While Catholic schools provide catechesis, they have not often been effective tools of the evangelization sadly lacking in the lives of American Catholics. Most attempt to explain this by appealing to the rather tenuous theory that grade-school and high-school-age children are incapable of any lasting commitment to Christ. We must also recognize that many of our pastoral educational efforts have centered on youth and young married people. We have generally neglected middle-aged, retired, and elderly people.

There are two factors which are forcing us to reevaluate our commitment to the parish and the parochial school as the most exclusive vehicle of pastoral renewal within the Church in the United States. The first is the so-called identity crisis surrounding priesthood and religious life in its present form. Due to lack of candidates in seminaries and convents, the number of those serving schools and parishes has had to be cut back. The second factor is the financial crisis presently being experienced by Catholic education. Many dioceses have been forced to close some of their schools due to inadequate funding.

What the charismatic covenant community will mean to the Church in the United States will depend on God's plan and not on human speculation. However, it seems to offer a viable option to the attempts of the parish to "create community" and to the attempts of schools to "evangelize." I think that it would be a mistake to view the covenant community as a parallel structure to the parish or school. It seems to complement these institutions rather than act as a substitute for them. In some cases it may be the Lord's desire that certain parishes become charismatic covenant communities. The Church of the Redeemer, an Episcopal parish in Houston, Texas, is a place where this has happened. However, it would be unwise to attempt to use covenant community as a basis of parish renewal. I believe that covenant communities should have an identity separate from the parish so as to facilitate the free development of both.

Conclusion

G. K. Chesterton once remarked to those who criticized Christianity for the rather dismal state of the world's affairs, "Christianity has not failed, it has never been tried." The question remains open. Are we willing to try the kind of Christian community that the Lord holds out to us? There has been much talk in recent years among Church reformers about "creating Christian community." One of man's most persistent concerns in the twentieth century is the existence of community, but the gap between words and deeds is often embarrassing, proving that the work must be God's. Throughout the history of salvation God has called his people to greater faithfulness by a communitarian reform of the Church. This was the case of the Benedictines in the sixth century, the Franciscans in the thirteenth century, the Jesuits in the sixteenth century, and many modern religious communities after the French Revolution. The nature of these communities varied according to the needs of the times. The charismatic covenant community can be seen as God's response to the current need for basic Christian communities to supplement the pastoral care of our overcrowded parishes.

The pastoral situation of the Church today is of course much more complex than these brief remarks have been able to communicate. Many assume that the kind of communitarian response appropriate to the situation of the early Church is what the Lord is again calling for today. We know that the best witness of the Lord's power and love in an unbelieving world is not some kind of spiritual elite, but a community of Christians who have been transformed by the Spirit of God, for God does not set a people apart as a privilege but because of the special mission and purpose that he would have them perform. However, just how common charismatic covenant communities are to become in the future depends on God's designs not on our own. We hope we will neither obstruct nor precipitate his activity. God's sovereign activity to win a people for the praise of his glory cannot be programmed.

To paraphrase the prayer of St. Paul, may we be filled with the knowledge of his will in all spiritual wisdom and understanding, so as to lead a life worthy of the Lord, fully pleasing to him, bearing fruit in every good work and increasing in the knowledge of God (cf. Col. 1:9-10).

Notes

1. Two other guests of The Word of God, *Fr. Dan Danielson and Fr. John Haughey, recently published their experiences of a covenant community, respectively in* Sisters Today *(Vol. 43, No. 4, December, 1971, pp. 215-224) and* America *(Vol. 126, No. 6, Feb. 12, 1972, pp. 142-145).*

2. G. Michonneau, Revolution in a City Parish. *London: Blackfriars, 1949.*

3. Karl Rahner, The Christian of the Future. *New York: Herder and Herder, 1967.*

4. Joseph Comblin, Théologie de la Ville *(Theology of the City) Editions Universitaires, 1968. We hope this interesting and important pastoral study will soon be translated into English. It includes an excellent summary of the development of the territorial parish.*

5. See Max Delespesse, The Church Community: Leaven and Life-Style. *Novalis Center, 1971.*

6. See Jeffrey L. Klaiber, "Pentecostal Breakthrough," in America, *January 31, 1970, and C. Peter Wagner, "The Street 'Seminaries' of Chile,"* Christianity Today, *August 6, 1971.*

Notes on the Contributors

Patti Gallagher Mansfield, now a member of the New Orleans community, attended the Duquesne weekend retreat in 1967.

Paul and Mary Ann Gray, then engaged to be married, were intimately involved in the Duquesne weekend. They are now leaders in the Light of the World Community in Erie, Pa.

James B. Manney is a member of the *New Covenant* editorial staff.

Fr. Val Gaudet is originally from western Canada. After serving six years as General Secretary for Pastoral Activities for the Oblate Fathers, and then working full time for the renewal in Rome, he retired to work for the renewal in Canada.

Cindy Conniff is a member of the *New Covenant* editorial staff.

Kevin Ranaghan, a married deacon, is one of the coordinators of the People of Praise, a charismatic community in South Bend. He is also a member of the North American Service Committee.

Mary Ann Jahr is a member of the *New Covenant* editorial staff.

Notes on the Contributors

Ralph Martin, former editor of *New Covenant,* is a member of the North American Service Committee. The article "God Is Restoring His People" is the edited text of the main address given at the 1974 International Conference on the Catholic Charismatic Renewal.

Bishop Joseph McKinney is auxiliary bishop of Grand Rapids, Mich.

The report of the American bishops in 1969 was presented to the National Conference of Catholic Bishops by **Bishop Alexander Zaleski** of Lansing, Mich.

Bishop Joseph Hogan is the Bishop of Rochester, N.Y. This article is based on a radio talk he gave in June, 1971.

Bishop Paul Anderson is the Bishop of Duluth, Minn.

Cardinal Leo Josef Suenens is the Archbishop of Malines-Brussels, Belgium, and the Primate of Belgium. The articles in this volume come from (1) a talk to the clergy of Milwaukee in March, 1973; (2) an interview with Ralph Martin that was published three months later.

George T. Montague, S.M., is editor of the *Catholic Biblical Quarterly* and rector of the Marianist Seminary in Toronto, Ontario. This testimony is condensed from the first chapter of his book *Riding the Wind,* published by Word of Life.

Fr. Heribert Mühlen is regarded by many persons as the leading theologian of the Holy Spirit in the Catholic Church today.

Fr. Salvador Carrillo Alday, M. Sp. S., studied at the Ecole Biblique in Jerusalem and took his doctorate in scripture in Rome. He is currently director of the Institute of Sacred Scripture in Mexico City, and he is the author of the first book in Spanish on the charismatic renewal. This is a condensed version of a talk he gave at the First International Leaders Conference on the Catholic Charismatic Renewal in Rome.

Fr. Basil Pennington is a Trappist monk at St. Joseph's Abbey in Spencer, Mass.

Fr. Francis Sullivan is a professor of theology at the Gregorian University in Rome.

Bert Ghezzi is the editor of *New Covenant* magazine.

Archbishop James Hayes is the Archbishop of Halifax, Nova Scotia.

Fr. Graham Pulkingham is the former rector of the (Episcopal) Church of the Redeemer in Houston, Tex. Subsequently he served the charismatic outreach in England. He is married and has six children.

Dr. Bill Burnett is the Anglican bishop of Capetown, South Africa. His article on "A Bishop, a

Diocese, and the Charismatic Renewal" is adapted from a two-part article that originally appeared in *Renewal* magazine, and is reprinted by permission.

Fr. Richard Jones, S.J., has worked extensively with the Sioux Indians.

Rev. Ken Pagard is pastor of the First Baptist Church in Chula Vista, Calif.

Rev. Charles Simpson is associated with Bread of Life Ministries in Mobile, Ala.

Fr. Michael Scanlan, T.O.R., is president of Steubenville College in Ohio. In 1976 he was elected chairman of the North American Service Committee. This article is excerpted, with permission, from his book *The Power of Penance: Confession and the Holy Spirit,* published by Ave Maria.

Fr. John O'Connor is a Holy Cross priest who has spent a considerable amount of time in Chile.